Lecture Notes in Computer Science   11967

More information about this series at http://www.springer.com/series/7410

Andrea Saracino · Paolo Mori (Eds.)

Emerging Technologies for Authorization and Authentication

Second International Workshop, ETAA 2019
Luxembourg City, Luxembourg, September 27, 2019
Proceedings

Springer

Editors
Andrea Saracino ⓘ
IIT-CNR
Pisa, Italy

Paolo Mori ⓘ
IIT-CNR
Pisa, Italy

ISSN 0302-9743   ISSN 1611-3349   (electronic)
Lecture Notes in Computer Science
ISBN 978-3-030-39748-7   ISBN 978-3-030-39749-4   (eBook)
https://doi.org/10.1007/978-3-030-39749-4

LNCS Sublibrary: SL4 – Security and Cryptology

This Springer imprint is published by the registered company Springer Nature Switzerland AG
The registered company address is: Gewerbestrasse 11, 6330 Cham, Switzerland

Preface

This book contains the papers which were selected for presentation at the Second International Workshop on Emerging Technologies for Authorization and Authentication (ETAA 2019), which was held in Luxembourg on September 27, 2019, and co-located with the 24th European Symposium on Research in Computer Security (ESORICS 2019).

The workshop program included 10 full papers and 1 invited paper concerning the workshop topics, in particular: new techniques for biometric and behavioral based authentication, authentication and authorization in the IoT and in distributed systems in general, techniques for strengthen password based authentication and for dissuading malicious users from stolen password reuse, an approach for discovering authentication vulnerabilities in interconnected accounts, and strategies to optimize the access control decision process in the Big Data scenario.

We would like to express our thanks to the authors who submitted their papers to the second edition of this workshop, thus contributing to making it again a successful event. A special thanks goes to Prof. Alessandro Aldini, who accepted being the invited speaker of ETAA 2019. We would like to thank the sponsors of the workshop, including the EU Commission funded projects: Collaborative and Confidential Information Sharing and Analysis for Cyber Protection (C3ISP) and European Network for Cyber Security (NeCS), Marie Sklodowska-Curie Actions (MSCA), and Innovative Training Networks (ITN). Last but not least, we would like to express our gratitude to the members of the Technical Program Committee for their valuable work in evaluating the submitted papers.

This workshop was supported by the EU Commission funded projects:

- **C3ISP**: Collaborative and Confidential Information Sharing and Analysis for Cyber Protection. Grant Agreement n. 700294.
- **NeCS**: European Network for Cyber Security, Grant Agreement n. 675320.

September 2019

Paolo Mori
Andrea Saracino

ETAA Workshop Introduction

IT devices are day by day becoming more pervasive in several application fields and in everyday life. The major driving factors are the ever increasing coverage of the Internet connectivity and the extreme popularity and capillarity of smartphones, tablets, and wearables, together with the consolidation of the Internet of Things (IoT) paradigm. As a matter of fact, interconnected devices directly control and take decisions on industrial processes, regulate infrastructures and services in smart cities, and manage quality of life and safety in smart homes, taking decisions with user interactions or even autonomously. The involvement of these devices in so many applications, unfortunately introduces a set of unavoidable security and safety implications, related to both the criticality of the aforementioned applications and to the privacy of sensitive information produced and exploited in the process. To address these and other related issues, there is an increasing need for instruments to control the access and the right to perform specific actions on devices or data. These instruments need to be able to cope with the high complexity of the considered applications and environments, being flexible and adaptable to different contexts and architectures, from centralized to fully-distributed ones, able to handle a high amount of information, as well as taking into account nonconventional trust assumptions. The considered technologies should regulate the actions of both human users and autonomous devices, being effective in enforcing security policies, still without introducing noticeable overhead, both on the side of performance and user experience. Hence, the design of advanced, secure, and efficient mechanisms for continuous authentication and authorization, requiring limited to no active interaction is solicited.

The ETAA workshop, which is now at its second edition, aims at being a forum for researchers and practitioners of security active in the field of new technologies for authenticating users and devices, and for enforcing security policies in new and emerging applications related to distributed systems, mobile/wearable devices, and IoT. ETAA 2019 saw the participation of Professor Alessandro Aldini from University of Urbino as invited speaker. It aimed to attract original research work covering both theoretical and practical aspects of authentication and authorization.

September 2019

Paolo Mori
Andrea Saracino

Organization

Workshop Chairs

Paolo Mori   Consiglio Nazionale delle Ricerche, Italy
Andrea Saracino   Consiglio Nazionale delle Ricerche, Italy

Technical Program Committee

Benjamin Aziz   University of Portsmouth, UK
Francesco Buccafurri   Universita Mediterranea di Reggio Calabria, Italy
Gabriele Costa   IMT Lucca, Italy
Francesco Di Cerbo   SAP Lab, France
Carmen Fernandez Gago   University of Malaga, Spain
Vasileios Gkioulos   Norwegian University of Science and Technology, Norway
Jatinder Singh   University of Cambridge, UK
Jens Jensen   Science and Technology Facilities Council, UK
Erisa Karafili   Imperial College London, UK
Georgos Karopulos   JRC, Italy
Hristo Koshutanski   ATOS, Spain
Gabriele Lenzini   University of Luxembourg, Luxembourg
Mirko Manea   HPE Italia, Italy
Charles Morisset   Newcastle University, UK
Silvio Ranise   Fondazione Bruno Kessler, Italy
Marco Tiloca   RISE, Sweden
Francesco Santini   Universita di Perugia, Italy
Daniele Sgandurra   Royal Holloway, University of London, UK
Debora Stella   Bird & Bird, Italy
Nicola Zannone   Eindhoven University of Technology, The Netherlands

Contents

Logics to Reason Formally About Trust Computation and Manipulation   1
    Alessandro Aldini and Mirko Tagliaferri

An Authorization Framework for Cooperative Intelligent
Transport Systems.   16
    Sowmya Ravidas, Priyanka Karkhanis, Yanja Dajsuren,
    and Nicola Zannone

A Framework for the Validation of Access Control Systems.   35
    Said Daoudagh, Francesca Lonetti, and Eda Marchetti

The Structure and Agency Policy Language (SAPL) for Attribute
Stream-Based Access Control (ASBAC)   52
    Dominic Heutelbeck

NoCry: No More Secure Encryption Keys for Cryptographic Ransomware   69
    Ziya Alper Genç, Gabriele Lenzini, and Peter Y. A. Ryan

Security Requirements for Store-on-Client and Verify-on-Server Secure
Biometric Authentication   86
    Haruna Higo, Toshiyuki Isshiki, Masahiro Nara, Satoshi Obana,
    Toshihiko Okamura, and Hiroto Tamiya

Reflexive Memory Authenticator: A Proposal for Effortless
Renewable Biometrics   104
    Nikola K. Blanchard, Siargey Kachanovich, Ted Selker,
    and Florentin Waligorski

Collaborative Authentication Using Threshold Cryptography   122
    Aysajan Abidin, Abdelrahaman Aly, and Mustafa A. Mustafa

MuFASA: A Tool for High-level Specification and Analysis of Multi-factor
Authentication Protocols   138
    Federico Sinigaglia, Roberto Carbone, Gabriele Costa,
    and Silvio Ranise

A Risk-Driven Model to Minimize the Effects of Human Factors
on Smart Devices   156
    Sandeep Gupta, Attaullah Buriro, and Bruno Crispo

A Formal Security Analysis of the $p \equiv p$ Authentication Protocol
for Decentralized Key Distribution and End-to-End Encrypted Email. 171
   Itzel Vazquez Sandoval and Gabriele Lenzini

Author Index 189

Logics to Reason Formally About Trust Computation and Manipulation

Alessandro Aldini$^{(\boxtimes)}$ and Mirko Tagliaferri

University of Urbino, Urbino, Italy
{alessandro.aldini,mirko.tagliaferri}@uniurb.it

Abstract. Trust represents a fundamental, complementary ingredient for the success of security mechanisms in computer science, as it goes beyond the intrinsic, technical aspects of cybersecurity, by involving the subjective perception of users, the willingness to collaborate and expose own resources and capabilities, and the judgement about the expected behavior of other parties. Computational notions of trust are formalized to support automatically the process of building and maintaining trust infrastructures, and mathematical logics provide the formal means to reason about the efficacy of such a process. In this work we advocate the use of two logical approaches to the modeling and verification of the two main tasks at the base of any trust infrastructure: the initial computation of trust values and the dynamic manipulation of such values.

Keywords: Computational trust · Modal logic · Conceptual analysis of trust

1 Introduction

Providing a secure environment on the Internet is a daunting task and a massive use of hard-security mechanisms does not guarantee the honest agents against outside attacks. Moreover, there is always a disparity in the resources required to offer proper defence mechanisms and the ones required to build successful attacks. Even admitting a completely safe environment, agents in the online community might still fall victims of deceit and scam. For these reasons, it has been argued [34] that social control mechanisms, employed as soft-security mechanisms, can integrate successfully the classical methodologies based, e.g., on encryption, access control policies, and authentication. First, they distribute the burden of protection on the whole community, therefore putting a balance in the amount of resources required to defend and to attack the system. Second, differently from hard-security mechanisms, which, if passed, often allow full access to the target of attack, soft-security mechanisms expect and even accept that there might be unwanted intruders in the system, but they help in identifying those intruders and then prevent them from harming the community at large, meanwhile limiting the amount of actions a given intruder might perform in the system.

© Springer Nature Switzerland AG 2020
A. Saracino and P. Mori (Eds.): ETAA 2019, LNCS 11967, pp. 1–15, 2020.
https://doi.org/10.1007/978-3-030-39749-4_1

Among the various typologies of social control mechanisms, trust is the best suited to foster positive behaviors and limit malevolent ones. However, digital environments lack the proper features that would allow a natural form of trust to emerge [31]. Therefore, computational notions of trust must be built artificially in the environment by using rigorous models that can be automated. Typically, trust is modeled as a relation between an agent/entity (the trustor) and another agent/entity (the trustee) *estimating* the expectation of the trustor about the future behavior of the trustee on which the trustor depends. Such a relation is always characterized by some degree of epistemic uncertainty, concerned with an unavoidable lack of knowledge, and, very often, nondeterminism, concerned with the subjectivity of the personal perception of trust, which may induce different reactions under the same conditions. These features are opposed to the notion of trustworthiness, which refers to the inherent, objective quality of the trustee [8]. Hence, trust is related to risk, but also opportunity.

There exists a strict, inherent relation between trust and hard-security policies and mechanisms such as authentication and authorization [11]. For instance, in pass-through authentication mechanisms, the trust relation between two domains enables user accounts as well as global groups to be employed in another domain other than the domain where accounts and groups are defined. In digital identity trusted ecosystems and federations, trust is part of the verification process of the attributes that work together to ensure identity authentication. Trust models can be also used in combination with emerging technologies supporting authentication [3], lightweight authentication protocols [19], or as a tool to trade between privacy issues and the intrusive nature of complex, multifactor authentication mechanisms [4]. Moreover, trust models can support authorization systems to deal with multiple domains of administrative control, partial knowledge of all users, highly volatile environments, dynamic mechanisms (such as delegation and revocation), need for flexibility and expressiveness in schemes purely based on identities [9,23,24,39,49].

In general, computational trust models have two fundamental, distinguished roles: explaining how trust is generated (see, e.g., [28]) and then explaining the dynamics of trust (see, e.g., [21,48]), which, respectively, amount to define a computing component and a manipulation component of trust. Even if the two components integrate with each other naturally to provide a comprehensive notion of trust, they rarely receive the same attention within a unique framework. In this paper, we advocate the use of two formal models of trust, one for each of such components, in a logical framework. In this setting, the formal modeling and verification of trust is not a novel research field. For instance, temporal trust properties can be model checked as CTL properties [14], thus providing a formal framework for the verification of the trust manipulation component. On the other hand, (modal) logics for trust (and notions of reputation), typically inspired by classical definitions of trust [10], have been defined to reason formally about trust and trust computation [18,30,38]. Our objective is to bridge the gap between the two components of trust by defining a formal, logical framework representing a step towards a uniform approach to trust analysis. To this aim, in the following we first summarize some elements characterizing different forms and aspects of the notion of trust that will be helpful to understand certain modeling choices (Sect. 2). Then we introduce two logical approaches to trust computation (Sect. 3) and trust manipulation (Sect. 4). Some conclusions follow (Sect. 5).

2 Trust: Origins and Varieties

Modeling the different aspects that affect the generation and maintenance of trust relationships is a task that requires a clear comprehension of the variables at play. Trust is a complex, multifaceted notion due to the several subjective elements contributing to its definition. Hence, before illustrating how to reason mathematically about a computational notion of trust, it is worth setting the context.

Navigating through the various definitions of trust given in the different disciplines is a burdensome task. First of all, disciplines as diverse as sociology [5,12,26,35], economy [13,15,36,47], political science [16,17,25] and evolutionary biology [6,44,45] dedicated some of their attention to trust, obviously prioritizing their specific needs and using their typical examination techniques. This produced many theoretical definitions of trust which diverge on the technical language employed to express the definitions and the principal features that are highlighted. More recently, in the last two decades, various and distinct formal, computational notions of trust have been developed to cope with the ever increasing necessity of implementing soft-security mechanisms in digital environments [20,22,29,32,37,41].

To classify trust, three dimensions emerge that describe in different ways the nature of the trust relation, the nature of the agents subject to trust and the context in which trust is evaluated [35,43,46]. The trust relation can be established according to strategic or moralistic considerations. A strategic approach to trust identifies the explicit knowledge and evaluation mechanisms that contribute to the decision making process. Such an approach typically relies on quantitative (e.g., probabilistic) methods to estimate trust. On the other hand, a moralistic approach relies on moral and ethical issues and, therefore, depends on psychological predispositions (due to, e.g., social norms and culture), which very often are necessary to initiate a trust relationship whenever past experience and significant knowledge are not available.

Trust definitions can be particular or general, depending on whether the phenomenon of trusting is modeled as a one-to-one relation or as a one-to-many relation, respectively. Notice that general trust can be placed on anonymous or unknown individuals whenever they belong to a group, organization, or institution with which a trust relationship exists by virtue of several, different motivations, either strategic or moralistic.

Trust may also refer to a specific context of evaluation (simplex notion of trust), meaning that trust is granted with respect to a specific task, so that different tasks require different trust estimations. Otherwise, it can be viewed as a context-free or multi-context phenomenon (multiplex notion of trust), where the trustee is evaluated without reference to any specific scenario or with respect to multiple, different tasks, respectively.

The three dimensions identify a space within which various notions of trust can be mapped and defined. Another important distinction that should be considered concerns whether trust must be computed or manipulated. The first task consists in computing trust on the basis of the belief and attitude that are specific in a given instant of time, including the special case of the startup phase. In practice, a computing component is fundamental for the trust bootstrap and depends strictly on the nature of trust as specified by the varieties surveyed above. The second task is related to the trust manipulation and the way in which trust evolves dynamically in time by virtue of the events and interactions that may affect the subjective perception of the trustor. Trust models covering these dynamics are typically used not only to update trust relationships but also to build the reputation of agents in their reference community [41]. In the following, we present two different logics for reasoning about these two tasks, respectively.

3   LCT: A Logic for Computing Trust

In this section we present a multi-agent modal logic for computing trust (LCT, for short). It relies on previous work on single-agent formalisms [40,42,43] and is inspired by neighborhood structures for the interpretation of the modal part [7,33], augmented with a machinery to estimate the relevance of beliefs[1] with respect to the problem of evaluating trust. Hence, the basic goal of this logic is to compute trust estimations on the base of the beliefs of the agents in a given instant of time.

3.1   Syntax

In LCT, the ground ingredients are a countable set At of atomic propositions $p, p', q, q' \ldots$, representing basic pieces of information (e.g., "Alice is trustworthy", "The access to Bob's LAN is SSL-VPN protected"), and a finite set Ag of agents $i, j, \ldots$. The language is defined by this grammar:

$$\phi ::= p \mid \neg\phi \mid \phi \wedge \phi \mid T(i, \phi)$$

where $i \in Ag$ and $p \in At$. Formula $T(i, \phi)$, called trust formula, should be intuitively read as "Agent i trusts that ϕ holds"; the set of trust formulas of the form $T(i, \phi)$ is denoted by Tf. In the following, we assume that the set $\mathcal{L}_{ct}$ of formulas generated by the grammar above is ranged over by $\phi, \psi, \ldots$, while $At \cup Tf$ is ranged over by $a, b, \ldots$.

---

[1] Notice that it is also possible to base the semantics of LCT on notions stronger than belief, like, e.g., classical definitions of knowledge from epistemic modal logic. However, we prefer using belief as it is a more general notion and it can capture better the cognitive states of human agents.

3.2 Semantics

The semantics of LCT is in truth-theoretical form and is based on formal models designed specifically to formalize trust and to allow reasoning about such a notion. Formally, $\mathcal{L}_{ct}$ formulas are interpreted in the following model.

Definition 1. *A **trust model** is a tuple* $M = (S, \pi, B, \Delta, \Theta)$, *where:*

- S *is a countable set of states, ranged over by* $s, s', \ldots$;
- $\pi : At \mapsto \mathcal{P}(S)$ *is the valuation function;*
- B *is the belief function set, which is a family of belief functions:*

$$b_i : S \mapsto (\mathcal{P}(S) \setminus \emptyset) \; \forall i \in Ag;$$

- Δ *is the trust relevance set, which is a family of quantitative trust relevance functions:*

$$\delta_{a,i} : \mathcal{P}(S) \mapsto [0,1] \; \forall a \in At \cup Tf, \; i \in Ag$$

such that $\sum_{X \subseteq S} \delta_{a,i}(X) = 1$;
- Θ *is the thresholds set, which is a family of trust threshold functions*

$$\theta_i : (At \cup Tf) \mapsto [0,1] \; \forall i \in Ag.$$

The set S of states of the system is defined as in standard modal logic; subsets of S are ranged over by $X, X', \ldots$. The valuation function π assigns to each atomic proposition p the set of states in which p holds.

The belief function b_i, with $i \in Ag$, assigns to every $s \in S$ the consistent set of states that are *compatible* with what is believed by i in s. More precisely, given the beliefs of i in the current state s, $b_i(s)$ is the set of all and only the states of S in which such beliefs hold. Notice that if i believes all the true statements identifying state s independently of the current state s', then i believes that s is the only possible current state, i.e., $b_i(s') = \{s\} \; \forall s' \in S$. Such an example emphasizes that it might be the case that a given state s is not included in $b_i(s)$, since an agent i can believe something that is actually false.

The quantitative trust relevance function $\delta_{a,i}$, with $a \in At \cup Tf$ and $i \in Ag$, assigns to every $X \subseteq S$ a value indicating the quantitative relevance of X for agent i to trust a. All such values are additive to 1. The interpretation is as follows. Each statement representing a piece of information that is relevant for trusting a (from the viewpoint of i) corresponds formally to the set X of states in which the statement holds. Hence, $\delta_{a,i}(X)$ expresses the contribution of the information given by such a statement to the computation of the trust of i towards a.

The threshold function θ_i, with $i \in Ag$, assigns to each $a \in At \cup Tf$ the threshold needed by i to trust a.

Before providing the truth definition for a formula in a trust pointed model, some additional functions must be defined. First of all, we extend functions θ_i to deal with any composed formula.

Definition 2. *Given a threshold function θ_i, the extended function θ_i^e is defined recursively as follows:*

- $\theta_i^e(a) = \theta_i(a), \forall a \in At \cup Tf$
- $\theta_i^e(\neg\phi) = 1 - \theta_i^e(\phi)$
- $\theta_i^e(\phi \wedge \psi) = max(\theta_i^e(\phi), \theta_i^e(\psi))$

The role of function θ_i^e is to assign a trust threshold value to all formulas of $\mathcal{L}_{ct}$. In particular, the case of negation captures the intuitive idea that when it is easy to trust a formula, then the negation of such a formula is hard to trust, and viceversa. Then, in order to trust a conjunction, it is necessary to consider the highest threshold value between the two conjuncts.

The next additional function is intended to establish the ideal value of trust in the current state s towards a statement in $At \cup Tf$. The computed value is ideal as it depends on the contributions of all the information relevant for trust that hold in s, independently on the beliefs of the agent involved.

Definition 3. *Given a trust model $M = (S, \pi, B, \Delta, \Theta)$, the trust value function $\tau_{a,i} : S \mapsto [0,1]$, with $a \in At \cup Tf$ and $i \in Ag$, is defined as:*

$$\tau_{a,i}(s) = \sum_{s \in X \subseteq S} \delta_{a,i}(X) \tag{1}$$

Function $\tau_{a,i}$ assigns to formula a the ideal trust value of agent i towards such a formula by assuming that i is aware of the fact that s is the current state of the world. Such a value is determined by summing up the weights of all the pieces of information that are considered to be relevant for trust from the viewpoint of i and that are satisfied in s. Notice that, as in the case of functions θ_i, both atomic propositions and trust formulas are treated atomically. This is because, in general, we assume that for both cases the estimations determined by i can depend only on the conditions assumed by i. For the other, composed formulas, the estimations can be derived depending on the semantics of the operators.

Definition 4. *The extended trust value function $\tau_{\phi,i}^e : S \mapsto [0,1]$, with $\phi \in \mathcal{L}_{ct}$ and $i \in Ag$, is defined recursively as follows:*

- $\tau_{a,i}^e(s) = \tau_{a,i}(s) \ \forall a \in At \cup Tf$
- $\tau_{\neg\phi,i}^e(s) = 1 - \tau_{\phi,i}^e(s)$
- $\tau_{\phi\wedge\psi,i}^e(s) = min(\frac{\tau_{\phi,i}^e(s) \cdot \theta_i^e(\phi\wedge\psi)}{\theta_i^e(\phi)}, \frac{\tau_{\psi,i}^e(s) \cdot \theta_i^e(\phi\wedge\psi)}{\theta_i^e(\psi)})$

The case of negation is managed according with the same intuition behind the definition of $\theta_i^e(\neg\phi)$. The case of conjunction is managed in a way inspired by probability theory and requires some special treatment in the limiting cases in which $\theta_i^e(\_) = 0$. In particular, if $\theta_i^e(\phi) = 0$, it holds that $\theta_i^e(\phi \wedge \psi) = \theta_i^e(\psi)$. Therefore, if $\tau_{\phi,i}^e(s) > 0$, then it is immediate to obtain $\tau_{(\phi\wedge\psi,i)}^e(s) = \tau_{\psi,i}^e(s)$, which captures the intuition that trust value and threshold of $\phi \wedge \psi$ depend on ψ only as ϕ is trivially trusted. On the other hand, if $\tau_{\phi,i}^e(s) = 0$ then we would have an indeterminate form that it is safe to manage by assuming $\tau_{(\phi\wedge\psi,i)}^e(s) = 0$, thus capturing the intuition that since there is no trust towards ϕ, there can be no trust towards $\phi \wedge \psi$. The symmetric case $\theta_i^e(\psi) = 0$ is analogous.

Given all the above functions, it is now possible to give a truth definition for LCT.

Definition 5 (Satisfiability relation). *Given a trust model* $M = (S, \pi, B, \Delta, \Theta)$ *and* $s \in S$, *it holds that formula* $\phi \in \mathcal{L}_{ct}$ *is true in a pointed trust model* (M, s) $((M, s) \models \phi)$ *if:*

- $(M, s) \models p$ *iff* $s \in \pi(p)$ $\forall p \in At$;
- $(M, s) \models \neg \phi$ *iff* $(M, s) \not\models \phi$;
- $(M, s) \models \phi \wedge \psi$ *iff* $(M, s) \models \phi$ *and* $(M, s) \models \psi$;
- $(M, s) \models T(i, \phi)$ *iff* $\forall s' \in b_i(s). \tau_{\phi,i}^e(s') > \theta_i^e(\phi)$.

The case of the trust operator emphasizes the subjective character of trust, as in order to trust ϕ, the agent has to consider the trust values related to all the states that are compatible with her beliefs, and to compare each of them with the trust threshold. The semantics of the T operator relies on the classical assumption that if the beliefs of the agent are partial and do not reveal the identity of the current state, then the worst case scenario is to be considered, by taking the minimum among all the possible trust values associated with the candidate states determined by the belief conditions of the agent.

Definition 6 (Satisfiability and validity). *A formula* $\phi \in \mathcal{L}_{ct}$ *is satisfiable in a trust model* M *iff there exists* $s \in S \in M$ *such that* $(M, s) \models \phi$. *If* $\forall s \in S \in M$ *it holds that* $(M, s) \models \phi$, *then* ϕ *is valid in* M $(M \models \phi)$. *If* $\forall M$ *it holds that* $M \models \phi$, *then* ϕ *is valid* $(\models \phi)$.

We notice that, as usual, a formula ϕ is valid if, and only if, the negation of the formula $\neg \phi$ is not satisfiable. We conclude the presentation of the semantics of LCT by showing the following decidability result about the problem of model checking $(M, s) \models \phi$.

Theorem 1. *The model checking problem* $(M, s) \models \phi$ *is decidable for LCT by using an algorithm with complexity* $\mathcal{O}(|\phi|^2 \cdot |S|)$.

In essence, LCT provides a formal framework in which it is possible to define and characterize quantitatively the trust relevant information for a given agent in order to trust a certain formula. Based on such a characterization, we have the formal means to compute the trust towards the formula in any state of the world and, depending on the threshold applied, decide whether the formula can be trusted or not. The computed trust is expressed in terms of the values $\tau_{\phi,i}^e(s)$ and, as we will see, represents the starting metric to consider whenever passing to the framework in which the dynamics of trust are evaluated as time goes on.

3.3 LCT and the Trust Taxonomy

By following the same lines of previous work [43], it is straightforward to extend LCT to make the model sensitive to specific contexts of evaluation. To this end, it is sufficient to add to the structure M the set of contexts C and to parameterize with respect to $c \in C$ the elements of Δ and of Θ. Accordingly, by using the extended function $\tau^e_{\phi,i,c}$, the satisfiability problem can consider such an additional aspect, by turning into $(M, s, c) \models \phi$.

By extending the notions of validity as well, we obtain interesting insights with respect to the taxonomy of the different notions of trust. For instance, the strategic notion of trust is characterized by the fact that in no context the·formula of interest turns out to be model-valid. The reason is that the information holding in the various states represents a key element for the satisfiability of trust. On the other hand, if it holds that there exists a context for which the formula of interest is model-valid, then what is known is not relevant for the attribution of trust. In other words, whatever the state of the system is, trust will be granted. This kind of behavior is typical of situations in which moralistic trust is taken into account, as well as cases in which the cost of distrusting is orders of magnitude higher than the potential benefit of trusting. If a trust formula is satisfied in a given state for each possible context, then the notion under consideration is that of multiplex trust, as opposite to the case in which the result of the evaluation depends on the chosen context (simplex trust). Notice that, model-validity with respect to both the set of states and the set of contexts captures intuitively a notion of moralistic multiplex trust. Finally, as far as the whom dimension of trust is concerned, the distinction between particular and general conceptions of trust is not explicitly characterized by any definition of satisfiability and validity. This is due to the fact that this dimension is not captured by these principles but, instead, by the meaning of the atomic propositions that are subject to trust evaluation. In fact, a proposition may refer to a single fact or agent, as well as an entity representing a class of agents.

4   LMT: A Logic for Trust Manipulation

The second logical language we present has been conceived to specify and then model check trust-based properties of dynamic networks of agents obeying the rules of the given trust model that governs the trust-based relationships among agents [1]. The underlying semantics of such a system is based on state/transition systems expressing both the behavior of the agents and the information required by the trust model. With respect to the varieties of trust, we introduce the theory for strategic, particular, simplex models. We start by introducing a classical notion of labeled transition system and then we extend it to deal with trust information.

Definition 7. *A labeled transition system (LTS) is a tuple* (Q, q_0, L, R), *where:*

- Q *is a finite set of states (with q_0 the initial one);*
- L *is a finite set of labels;*
- $R \subseteq Q \times L \times Q$ *is a finitely-branching transition relation.*

We assume that each $q \in Q$ represents a global state of the system expressed as a vector of local states, each one denoting the local behavior of every agent composing the system. The transitions in R represent the execution of events, and the labels in L range over the names of such events, each one denoting either an autonomous move of an agent, or an interaction between agents. The LTS representation of the behavior of the system needs to be extended with pieces of information needed to feed the trust model regulating the trust-based interactions among agents. To this aim, we enrich the states with such additional information.

Definition 8. *Let V be the domain of trust variables and $\mathbb{T}$ the domain of trust values. A trust labeled transition system (tLTS) is a tuple $(Q, q_0, L, R, \mathcal{T}, P)$ where:*

- *(Q, q_0, L, R) is a LTS;*
- *$\mathcal{T}$ is a finite set of trust predicates of the form $v = k$, with $v \in V$ and $k \in \mathbb{T}$;*
- *$P : Q \rightarrow (\mathcal{T} \rightarrow \mathbb{N})$ is a labeling function that associates a multiset of $\mathcal{T}$ to each state of the tLTS.*

Set V contains all the variables needed by the trust model to compute trust metrics. In practice, each $v \in V$ represents a trust-relevant piece of information feeding the trust model. For instance, in several trust models (see, e.g., [27] and the references therein), in order to compute the trust metric t_{ij}, denoting the trust of agent i towards agent j, it is necessary to collect all the rates i has assigned to j by virtue of the evaluation of the interactions occurred between them. Denoted by e_{ij} such an evaluation, predicate $e_{ij} = 1$ may represent a positive feedback reported by i after a satisfactory interaction with j. Notice that i may experience several such interactions, thus motivating the need for dealing with multisets of predicates. As another example, a typical class of variables feeding the trust model is that expressing recommendations provided by the agents.

In order to allow for the representation of several different trust models, here we consider a very general and abstract definition that considers the basic ingredients shared by the majority of trust models in the literature.

Definition 9. *A trust model is a mathematical structure encompassing:*

- *a black box taking in input trust-relevant information encoded in the current state of the tLTS and updating the trust metrics expressing the trust relations among agents;*
- *a trust threshold function that, for each agent, returns the minimum value required by the agent to trust other agents;*
- *initial estimations of the trust metrics, known as dispositional trust values.*

For the sake of simplicity, in the following we assume that trust thresholds and trust metrics expressing the trust relations among agents are represented by values in the domain $[0, 1]$. Notice that for several sophisticated models of trust, the threshold function can be accompanied by further parameters configured at the level of each single agent. However, it is worth observing that usually in the literature on models for trust manipulation, it is not specified the way in which the dispositional trust must be assessed, sometimes as an intermediate value in the range of trust values, sometimes as the combination of prefetched information collected through alternative ways or by employing pre-existing, unspecified relations among agents, sometimes chosen by the agent, probably on the basis of her attitude to initiate new interactions with unknown users. In our setting, we propose to solve formally such a lack by employing the values returned by model checking LCT formulas. In fact, given $\phi \in \mathcal{L}_{ct}$ the formula concerning the trustworthiness of an agent $j \neq i$, the truth value of the formula $T(i, \phi)$ establishes whether i trusts j, and the values $\tau^e_{\phi,i}(s)$, which are used to determine such a truth value, can be employed to determine the initial value of the trust metric t_{ij}. In particular, if we follow the same intuition behind the semantics of $T(i, \phi)$, among all the $\tau^e_{\phi,i}(s)$ that contribute to the evaluation of $T(i, \phi)$, we take the minimum value to initialize t_{ij}.

Until now we have defined the ingredients of the formal semantic model underlying the behavior of a network of interacting agents, without specifying how such a model is derived. This is typically done by employing formal specification languages with a translation semantics towards state/transition systems, thus enabling verification techniques like model checking. Among the various possibilities, process algebra represent a well-established approach. Instead of proposing a specific language (see, e.g., [1,2], where two different process algebraic languages are defined with an underlying semantics compatible with the notion of tLTS), here we list three basic features that must be possessed to model properly a trust-based system with a tLTS based semantics:

- capability of expressing interacting agents (parallel composition, communication, synchronization);
- semantic rules, expressing the execution of trust-relevant events, with conclusions that allow for the update of the set of trust predicates that label the tLTS states and feed the trust model;
- semantic rules, expressing the execution of trust-relevant events, with premises checking the trust metrics against the trust thresholds as returned by the trust model (in order to model trust-based alternative choices).

Once the behavior of a system is formally given in terms of a tLTS, trust-based properties can be specified through a logic for trust manipulation (LMT, for short). The syntax of LMT is defined as follows:

$$\Phi ::= \ true \mid \alpha \mid w > k \mid \Phi \wedge \Phi \mid \neg \Phi \mid A\Psi \mid E\Psi$$
$$\Psi ::= \ \Phi \, _{\mathcal{A}_1} U \, \Phi \mid \Phi \, _{\mathcal{A}_1} U_{\mathcal{A}_2} \, \Phi$$

where $\mathcal{A}_1, \mathcal{A}_2 \subseteq L$, $\alpha \in L$, $k \in \mathbb{T}$, and w ranges over $V \cup$ the set of mathematical combinations of the trust variables satisfying some predicate (e.g., the sum of all the e_{ij} for some given i and j) $\cup$ the set of trust metrics t_{ij}. Therefore, we have two types of state-based statements: either events or predicates about trust variables, mathematical combinations of selected trust variables, and trust metrics. State formulas, which range over Φ, include atomic statements, logical combinations of state formulas, universally (A) and existentially (E) quantified path formulas. Path formulas, which range over Ψ, include two types of indexed until operator, where the indexes $\mathcal{A}_1, \mathcal{A}_2$ are sets of events.

The intuitive interpretation of the operators is given as follows with respect to a tLTS $(Q, q_0, L, R, \mathcal{T}, P)$. A state $q \in Q$ satisfies an event-based predicate α if it enables a transition labeled with α. On the other hand, q satisfies a trust-based predicate $w > k$ if the evaluation of w in q, denoted by w_q, satisfies the condition $>k$. The evaluation of w in q depends on the trust predicates labeling q, i.e., $P(q)$. If w is a trust metric, then it is computed by the trust model that takes as input values the trust information encoded in $P(q)$. The logical connectives and the quantifiers over the paths have the usual interpretation. In particular, a path satisfies the until formula $\Phi_{\mathcal{A}_1} U \Phi'$ if along the path a state satisfying Φ' is visited, while until reaching such a state, all the visited states satisfy Φ and all the executed events belong to $\mathcal{A}_1$. The only difference in the interpretation of the until formula $\Phi_{\mathcal{A}_1} U_{\mathcal{A}_2} \Phi'$ is that the event leading to the state satisfying Φ' belongs to $\mathcal{A}_2$. Such a difference emphasizes that a path satisfying $\Phi_{\mathcal{A}_1} U_{\mathcal{A}_2} \Phi'$ includes at least a transition. Instead, a state q satisfying Φ' satisfies also $\Phi_{\mathcal{A}_1} U \Phi'$ independently of its outgoing transitions, if any.

In order to introduce the formal semantics of the operators, we recall some notations. A path σ is a (possibly infinite) sequence of transitions of the form:

$$q_0 \xrightarrow{\alpha_0} q_1 \ldots q_{j-1} \xrightarrow{\alpha_{j-1}} q_j \ldots$$

where $q_{j-1} \xrightarrow{\alpha_{j-1}} q_j$ denotes the transition $(q_{j-1}, \alpha_{j-1}, q_j) \in R$, for each $j > 0$. Every state q_j in the path is denoted by $\sigma(j)$. Moreover, $q_j \xrightarrow{\mathcal{A}} q_{j+1}$ can be used in the case $\alpha_j \in \mathcal{A} \subseteq L$. We denote with $Path(q)$ the set of paths starting in state $q \in Q$. Then, the formal semantics of LMT is shown in Table 1.

As a shorthand, the derived operators of Table 2 are defined. Such abbreviations allow for the definition of compact patterns that represent trust-based variants of classical formulas used in the setting of safety analysis. Some examples are given by reachability:

$$EF(t_{ij} > k \wedge \alpha)$$

and its variants given by conditional and extended reachability:

$$E(t_{ij} > k \ _{\mathcal{A}_l} U \ \alpha)$$
$$AGEF(t_{ij} > k)$$
$$EFEG_{\mathcal{A}_1}.$$

As an example, the first conditional reachability pattern can be used to define a property stating whether eventually a certain (trust-based) action α is executed, provided that along the path preceding it, while executing actions in $\mathcal{A}_1$ only, j is trusted by i if the trust threshold is k. Another interesting class of properties is related to liveness:

$$AG(t_{ij} > k \rightarrow AF\alpha)$$
$$AG(\alpha \rightarrow AG(t_{ij} > k))$$

Table 1. Semantics of LMT.

$$
\begin{aligned}
&q \models \textit{true} && \textit{holds always} \\
&q \models \alpha && \textit{iff } \exists q' : q \xrightarrow{\alpha} q' \in R \\
&q \models w > k && \textit{iff } w_q > k \\
&q \models \Phi \wedge \Phi' && \textit{iff } s \models \Phi \textit{ and } s \models \Phi' \\
&q \models \neg \Phi && \textit{iff } s \not\models \Phi \\
&q \models A\Psi && \textit{iff } \forall \sigma \in \textit{Path}(q) : \sigma \models \Psi \\
&q \models E\Psi && \textit{iff } \exists \sigma \in \textit{Path}(q) : \sigma \models \Psi \\[1em]
&\sigma \models \Phi \,_{\mathcal{A}_1}U\, \Phi' && \textit{iff } \exists n \geq 0 : \\
&&& \sigma(n) \models \Phi' \wedge (\textit{for all } 0 \leq i < n : \sigma(i) \models \Phi \wedge \sigma(i) \xrightarrow{\mathcal{A}_1} \sigma(i+1)) \\[0.5em]
&\sigma \models \Phi \,_{\mathcal{A}_1}U_{\mathcal{A}_2}\, \Phi' && \textit{iff } \exists n > 0 : \\
&&& \sigma(n) \models \Phi' \wedge (\textit{for all } 0 \leq i < n-1 : \sigma(i) \models \Phi \wedge \\
&&& \sigma(i) \xrightarrow{\mathcal{A}_1} \sigma(i+1)) \wedge \sigma(n-1) \models \Phi \wedge \sigma(n-1) \xrightarrow{\mathcal{A}_2} \sigma(n)
\end{aligned}
$$

which can be used to state whether certain conditions about trust are sufficient to enable the execution of certain (trust-based actions), or viceversa.

By considering that the granularity of the trust-based information and of the trust model parameters is at the level of the single agent, these patterns can be used to perform sensitivity analysis with respect to the parameters governing the trust model. Moreover, it is possible to verify the effects of pro-social attitudes of the agents, malicious behaviors of single agents or coalitions of agents, fake information injected by such malicious agents in order to execute bad mouthing (false negative recommendations about honest agents), ballot stuffing (false positive recommendations about dishonest agents), collusion, and so on. Analogously, since the model can easily capture dynamic behaviors, even the related attacks can be model checked, such as on-off (agents alternating good and bad behaviors), sybil (adversaries creating multiple fake colluding agents), white-washing (change of identity when reputation is compromised), and so on. For instance,

Table 2. Derived operators of LMT.

$$
\begin{aligned}
X\Phi &= \textit{false} \,_0U_L\, \Phi \\
X_{\mathcal{A}_1}\Phi &= \textit{false} \,_0U_{\mathcal{A}_1}\, \Phi \\
EF\Phi &= E(\textit{true} \,_LU\, \Phi) \\
EF_{\mathcal{A}_1}\Phi &= E(\textit{true} \,_LU_{\mathcal{A}_1}\, \Phi) \\
AF\Phi &= A(\textit{true} \,_LU\, \Phi) \\
AF_{\mathcal{A}_1}\Phi &= A(\textit{true} \,_LU_{\mathcal{A}_1}\, \Phi) \\
EG\Phi &= \neg AF \neg \Phi \\
EG_{\mathcal{A}_1} &= \neg AF_{L-\mathcal{A}_1} \textit{true} \\
AG\Phi &= \neg EF \neg \Phi \\
AG_{\mathcal{A}_1} &= \neg EF_{L-\mathcal{A}_1} \textit{true}
\end{aligned}
$$

examples of trust models that have been modeled formally are Eigentrust and Subjective Logic; more specific trust systems that have been modeled, compared, and analyzed are Trust-Incentive Service Management, Reputation-based Framework for Sensor Networks, Robust Reputation System [1,2].

5   Conclusion

Two logical languages have been discussed that propose a formal framework for the modeling and analysis of a general notion of trust and of its operational components.

The language LCT is general enough to capture a wide range of trust notions. Certain semantic choices can be further generalized to obtain a meta-theory of trust in which any desired form of trust computation (e.g., based on knowledge rather than belief) and trust property can be formalized. To this aim, it is worth studying axiomatizations in order to investigate potential properties of interest, like, e.g., trust transitivity. Second, it is worth comparing the notions of trust and knowledge/belief, with respect to the typical properties that are considered in the literature of modal logics, like, e.g., soundness and introspection.

The language LMT, as presented in this paper, offers a meta-theory for the specification and analysis of computational trust models. Model checking techniques have been used to test its expressiveness and flexibility in estimating the properties of real-world trust systems and their robustness against several classes of attacks. As a fundamental future work, the bridge between the two logics still requires the definition of an algorithmic process enabling the two-steps automated analysis of the computing and manipulating components of trust.

References

1. Aldini, A.: Modeling and verification of trust and reputation systems. J. Secur. Commun. Netw. 8(16), 2933–2946 (2015)
2. Aldini, A.: Design and verification of trusted collective adaptive systems. Trans. Model. Comput. Simul. (TOMACS) 28(2), Article no. 9 (2018). https://doi.org/10.1145/3155337
3. Alexopoulos, N., Daubert, J., Mühlhäuser, M., Habib, S.M.: Beyond the hype: on using blockchains in trust management for authentication. In: IEEE Trustcom/BigDataSE/ICESS, pp. 546–553. IEEE (2017)
4. Anakath, A., Rajakumar, S., Ambika, S.: Privacy preserving multi factor authentication using trust management. Clust. Comput. 22, 10817–10823 (2019)
5. Barber, B.: The Logic and Limits of Trust. Rutgers University Press, New Brunswick (1983)
6. Bateson, P.: The biological evolution of cooperation and trust. In: Gambetta, D. (ed.) Trust: Making and Breaking Cooperative Relations, pp. 31–48. Blackwell, New York (1988)
7. van Benthem, J., Fernández-Duque, D., Pacuit, E.: Evidence logic: a new look at neighborhood structures. Adv. Modal Log. 9, 97–118 (2012)

8. Solhaug, B., Stølen, K.: Uncertainty, subjectivity, trust and risk: how it all fits together. In: Meadows, C., Fernandez-Gago, C. (eds.) STM 2011. LNCS, vol. 7170, pp. 1–5. Springer, Heidelberg (2012). https://doi.org/10.1007/978-3-642-29963-6_1

9. Blaze, M., Feigenbaum, J., Ioannidis, J., Keromytis, A.D.: The role of trust management in distributed systems security. In: Vitek, J., Jensen, C.D. (eds.) Secure Internet Programming. LNCS, vol. 1603, pp. 185–210. Springer, Heidelberg (1999). https://doi.org/10.1007/3-540-48749-2_8

10. Castelfranchi, C., Falcone, R.: Principles of trust for MAS: cognitive anatomy, social importance, and quantification. In: International Conference on Multi Agent Systems (ICMAS), pp. 72–79. IEEE (1988)

11. Chapin, P.C., Skalka, C., Wang, X.S.: Authorization in trust management: features and foundations. Comput. Surv. **40**(3), 9:1–9:48 (2008)

12. Coleman, J.: Foundations of Social Theory. Harvard University Press, Cambridge (1990)

13. Dasgupta, P.: Trust as a commodity. In: Gambetta, D. (ed.) Trust: Making and Breaking Cooperative Relations, pp. 49–72. Blackwell, New York (1988)

14. Drawel, N., Bentahar, J., Laarej, A.: Verifying temporal trust logic using CTL model checking. In: 20th International Workshop on Trust in Agent Societies. CEUR-WS (2018)

15. Fehr, E.: On the economics and biology of trust. J. Eur. Econ. Assoc. **7**, 235–266 (2009)

16. Hardin, R.: The street-level epistemology of trust. Polit. Soc. **21**, 505–529 (1993)

17. Hardin, R.: Trust and Trustworthiness. Russell Sage Foundation, New York (2002)

18. Herzig, A., Hübner, J.F., Lorini, E., Vercouter, L.: A logic of trust and reputation. Log. J. IGPL **18**(1), 214–244 (2010)

19. Husseini, A., M'Hamed, A., ElHassan, B.A., Mokhtaari, M.: A novel trust-based authentication scheme for low-resource devices in smart environments. Pers. Ubiquit. Comput. **5**(5), 362–369 (2011)

20. Jøsang, A.: Trust and reputation systems. In: Aldini, A., Gorrieri, R. (eds.) FOSAD 2006-2007. LNCS, vol. 4677, pp. 209–245. Springer, Heidelberg (2007). https://doi.org/10.1007/978-3-540-74810-6_8

21. Jøsang, A.: Subjective Logic. Springer, Cham (2016). https://doi.org/10.1007/978-3-319-42337-1

22. Jøsang, A., Ismail, R., Boyd, C.: A survey of trust and reputation systems for online service provision. Decis. Support Syst. **43**(2), 618–644 (2007)

23. Kim, H., Lee, E.A.: Authentication and authorization for the Internet of Things. IEEE IT Prof. **19**(5), 27–33 (2017)

24. Koshutanski, H., Massacci, F.: An interactive trust management and negotiation scheme. In: Dimitrakos, T., Martinelli, F. (eds.) Formal Aspects in Security and Trust. IIFIP, vol. 173, pp. 115–128. Springer, Boston (2005). https://doi.org/10.1007/0-387-24098-5_9

25. Levi, M.: A state of trust. In: Braithwaite, V., Levi, M., Cook, K., Hardin, R. (eds.) Trust and Governance, pp. 77–101. Russell Sage Foundation, New York (1998)

26. Luhmann, N.: Trust and Power. Wiley, New York (1979)

27. Mármol, F.G., Pérez, G.M.: Trust and reputation models comparison. Internet Res. **21**(2), 138–153 (2011)

28. Marsh, S.: Formalising Trust as a Computational Concept. University of Stirling, Scotland (1994)

29. Mousa, H., Mokhtar, S.B., Hasan, O., Younes, O., Hadhoud, M., Brunie, L.: Trust management and reputation systems in mobile participatory sensing applications: a survey. Comput. Netw. **90**, 49–73 (2015)

30. Muller, T.: Semantics of trust. In: Degano, P., Etalle, S., Guttman, J. (eds.) FAST 2010. LNCS, vol. 6561, pp. 141–156. Springer, Heidelberg (2011). https://doi.org/10.1007/978-3-642-19751-2_10
31. Nissenbaum, H.: Securing trust online: wisdom or oxymoron. Boston Univ. Law Rev. **81**(3), 635–664 (2001)
32. Nunoo-Mensah, H., Boateng, K.O., Gadze, J.D.: The adoption of socio- and bio-inspired algorithms for trust models in wireless sensor networks: a survey. Int. J. Commun. Syst. **31**(7), e3444 (2018)
33. Pacuit, E.: Neighborhood Semantics for Modal Logic. Springer, Cham (2017). https://doi.org/10.1007/978-3-319-67149-9
34. Rasmusson, L., Jansson, S.: Simulated social control for secure Internet commerce. In: Proceedings of the Workshop on New Security Paradigms, pp. 18–25 (1996)
35. Robbins, B.G.: What is trust? A multidisciplinary review, critique, and synthesis. Sociol. Compass **10**(10), 972–986 (2016)
36. Schelling, T.: The Strategy of Conflict. Harvard University Press, Cambridge (1960)
37. Seigneur, J.-M., Ahram, T., Taiar, R.: A survey on trust in augmented human technologies. In: Ahram, T., Karwowski, W., Taiar, R. (eds.) IHSED 2018. AISC, vol. 876, pp. 1033–1037. Springer, Cham (2019). https://doi.org/10.1007/978-3-030-02053-8_157
38. Singh, M.P.: Trust as dependence: a logical approach. In: 10th International Conference on Autonomous Agents and Multiagent Systems (AAMAS), pp. 863–870 (2011)
39. Singh, S., Bawa, S.: A privacy, trust and policy based authorization framework for services in distributed environments. Int. J. Comput. Sci. **2**(2), 85–92 (2007)
40. Tagliaferri, M., Aldini, A.: From knowledge to trust: a logical framework for pre-trust computations. In: Gal-Oz, N., Lewis, P.R. (eds.) IFIPTM 2018. IAICT, vol. 528, pp. 107–123. Springer, Cham (2018). https://doi.org/10.1007/978-3-319-95276-5_8
41. Tagliaferri, M., Aldini, A.: A taxonomy of computational models for trust computing in decision-making procedures. In: 17th European Conference on Cyber Warfare and Security (ECCWS), pp. 571–578. ACPI (2018)
42. Tagliaferri, M., Aldini, A.: A trust logic for pre-trust computations. In: 21th International Conference on Information Fusion (FUSION). IEEE (2018)
43. Tagliaferri, M., Aldini, A.: A trust logic for the varieties of trust. In: Camara, J., Steffen, M. (eds.) SEFM 2019. LNCS. Springer (2019, to appear)
44. Trivers, R.L.: The evolution of reciprocal altruism. Q. Rev. Biol. **46**(1), 35–57 (1971)
45. Trivers, R.L.: Natural Selection and Social Theory: Selected Papers of Robert Trivers. Oxford University Press, New York (2002)
46. Uslaner, E.M.: Who do you trust? In: Shockley, E., Neal, T.M.S., PytlikZillig, L.M., Bornstein, B.H. (eds.) Interdisciplinary Perspectives on Trust, pp. 71–83. Springer, Cham (2016). https://doi.org/10.1007/978-3-319-22261-5_4
47. Williamson, O.: Calculativeness, trust, and economic organization. J. Law Econ. **36**(2), 453–486 (1993)
48. Yu, B., Singh, M.P.: Detecting deception in reputation management. In: 2nd International Joint Conference on Autonomous Agents and Multiagent Systems (AAMAS), pp. 73–80. ACM (2003)
49. Zhang, C.C., Winslett, M.: Distributed authorization by multiparty trust negotiation. In: Jajodia, S., Lopez, J. (eds.) ESORICS 2008. LNCS, vol. 5283, pp. 282–299. Springer, Heidelberg (2008). https://doi.org/10.1007/978-3-540-88313-5_19

An Authorization Framework
for Cooperative Intelligent Transport
Systems

Sowmya Ravidas, Priyanka Karkhanis, Yanja Dajsuren, and Nicola Zannone$^{(\boxtimes)}$

Eindhoven University of Technology, Eindhoven, The Netherlands
{s.ravidas,p.d.karkhanis,y.dajsuren,n.zannone}@tue.nl

Abstract. Cooperative Intelligent Transport Systems (C-ITS) aims to enhance the existing transportation infrastructure through the use of sensing capabilities and advanced communication technologies. While improving the safety, efficiency and comfort of driving, C-ITS introduces several security and privacy challenges. Among them, a main challenge is the protection of sensitive information and resources gathered and exchanged within C-ITS. Although several authorization frameworks have been proposed over the years, they are unsuitable to deal with the demands of C-ITS. In this paper, we present an authorization framework that addresses the challenges characterizing the C-ITS domain. Our framework leverages principles of both policy-based and token-based architectures to deal with the dynamicity of C-ITS while reducing the overhead introduced by the authorization process. We demonstrate our framework using typical use case scenarios from the C-ITS domain on location tracking.

1 Introduction

Intelligent Transport Systems (ITS) are *"systems in which information and communication technologies are applied in the field of road transport, including infrastructure, vehicles and users, in traffic management and mobility management, as well as for interfaces with other modes of transport"* [4]. Cooperative Intelligent Transport Systems (C-ITS) aims to improve the quality of ITS through the use of sensing capabilities and advanced information and communication technologies [13].

Significant developments have taken place over the past few years in the C-ITS domain. Several initiatives and projects have been established all over the world (e.g., DITCM [34], CONVERGE [1], US-ITS [2]) to enable the development of a cooperative architecture to support the communication of vehicles with the transport infrastructure, service providers and other vehicles. While these initiatives provide a foundation for the design and development of C-ITS,

---

S. Ravidas and P. Karkhanis—Equal contribution to this manuscript.

© Springer Nature Switzerland AG 2020
A. Saracino and P. Mori (Eds.): ETAA 2019, LNCS 11967, pp. 16–34, 2020.
https://doi.org/10.1007/978-3-030-39749-4_2

their results can be deployed at a large scale only if the developed infrastructure and services meet the requirements posed by the C-ITS domain, including scalability, performance and security.

Security is particularly challenging to achieve within C-ITS as it encompasses multiple systems, such as automotive systems, road infrastructure, services and applications, and requires addressing attackers with various motivations and levels of skills, and diversity of threats and countermeasures [22]. Among the several security concerns, the protection of information gathered and shared within C-ITS is of utmost importance to enable its deployment at a large scale. Typically, sensitive data are protected through the adoption of authorization mechanisms that guarantee that only authorized parties can gain access to the data. While several authorization frameworks have been proposed to address authorization concerns in several application domains, there has been very little attention towards authorization in the C-ITS domain. Given the critical and dynamic nature of C-ITS, authorization mechanisms should not affect the functioning and performance of the system as well as provide fine-grained protection of sensitive information and resources. Specifically, an authorization framework for C-ITS should allow the specification and evaluation of context-aware policies to deal with the dynamicity of C-ITS, minimizing the overhead of the authorization process, and guaranteeing its reliability [30].

In this paper, we present an authorization framework that addresses the unique challenges of the C-ITS domain. The design of our framework leverages principles of both policy-based [26] and token-based [3,11] architectures to deal with the dynamicity of C-ITS while minimizing the overhead introduced by the authorization process. Specifically, we decouple the evaluation of policies from their enforcement. Our solution encompasses a policy-based authorization server that is used off-line to generate tokens encoding user permissions based on the policies provided by the resource owner. Tokens are then locally validated by the resource server at request time to determine whether access should be granted. While this decoupling allows minimizing the overhead introduced by the authorization process at request time, relying only an off-line policy evaluation does not make it possible to account for access constraints based on the run-time environment. To this end, we devise authorization tokens that encompass constraints to be verified at request time. For the design of our authorization framework, we leverage a C-ITS reference architecture as a baseline. The adoption of a C-ITS reference architecture helps identifying the C-ITS systems involved in the authorization process and, thus, facilitate the realization and integration of our authorization framework within existing C-ITS deployment sites.

The paper is organized as follows. Section 2 provides background on the C-ITS domain and authorization. Section 3 discusses related work. Section 4 introduces the C-ITS reference architecture used in this work and Sect. 5 proposes an authorization framework conforming to such an architecture. Section 6 presents an application of the proposed authorization framework in the context of location tracking services. Finally, Sect. 7 discusses design choices, and Sect. 8 concludes the paper and presents directions for future work.

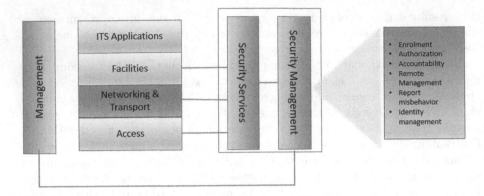

Fig. 1. ETSI security services within C-ITS

2 Background

Cooperative Intelligent Transport System (C-ITS) is emerging to improve the quality of existing ITS infrastructure by making transportation more safe and economical by combining data from vehicles and other sensors [13]. In particular, C-ITS applies information and communication technologies to the field of road transportation, including infrastructures, vehicles and users, for efficient traffic management and mobility management. While bringing several advantages to individuals, industry and society, the deployment of C-ITS also opens new challenges. To be adopted at a large scale, C-ITS should facilitate the addition and management of a large range of heterogeneous devices, allow for transferring data at high rate and provide real-time response.

On top of these issues, security is a critical success factor for the adoption of C-ITS. This has spurred several efforts from both industry and academia to enable and improve security within the C-ITS domain. Standardization bodies such as the European Telecommunication Standards Institute (ETSI), have defined guidelines towards the design and development of secure services for C-ITS [5]. Specifically, ETSI has identified key secure functionalities to be provided by C-ITS, including identification, authentication, authorization and enrolment. These functionalities are positioned within security management services, as illustrated in Fig. 1.

Authorization services (the focus of this work) aim at the protection of sensitive information exchanged within C-ITS (e.g., location data). A typical solution to protect sensitive information and resources is through the adoption of access control solutions that guarantee that only authorized parties can gain access. Access is regulated using policies that specify which actions an entity can perform on a certain object. In the remainder of the section, we provide an overview of the reference architectures commonly adopted for the design of authorization frameworks and discuss the main challenges to be addressed in the design of an authorization framework tailored to C-ITS.

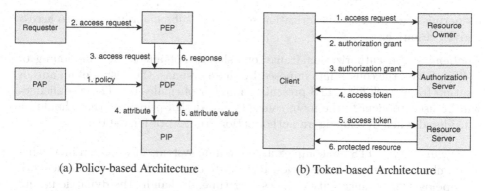

(a) Policy-based Architecture   (b) Token-based Architecture

Fig. 2. Authorization reference architectures

Authorization Reference Architectures: Several architectures have been proposed for the design of authorization mechanisms. Two widely adopted architectures are the *policy-based* and *token-based* architectures. Policy-based architectures can be exemplified by the reference architecture proposed by XACML [26], the de facto standard for the specification and enforcement of attribute-based access control policies. This architecture comprises four main components: *Policy Enforcement Point* (PEP), which provides an interface with the system and is responsible for enforcing access decisions; *Policy Decision Point* (PDP), which evaluates access requests against access control policies and determines whether access should be granted or denied; *Policy Administration Point* (PAP), which acts as a policy repository and offers facilities for policy management; *Policy Information Point* (PIP), which denotes the source of information (e.g., context information) needed for policy evaluation. Figure 2a shows the interaction between these components. The PAP makes the policies available to the PDP (1). Upon receiving an access request (2), the PEP forwards the request to the PDP (3), which evaluates the request against the policies fetched from the PAP. If additional information is required for policy evaluation, the PDP queries the PIP (4, 5). The PDP evaluates the request against the policies and returns a response specifying the access decision to the PEP (6), which enforces the decision.

Authorization mechanisms adopting a policy-based architecture typically provide a single, centralized point for the evaluation and enforcement of access control policies [18]. This solution may not be suitable when resources are distributed across different nodes, which is a typical situation in C-ITS. The last years have seen the emergence of token-based architectures as an alternative to policy-based architectures to deal with the needs of open and decentralized systems. Various standards have defined reference token-based architectures and authorization protocols [3, 11]. Although these architectures and protocols vary in the way tokens are generated and in the flow of the authorization process, they share the same underlying principles. As an example, Fig. 2b presents the OAuth protocol [11], in which a client application first obtains a token encoding its permissions from an authorization server and subsequently uses it to access a given resource.

Challenges: An authorization framework should not affect the functioning of C-ITS. Given the constraints imposed by these systems, the design of an authorization framework for C-ITS presents a number of challenges. These challenges will be used to identify the main concepts and design principles that should be considered when developing an authorization framework for C-ITS.

- *Dynamicity:* C-ITS are complex and dynamic systems in which an increasing number of entities (e.g., vehicles, RSUs) are connected and in which network topology and connectivity changes over time. To handle the dynamic nature of C-ITS, an authorization framework should support the specification and evaluation of context-aware access control policies that impose conditions on the C-ITS ecosystem such as access time and location.
- *Management:* The dynamicity of the C-ITS ecosystem can also affect policy management. In such systems, the resources of an entities can be stored and managed by different administrative domains interacting together. Therefore, an authorization framework should be able to support the management of access control policies for devices and resources across multiple domains.
- *Automation:* A main characteristic of C-ITS is collaboration, which is achieved through interactions between entities involved in the C-ITS (e.g., vehicles, RSUs). These interactions involve the sharing of real-time safety critical information. Hence, C-ITS systems require a high level of automation, possibly without any user involvement. This need for automation also reflects in the authorization process.
- *Performance:* C-ITS are critical systems in which delays can have serious consequences and even result in human loss. Therefore, services deployed within the C-ITS should not introduce latency both in terms of computation and communication. This constraint extends to the authorization process. In particular, the authorization process should not inhibit performance with significant overhead, which violates the timing constraints imposed by the C-ITS.
- *Reliability:* The critical nature of C-ITS also poses high demands for business continuity, even in cases of system failures. On the other hand, the highly sensitive information gathered and exchanged within the C-ITS requires protection and its disclosure to unauthorized parties should be prevented. Meeting these (apparently conflicting) demands requires the authorization process to be reliable. Even in cases where failures or loss of connectivity occur, the authorization framework must still be operational.

3 Related Work

Several security services for ITS have been proposed in the literature [6,22,30, 31,36,37]. However, they typically focus either on authentication alone or on the protection of communication using cryptographic techniques. To the best of our

Table 1. Analysis of existing authorization frameworks for ITS. Symbol ● denotes that a challenge is *addressed*, ◐ that it is *partially addressed*, and ○ that its is *not addressed*

	Ref. Arch.	Dynamicity	Management	Automation	Performance	Reliability
Salonikias et al. [33]	Policy-based	●	●	●	◐	◐
Gupta et al. [15]	Policy-based	◐	●	●	◐	◐
Dorri et al. [12]	Blockchain	○	○	●	○	◐
Albouq et al. [8]	Policy-based	◐	●	●	◐	◐
Riabi et al. [32]	Policy-based	○	◐	●	◐	○

knowledge, only a few authorization frameworks have been proposed in the ITS context. Salonikias et al. [33] propose a policy-based authorization mechanism tailored to vehicular infrastructures based on fog computing. This mechanism comprises multiple PDPs and PEPs located at the edge, while a single PAP (which also encompasses a PIP) deployed in the cloud is responsible to maintain and propagate access control policies to the PDPs. Gupta et al. [15] present an authorization framework for Internet of Vehicles. This framework proposes the deployment of authorization components (PEP, PDP, PAP, PIP) at different layers – object, virtual object and cloud level layer – to deal with different types of interactions. Dorri et al. [12] propose an authorization framework for vehicular networks based on blockchain. In this framework, interactions between vehicles are stored in the blockchain as transactions, which are verified by powerful nodes acting as miners. Albouq et al. [8] propose a policy-based framework for ITS infrastructures based on fog computing. Service providers deploy their services in fog nodes and vehicles can connect to these nodes through RSUs acting as edge network units. RSUs rely on the publish-subscribe paradigm to enable vehicles to subscribe to the services deployed in fog nodes. In this respect, the authorization framework resides within RSUs to control which services can be published whereas vehicles can subscribe to any (allowed) service. Riabi et al. [32] propose the use of a distributed hash table (DHT) to handle authorization within ITS. Resources are stored in fog nodes and each fog node maintains a DHT specifying the mapping between fog nodes and the Access Control List (ACL) maintained by them. Upon receiving an access request for a given resources, fog nodes use the DHT to identify the node handling the requested resource and forward the request to such a node, which makes an access decision by evaluating the request against its ACL.

Discussion: Despite the number of authorization mechanisms for ITS proposed by both industry and academia, existing authorization mechanisms are inadequate to deal with the open and dynamic nature of C-ITS systems. Table 1 presents an analysis of existing authorization frameworks for ITS with respect to the challenges discussed in Sect. 2.

An authorization framework for C-ITS should cope with the dynamic nature of ITS. While some frameworks (e.g., [15,33]) support the definition of context constraints in policies and their evaluation, many frameworks (e.g., [8,12,32]) do not, thereby not addressing this challenge. Nonetheless, most frameworks [8,15,33] provide a single point for policy administration, thus facilitating policy administration. An exception is the frameworks in [12], in which policies reside within vehicles. It is worth noting that the framework in [32] allows resource owners to deploy their policies to a single fog node and uses a DHT to identify which nodes should evaluate a request for a given resource. However, the DHT stored in each node has to be updated whenever an ACL is modified. The automation of the authorization process is satisfied by all frameworks as they do not require user involvement in the authorization process.

To be effective in C-ITS, an authorization framework should not introduce significant overhead and latency and, in general, should not affect the overall performance of the C-ITS [30]. None of the existing frameworks fully satisfies this requirement. Existing authorization frameworks typically perform policy evaluation upon receiving an access request, thus delaying service provision. In addition, some frameworks require additional communication to retrieve the context information needed for policy evaluation [33], or rely on technology that is computational expensive like blockchain [12]. Other frameworks [8,15,32] adopt a centralized architecture where all authorization components reside within the cloud, a fog node or the vehicle. However, assuming that all (context) information needed for policy evaluation is available from a single source limits the constraints on the context that can be verified.

Existing authorization frameworks partially address the reliability of the authorization process by placing authorization components within the cloud [15,33], which typically provides recovery measures to ensure business continuity. In addition, Salonikias and colleagues envision redundancy for those components deployed at the edge. Similarly, the frameworks in [12] and in [8] can theoretically ensure the reliability of authorization components by replicating them in blockchain nodes and RSUs, respectively. However, for both frameworks, scenarios of node failure or loss of connectivity are not analyzed. In [32], the request can be sent to any fog node, which forwards it to the node that has the requested resource. However, ACLs are not replicated among nodes, leading to reliability issues in case of connectivity loss or node failure.

In summary, existing authorization frameworks fail to fully address all challenges posed by C-ITS. A main drawback is given by latency due to the choice of a policy-based architecture for their design. In this work, we present an authorization framework for C-ITS that adopt principles underlying the token-based architecture as a baseline for its design (Sect. 5). This architecture provides a foundation to deal with the dynamicity and performance constraints typical of C-ITS scenarios.

4   C-ITS Reference Architecture

For the design of our authorization framework for C-ITS and its realization and integration in existing C-ITS sites, we adopt a C-ITS reference architecture as a baseline for our design. A reference architecture is typically used to facilitate

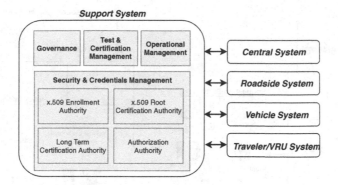

Fig. 3. C-ITS reference architecture

communication and cooperation between different stakeholders during the design and development of complex systems. A reference architecture for the C-ITS domain addresses not only demands in the software/system engineering field, but also in traffic engineering, civil engineering, information technology, etc. Moreover, its design should account not only for new systems but also taking into account the infrastructure and systems already in place.

In the recent years, several C-ITS reference architectures have been proposed to address the interdisciplinary concerns and to enable the large scale deployment of region or nation wide C-ITS services. In this work, we adopt the C-ITS reference architecture proposed in the C-MobILE project (http://c-mobile-project.eu) as a baseline for the design of our authorization framework. The C-MobILE reference architecture provides a baseline for the design of a C-ITS infrastructure mainly targeting traffic related concerns [9,20]. The C-MobILE reference architecture is based on the generalization of existing C-ITS architectures while addressing the main concerns of the C-ITS stakeholders.

The C-MobILE reference architecture categorizes C-ITS systems into five main types based on the functionalities they provide, as illustrated in Fig. 3. Below we present a brief description of the main systems and refer to [9] for details:

- *Support system* consists of systems supporting the governance and management of C-ITS services. Support systems influence all other systems of the C-ITS.
- *Central system* comprises systems that support connected vehicles and roadside units by capturing data from vehicles and roadside units, and providing such data to C-ITS applications. Central systems can be aggregated together or can be geographically or functionally distributed.
- *Roadside system* consists of systems forming the physical road infrastructure such as roadside units, traffic light controllers, and cameras.
- *Vehicle system* comprises systems integrated within vehicles such as a Vehicle On-Board Unit (V-OBU).

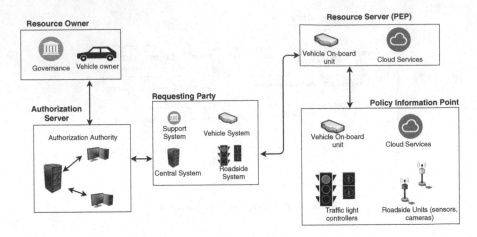

Fig. 4. Authorization framework and mapping of its components to C-ITS systems

- *Traveler/VRU system* consists of personal devices, typically a smart phone or personal navigation device used by a traveler or Vulnerable Road User (VRU).

Security services are provided by the support system. Below we describe its sub-systems.

- *Governance* comprises systems and entities that are responsible for the functioning and security of the C-ITS.
- *Operational Management* comprises systems enabling operational processes such as fault, performance and configuration management of C-ITS systems.
- *Test and Certification Management* supports the registration and management of tested and certified communication systems for ITS (safety) applications.
- *Security and Credentials Management* provides a high-level representation of the systems that enable trusted communications between mobile devices, roadside devices and centres, and protect data from unauthorized access. A sub-systems is the *Authorization Authority*, which is in charge of issuing authorization tickets to ITS entities.

In the next section, we present the design of our authorization framework and show how its components are mapped to the systems of the C-ITS reference architecture. This mapping will help understand the external interfaces, high level functional capabilities of the authorization components within the C-ITS architecture.

5   Authorization Framework

Existing authorization frameworks are usually based on either a policy-based or a token-based architecture. As discussed in Sect. 2, policy-based frameworks

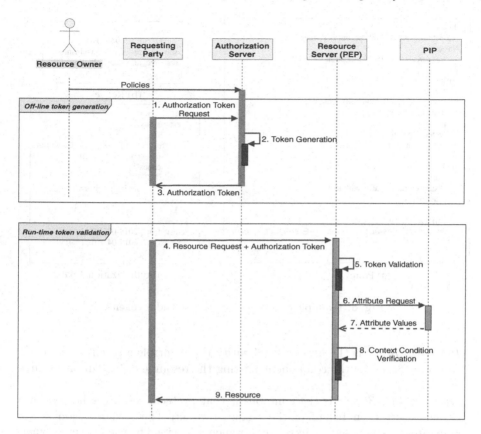

Fig. 5. Authorization process

often introduce delays that cannot be tolerated by the C-ITS. While existing token-based frameworks address this issue by limiting the operations to be performed at run-time to token validation, they usually require user involvement to determine whether access should be granted, thus providing no automation of the authorization process. In this work, we propose a *hybrid* authorization framework that leverages the advantages of both these architectures. In particular, we divide the authorization process into two main stages: an *off-line* process in which tokens are automatically generated based on policies (without any user involvement) and a *run-time* process in which tokens are validated. Such an approach provides the flexibility and performance necessary to deal with the dynamic and critical nature of C-ITS while providing a high degree of automation. In the remainder of the section, we present the main components of the framework along with the authorization process.

Authorization Components: The authorization framework encompasses the following entities and components:

```
policy {
  "Combining Algorithm": permit-overrides
  "target": {
    "resource": vehicle7282:location
  }
  "rule":{
    "target": {
      "subject_organization": MyInsurance
      "action": GET
    }
    "effect": permit
    "constraint":Driver=A120223
  }
  "rule":{
    "target": {
      "subject_role": traffic authority
      "action": GET
    }
    "effect": permit
    "constraint": resource_location ∈ subject_region
  }
}
```

(a) Policy

```
request: {
  subject_id: AI094520
  subject_organization: MyInsurance
  resource_id: vehicle7282:location
}
```

(b) Request

```
token{
  "permissions": [
    {
      "resource_id": vehicle7282:location
      "subject_id": AI094520
      "scopes": [
        "GET"
        "constraint": Driver=A120223
      ],
    }
  ]
  "created_at": 2019-03-10T11:55:00
  "expires_at": 2019-04-10T11:54:59
}
```

(c) Authorization Token

Fig. 6. Example of a policy, a request and a token

- *Resource Owner* is the user or legal entity that controls a given resource.
- *Resource Server* is the component hosting the resource on behalf of resource owner.
- *Authorization Server* is the component that protects resources hosted on a resource server on behalf of the resource owner. The authorization server generates tokens based on access requirements specified by the resource owner, thus acting as the PDP.
- *Policy Information Point* denotes the source of context information.
- *Requesting Party* is a user or a legal entity that uses a client application to access resources.

Figure 4 shows these components along with their interactions. It also provides their mapping to the systems of the C-ITS reference architecture in Fig. 3. This mapping identifies which C-ITS systems can play a role in the authorization process.

Authorization Process: The authorization process supported by our hybrid authorization framework is performed in two stages. First, the authorization server evaluates the policies off-line and generates an authorization token asserting the permissions of the requesting party. Then, when requesting access to a resource, the requesting party provides the token along with request to the resource server, which validates the token and verifies additional constraints on the context (if any). The procedures for off-line token generation and run-time token validation are represented in Fig. 5.

We assume that the resource owner stores her resources in a resource server. Moreover, she has provided the authorization server with access control policies

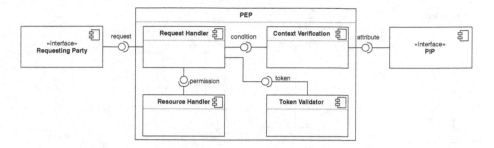

Fig. 7. Component diagram of PEP

defining who can access her resources. It is worth noting tha resources can be under the control of multiple entities or negotiation between entities may be necessary to determine how resources can be used and with whom they can be shared. In this settings, data sharing agreements [19,25] should be established between the involved parties to determine provisions concerning access and dissemination. How data sharing agreements and collaborative policies [10,23] can be defined is out of the scope of this work and here we simply assume that the policies to be enforced are provided to the authorization server. Interested readers can refer to [28] for a thorough discussion on this issue.

In this work, we consider policies specified in attribute-based access control (ABAC) as this paradigm provides a means for the specification of fine-grained access control policies. In ABAC, access requests and policies are defined in terms of attribute name-value pairs. Policies have a *target*, which defines the applicability of the policy by specifying to which requests the policy applies, and an *effect*, which specifies whether the subject has the permission to perform the specified action on the resource (permit) or not (deny). Figure 6a shows an example policy expressed in (a compact representation of) the XACML policy language [26]. This example policy is used to regulate the access to the location information of a given vehicle and consists of two rules combined using permit-override combining algorithm. The first rule states that subjects working in a certain insurance company are allowed to perform a *GET* operation to retrieve location information, whereas the second rule is used to restrict the access to the traffic authority operating in the region in which the vehicle is passing through. Note that policies, being evaluated off-line, can only be used to verify constraints on static properties of the subjects and resources. To account for context-depended properties (e.g., location, current time), policies also include *constraints* that are returned along with the authorization token and verified at run-time time (see below).[1] For instance, in our example, the constraint of the first rule allows the insurance company to retrieve location information of the vehicle only when a given individual is driving the vehicle.

---

[1] Constraints can be specified in XACML using element `<Obligations>`. In XACML, obligations are returned along with the access decision (either *permit* or *deny*) to enrich the decision.

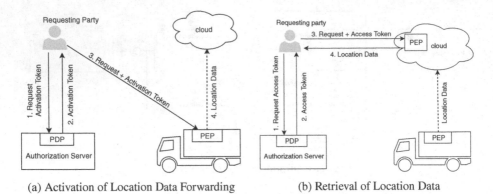

(a) Activation of Location Data Forwarding   (b) Retrieval of Location Data

Fig. 8. Deployment of the authorization framework for location tracking

Off-line Token Generation: The authorization process starts with the off-line generation of an authorization token (top of Fig. 5). The requesting party requests the authorization token from the authorization server to access a resource (1). The authorization server determines the permissions of the requesting party on the resource on the basis of the policies provided by the resource owner and generates an authorization token listing all permissions the requesting party has over the resource (2). The token is then sent to the requesting party (3). Figure 6c shows the authorization token generated by evaluating the access request in Fig. 6b against the policy in Fig. 6a. The token contains the *permissions* of the requesting party on the resource along with the validity period of the token. It is worth noting that the *constraint* specified in the policy is passed, together with the permissions, to the authorization token in order to prevent application overprivilege [17,35]. This constraint is then verified at run-time to determine whether access should be granted.

Run-Time Token Validation: When the requesting party wants to access a resource, she sends a request to the PEP located in the resource server along with the authorization token (4). The resource server verifies whether the token is valid (5). In addition, the resource server verifies the constraints provided in the token. If additional information is needed to verify the constraints on the context, the resource server retrieves it from the appropriate sources (PIPs), which can be located within the resource server or in a different component (6 and 7). For example, the resource server could be vehicle which may have to retrieve context information from the nearby RSUs. If the verification of the constraint (8) is successful, the resource is disclose to the requesting party (9). Figure 7 provides a detailed view of the components and interfaces involved in the run-time token validation process.

Note that authorization tokens needs to be protected against tampering or relay attacks. How tokens can be protected against those attacks is out of the scope of this work and we refer to [11] for approaches commonly used to secure authorization tokens.

6   Application to Location Tracking Services

This section presents typical C-ITS use case scenarios and discusses how our authorization framework can be deployed to deal with such scenarios.

6.1   Location Tracking Services

Location information is an enabler for several services in the C-ITS domain [5]. For instance, location information can be used to increase vehicular safety (such as notification of nearby accident), tracking of stolen vehicle, pay-per-drive insurance, car sharing, toll payment, etc. To enable the retrieval of location information from a vehicle, the vehicle owner typically has to activate the forwarding of location information within the vehicle, including setting the time interval data are transmitted. Since this might generate a large amount of data, it is not ideal to forward the data to the requester directly. To this end, in our scenarios, we envision that data are transmitted to one of the C-ITS central systems (e.g., a Data Provider Back Office in the cloud), from which data can be retrieved when needed. Below we present typical use case scenarios relying on location tracking. These scenarios are an adaptation of the ones defined in the ETSI standard [5].

Scenario 1: Pay Per Drive Insurance. Consider two sibyls, Alice and Bob, who co-own a car. They want to insure their car, but they would like different types of insurance. While Bob prefers a fixed premium, Alice wants a pay-per-drive insurance where the premium of the insurance policy is based on the kilometers traveled. In order to calculate the premium, the insurance company should be able to retrieve the location information from the vehicle when it is driven by Alice.

Scenario 2: Stolen Car. Alice and Bob's car was stolen and, thus, the two sibyls alert the police. Assuming that Bob has previously activated the forwarding of location information from the vehicle to the cloud, he can retrieve the exact location of his car in real time. Bob shares this information with the police to assist them in retrieving the car.

While enabling a variety of services, location information is sensitive and, thus, should be protected from unauthorized accesses. Next, we present how the authorization framework in Sect. 5 can be used to enable the selective sharing of location information.

6.2   Authorization Framework for Location Tracking Services

The first step for adapting our authorization framework to the scenarios above is to identify the C-ITS systems to which its components are deployed. In the scenarios, the owner of the vehicle represents the resource owner as he is the entity to whom information refers and, thus, he has the control on how the information is processed and to whom it can be disclosed [14]. The authorization server is handled by the Authorization Authority within the support system (cf. Fig. 3). The insurance company (scenario 1) and the police (scenario 2), which can be seen as two instances of the service provider back office (SP-BO) within the central system, are the requesting parties.

The scenarios involve two main phases: a first phase in which the forwarding of location information is activated and a second phase in which the information is retrieved from the Data Provider Back Office (DP-BO) that the vehicle owner used to store its data. Accordingly, the C-ITS system acting as the resource server varies in the two steps; in the first step the V-OBU acts as the resource server whereas in the second step the DP-BO acts as the resource server. We also distinguish two types of authorization tokens based on their purpose, namely *activation tokens* and *access tokens*. Activation tokens are used to enable the forwarding of location data from vehicle to the cloud. Access tokens are used to enable the retrieval of location information from the cloud.

Forwarding of Location Information: Alice wants to activate the gathering of the location of her vehicle, e.g., to enable vehicle tracking as demanded by her insurance company. To this end, she enables the forwarding of location information from the vehicle to the cloud. Figure 8a depicts the forwarding activation process. The requesting party (acting on behalf of Alice) requests an activation token to the authorization server (1). The authorization server provides Alice with an activation token listing her permissions on the vehicle (2). These steps are performed during the off-line phase. At run-time, the requesting party provides the activation token to the V-OBU (3). The PEP in the vehicle validates the token as well as verifies the constraints on the context (if any). Upon successful validation, the vehicle starts forwarding location information to the cloud (4).

Retrieval of Location Information: Suppose that Alice has specified a policy that allow the insurance company to access location information of her car but only under the condition that she is driving (see Fig. 6a). To comply with Alice's access requirements, the resource server (i.e., the cloud) has to verify this constraint at run-time before disclosing location data. This means that the resource server might have to retrieve additional information from the vehicle or roadside units in order to evaluate such constraints. Figure 8b depicts the information retrieval process. In the off-line phase, the requesting party (acting on behalf of the insurance company) requests an access token to the authorization server (1). The authorization server verifies the permissions of the insurance company and provides it with an access token (2). When requesting access to the location information of Alice's vehicle, the insurance company attaches the access token to the request (3). The resource server validates the token and verifies the constraints on the context conditions (i.e., whether Alice is driving). Upon successful validation, the location information is disclosed to the insurance company (4).

7   Discussion

This section discusses the feasibility of our framework and provides a qualitative analysis of the main design choices with respect to the challenges presented in

Sect. 2. These choices encompass the use of a hybrid authorization framework, the use of a centralized authorization server and the handling of contextual information.

We have adopted a hybrid authorization framework that combines principles of both policy-based and token-based frameworks. As discussed previously, policy-based frameworks perform policy evaluation at request time, introducing delay in service provisions. This, however, might be problematic in critical systems as C-ITS. In our design of the authorization framework, we leverage a token-based architecture where a token is generated off-line and then validated (along with the constraints on the context) at run-time, when access to a resource is requested. This allows performing policy evaluation off-line, thus reducing overhead and latency [24]. However, differently from existing token-based frameworks like OAuth [11], which require the resource owner to authorize an application the first time it requires access to a resource, we automate the generation of tokens by exploiting the use of policies. Although there have already been efforts to integrate the use of policies in the token-based architecture [3], existing framework usually do not support the verification of context conditions, making them unsuitable to deal with the dynamicity of C-ITS. It is worth noting that token validation along with verification of context conditions does not introduce a significant overhead as this operation is significantly less expensive than policy evaluation and token generation [16].

Our framework employs a centralized component for token generation (i.e., the authorization server). This provides resource owners with a single point for policy administration where they can efficiently manage their policies [7,18]. The use of a centralized authorization server can also bring other advantages compared to deploying the policy decision point into (multiple) edge nodes (e.g. [32]) or within vehicles (e.g. [12]). For example, it allows exploiting the benefits of cloud computing in terms of scalability and reliability. It is worth noting that, in C-ITS, entities can rely on several resource servers to store and manage their data and resources. Therefore, an approach based on sticky policies [29], in which the resource server is required to attach policies to the data, is not particularly suitable as an entity would be required to configure their policies in each resource server in which her resources are stored.

In C-ITS, the information needed to verify context conditions may have to be retrieved from different sources, e.g. vehicles, road-side units or cloud. Thus, assuming that the resource server is the only source of context information as in [8,15] restricts the types of context conditions that can be verified, thus limiting the level of granularity for access control. However, retrieving context information from different sources can have an impact on latency as it requires additional interactions between parties. Hence, one has to make a trade-off between the expressiveness of context conditions and the latency introduced by the retrieval of the information necessary for their verification.

Unlike other authorization frameworks, our framework has been designed to address the challenges characterizing the C-ITS domain. In this work, we have looked into these challenges from a design perspective. However, in practical deployments, other factors such as communication protocols (CoAP, MQTT) [21, 27], data format (JSON, XACML), handling of token refreshing and revocation, should be taken into account. Nevertheless, we believe that our hybrid authorization framework makes a step forward to the development of practical authorization mechanisms tailored to C-ITS. Moreover, the adoption of a C-ITS reference architecture as a baseline for our framework facilitates its integration and realization in existing C-ITS deployment sites.

8   Conclusions and Future Work

In this paper, we have designed an authorization framework tailored to the C-ITS domain. Our framework leverages principles of both policy-based and token-based architectures to minimize the overhead introduced by the authorization process while providing fine-grained protection. We have adopted the C-MobILE reference architecture as a baseline for the design of our hybrid authorization framework. This will help identifying the C-ITS systems involved in the authorization process for a specific application scenario and, thus, realizing the framework at various C-ITS deployment sites. We have also provided a qualitative analysis of our framework by demonstrating its application to typical C-ITS scenarios and showing how it addresses the challenges characterizing the C-ITS domain.

In the future, we plan to implement, integrate and validate our authorization framework within existing C-ITS deployment sites. To this end, we will further refine the design of our framework by investigating communication and implementation aspects.

Acknowledgements. This work is funded by the Horizon 2020 C-MobILE project (723311) and the ITEA3 project APPSTACLE (15017).

References

1. CONVERGE. https://converge-online.de. Accessed 25 June 2019
2. US-ITS. https://local.iteris.com/arc-it. Accessed 25 June 2019
3. User-Managed Access (UMA) 2.0 Grant for OAuth 2.0 Authorization. https://kantarainitiative.org/file-downloads/rec-oauth-uma-grant-2-0-pdf/. Accessed 25 June 2019
4. Directive 2010/40/EU of the European Parliament and of the Council. Official Journal of the European Union, vol. 50, p. 207 (2010)
5. Intelligent Transport Systems (ITS); Security; ITS communications security architecture and security management. ETSI TS 102 940, ETSI (2018)
6. Abrougui, K., Boukerche, A.: Efficient group-based authentication protocol for location-based service discovery in intelligent transportation systems. Secur. Commun. Netw. **6**(4), 473–484 (2013)
7. Ahmad, T., Morelli, U., Ranise, S., Zannone, N.: A lazy approach to access control as a service (ACaaS) for IoT: an AWS case study. In: Proceedings of Symposium on Access Control Models and Technologies, pp. 235–246. ACM (2018)

8. Albouq, S.S., Fredericks, E.M.: Securing communication between service providers and road side units in a connected vehicle infrastructure. In: Proceedings of International Symposium on Network Computing and Applications, pp. 1–5. IEEE (2017)
9. Dajsuren, Y., Karkhanis, P., Kadiogullary, D., Fuenfrocken, M.: C-MobILE D3.1 reference architecture. Technical report (2017). http://c-mobile-project.eu/library/
10. Damen, S., den Hartog, J., Zannone, N.: Collac: collaborative access control. In: Proceedings of International Conference on Collaboration Technologies and Systems, pp. 142–149. IEEE (2014)
11. Denniss, W., Bradley, J.: OAuth 2.0 for Native Apps. RFC 8252, IETF (2017). https://tools.ietf.org/html/rfc6749
12. Dorri, A., Steger, M., Kanhere, S.S., Jurdak, R.: Blockchain: a distributed solution to automotive security and privacy. IEEE Commun. Mag. 55(12), 119–125 (2017)
13. Festag, A.: Cooperative intelligent transport systems standards in Europe. IEEE Commun. Mag. 52(12), 166–172 (2014)
14. Guarda, P., Zannone, N.: Towards the development of privacy-aware systems. Inf. Software Technol. 51(2), 337–350 (2009)
15. Gupta, M., Sandhu, R.: Authorization framework for secure cloud assisted connected cars and vehicular internet of things. In: Proceedings of Symposium on Access Control Models and Technologies, pp. 193–204. ACM (2018)
16. Hernández-Ramos, J.L., Jara, A.J., Marin, L., Skarmeta, A.F.: Distributed capability-based access control for the internet of things. J. Internet Serv. Inf. Secur. 3(3/4), 1–16 (2013)
17. Jia, Y.J., et al.: ContexIoT: towards providing contextual integrity to appified IoT platforms. In: Proceedings of Network and Distributed System Security Symposium (2017)
18. Kaluvuri, S.P., Egner, A.I., den Hartog, J., Zannone, N.: SAFAX - anextensible authorization service for cloud environments. Front. ICT (2015)
19. Karafili, E., Lupu, E.C.: Enabling data sharing in contextual environments: Policy representation and analysis. In: Proceedings of Symposium on Access Control Models and Technologies, pp. 231–238. ACM (2017)
20. Karkhanis, P., van den Brand, M., Rajkarnikar, S.: Defining the C-ITS reference architecture. In: Proceedings of International Conference on Software Architecture Companion, pp. 148–151. IEEE (2018)
21. Laaroussi, Z., Morabito, R., Taleb, T.: Service provisioning in vehicular networks through edge and cloud: an empirical analysis. In: Proceedings of Conference on Standards for Communications and Networking. IEEE (2018)
22. Le, V.H., den Hartog, J., Zannone, N.: Security and privacy for innovative automotive applications: a survey. Comput. Commun. 132, 17–41 (2018)
23. Mahmudlu, R., den Hartog, J., Zannone, N.: Data governance and transparency for collaborative systems. In: Ranise, S., Swarup, V. (eds.) DBSec 2016. LNCS, vol. 9766, pp. 199–216. Springer, Cham (2016). https://doi.org/10.1007/978-3-319-41483-6_15
24. Martinez, J.A., Ruiz, P.M., Marin, R.: Impact of the pre-authentication performance in vehicular networks. In: Proceedings of Vehicular Technology Conference-Fall. IEEE (2010)
25. Matteucci, I., Petrocchi, M., Sbodio, M.L.: CNL4DSA: a controlled natural language for data sharing agreements. In: Proceedings of Symposium on Applied Computing, pp. 616–620. ACM (2010)
26. OASIS: eXtensible Access Control Markup Language (XACML) v. 3.0. OASIS Standard (2013)

27. Ojanperä, T., Mäkelä, J., Mämmelä, O., Majanen, M., Martikainen, O.: Use cases and communications architecture for 5G-enabled road safety services. In: Proceedings of European Conference on Networks and Communications, pp. 335–340. IEEE (2018)

28. Paci, F., Squicciarini, A.C., Zannone, N.: Survey on access control for community-centered collaborative systems. ACM Comput. Surv. 51(1), 6:1–6:38 (2018)

29. Pearson, S., Casassa-Mont, M.: Sticky policies: an approach for managing privacy across multiple parties. Computer 44(9), 60–68 (2011)

30. Ravidas, S., Lekidis, A., Paci, F., Zannone, N.: Access control in internet-of-things: a survey. J. Netw. Comput. Appl. 144, 79–101 (2019)

31. Raya, M., Papadimitratos, P., Hubaux, J.P.: Securing vehicular communications. IEEE Wirel. Commun. 13(5), 8–15 (2006)

32. Riabi, I., Saidane, L.A., Ayed, H.K.B.: A proposal of a distributed access control over Fog computing: the ITS use case. In: Proceedings of International Conference on Performance Evaluation and Modeling in Wired and Wireless Networks. IEEE (2017)

33. Salonikias, S., Mavridis, I., Gritzalis, D.: Access control issues in utilizing fog computing for transport infrastructure. In: Rome, E., Theocharidou, M., Wolthusen, S. (eds.) CRITIS 2015. LNCS, vol. 9578, pp. 15–26. Springer, Cham (2016). https://doi.org/10.1007/978-3-319-33331-1_2

34. van Sambeek, M., et al.: Towards an architecture for cooperative-intelligent transport system (C-ITS) applications in the Netherlands. Technical report, DITCM Innovations (2015)

35. Schuster, R., Shmatikov, V., Tromer, E.: Situational access control in the internet of things. In: Proceedings of Conference on Computer and Communications Security, pp. 1056–1073. ACM (2018)

36. Sha, K., Xi, Y., Shi, W., Schwiebert, L., Zhang, T.: Adaptive privacy-preserving authentication in vehicular networks. In: Proceedings of International Conference on Communications and Networking in China, pp. 1–8. IEEE (2006)

37. Sucasas, V., Mantas, G., Saghezchi, F.B., Radwan, A., Rodriguez, J.: An autonomous privacy-preserving authentication scheme for intelligent transportation systems. Computers & Security 60, 193–205 (2016)

A Framework for the Validation of Access Control Systems

Said Daoudagh[1,2]([✉]) [iD], Francesca Lonetti[1] [iD], and Eda Marchetti[1] [iD]

[1] Istituto di Scienza e Tecnologie dell'Informazione "A. Faedo" (ISTI), CNR,
via G. Moruzzi 1, 56124 Pisa, Italy
{said.daoudagh,francesca.lonetti,eda.marchetti}@isti.cnr.it
[2] Computer Science Department, University of Pisa, Pisa, Italy
said.daoudagh@di.unipi.it

Abstract. In modern pervasive applications, it is important to validate Access Control (AC) mechanisms that are usually defined by means of the XACML standard. Mutation analysis has been applied on Access Control Policies (ACPs) for measuring the adequacy of a test suite.

This paper provides an automatic framework for realizing mutations of the code of the Policy Decision Point (PDP) that is a critical component in AC systems. The proposed framework allows the test strategies assessment and the analysis of test data by leveraging mutation-based approaches. We show how to instantiate the proposed framework and provide also some examples of its application.

Keywords: Access Control Systems · Mutation analysis · Testing · XACML

1 Introduction

Security is among the top most pressing concerns of both developers and consumers of modern software systems. In today's highly connected and pervasive software-intensive systems, preventing unauthorized, erroneous or even malicious usage of critical resources is imperative. Thus, secure software engineering relies on sophisticated control and protection mechanisms to ensure the proper behavior of software systems at each implementation level and against any potential threat.

Among security mechanisms, a critical role is played by Access Control (AC) systems, which aim to ensure that only the intended subjects can access the protected data and get only the permission levels required to accomplish their tasks and no much more. An Access Control Policy (ACP) specifies the level of confidentiality of data, the procedures for managing data and resources, and the classification of resources into category sets yielding different security requirements.

Supported by CyberSec4Europe Grant agreement ID: 830929.

A. Saracino and P. Mori (Eds.): ETAA 2019, LNCS 11967, pp. 35–51, 2020.
https://doi.org/10.1007/978-3-030-39749-4_3

Into the AC systems, the Policy Decision Point (PDP) is one of the most critical components. It is in charge of implementing the evaluation logic of *ACPs*, i.e., the rules for accessing data and resources. Then, any error or overlook of the PDP could result either in forbidding due access rights, or worse in authorizing accesses that should be denied, thus jeopardizing the security of the protected data.

In this paper, we focus on the testing of the PDP. Different PDP implementations, and in general AC systems, usually rely on the eXtensible Access Control Markup Language (XACML) [20], the de facto standard for the specification of policies and requests. It is an XML-based language conceived with interoperability, extensibility, and distribution in mind, thus enabling the specification of very complex rules.

Due to the complexity of the XACML language as well as the criticality of the PDP role, for assuring the required security level a key factor becomes the application of effective and efficient testing approaches; indeed, generated test cases should exercise all the security-critical aspects discovering all the possible faults. Therefore, knowing in advance the peculiarities of each available test strategy and its level of fault detection effectiveness it is important for a proper selection of the most promising testing approach and consequently for developing a successful testing phase.

Testing of the PDP consists of probing the PDP with a set of test cases (i.e., XACML requests) and checking its responses against the expected decisions. Available proposals for generation of test cases can be divided into three categories: *(i)* those that focus on the application of the combinatorial approaches to XACML policies values for generating test inputs, as, for instance X-CREATE [2,8] and Targen [17]; *(ii)* those that exploit change-impact analysis for test cases generation starting from policies specification [18]; and *(iii)* those that are based on the representation of policy-implied behavior by means of models [13,19].

However, even though there is an increasing research interest in defining new testing strategies and automatic testing facilities for AC systems validation, few proposals are targeting the analysis of test data and provide support for repeatable experiments in the context of AC systems. This paper would like to provide a contribution in this direction by presenting an automated testing framework, called *XACML Mutation Framework (XMF)*, useful for both testing the PDP component and assessing the test suite effectiveness. Specifically, with the intent to join together automation and replication, this paper would like to target the development of an automatic framework for test strategies selection and assessment as well as analysis of test data, also providing some examples of application.

The proposed framework leverages the application of the classical approach of mutation testing. Briefly, mutation testing is a technique in which syntactic faults, simulating typical programmer's mistakes, are seeded in the original program in order to produce a set of faulty programs, called *mutants*, each one containing one fault. The ratio of the number of detected faults over the total number of seeded faults indicates the effectiveness of the test suite. We refer to [12,21] for an extensive survey of software mutation testing.

Many existing mutation-based proposals [4,16,19] rely on mutations applied directly on the ACPs. A first attempt to realize mutations of the code of the PDP implementation is presented in [9]. The proposal of this paper includes and extends the work in [9] realizing an automated framework for assessing the effectiveness of the test suites by applying a set of classical code-based mutation operators of the PDP.

Indeed, even though some case studies show that the existing methodologies are quite effective in the simulation of many common faults in the XACML policy specification [4,16], due to the complexity of PDP functional realization and the specific characteristics of the adopted implementation language, the proposed mutations do not exhaustively cover all the important criticalities of the PDP specification.

XMF tries to overcome the above mentioned limitations integrating facilities for testing the PDP engine and assessing the different test strategies. The main goal of the proposed framework is to provide an automated solution for analysis and assessment of test strategies in the context of AC systems. Indeed, the framework provides test data storage and analysis capabilities supporting the tester into an easy replication of the experiments as well as a better addressing of the testing activities. The framework allows different kinds of test data analysis such as comparison of test strategies in terms of fault detection and cardinality of the test suites, mutants distribution and number of distinct executions of the mutated PDPs, among the others.

For the sake of simplicity, we report only two examples of the framework application: (i) the assessment of two different test generation strategies in terms of cardinality of the derived test suites; and (ii) the analysis of the distribution of the mutants in the PDP code. In the first example we consider real-world ACPs based on the Attribute-Based Access Control (ABAC) model encoded in XACML.

Outline. We recall XACML based AC and mutation testing in Sect. 2. In Sect. 3 we present the proposed framework and describe its components, whereas Sect. 4 contains examples of the application of the framework. Section 5 presents related works. Finally, in Sect. 6 we conclude and point out the future work.

2 Background

In the following subsections, basic details about XACML-based access control systems and mutation testing are provided.

2.1 XACML-Based Access Control System

XACML [20] is a platform-independent XML-based language for the specification of Access Control Policies (ACPs). The main purpose of an XACML policy

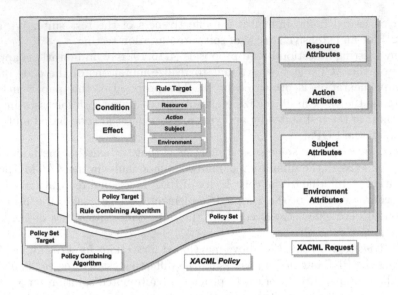

Fig. 1. Anatomy of an XACML policy and an XACML request.

is to define the constraints that a subject needs to comply with for accessing a resource and doing an action in a given environment.

Briefly, an XACML policy has a tree structure whose main elements are: *PolicySet*, *Policy*, *Rule*, *Target* and *Condition*. The *PolicySet* includes one or more policies. A *Policy* contains a *Target* and one or more rules. The *Target* specifies a set of constraints on *attributes* of a given request. Typical categories of *attributes* are *Subject*, *Resource*, *Action* and *Environment*. The *Rule* specifies a *Target* and a *Condition* containing one or more boolean functions. If the *Condition* evaluates to true, then the Rule's *Effect* (a value of *Permit* or *Deny*) is returned, otherwise a *NotApplicable* decision is formulated. If an error occurs during the evaluation of a policy against a request, *Indeterminate* value is returned. The *PolicyCombiningAlgorithm* and the *RuleCombiningAlgorithm*

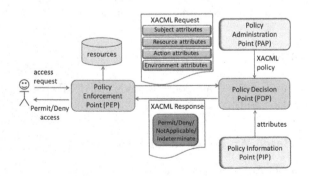

Fig. 2. Access control system architecture.

define how to combine the results from multiple policies and rules respectively in order to derive a single authorization access decision.

The structure of an ACP and an AC request is sketched in Fig. 1. The main actors in the XACML domain are shown in Fig. 2: the Policy Administration Point (PAP) is the system entity in charge of managing the policies; the Policy Enforcement Point (PEP), usually embedded into an application system, receives the access request in its native format, constructs an XACML request and sends it to the Policy Decision Point (PDP); the Policy Information Point (PIP) provides the PDP with the values of subject, resource, action and environment attributes; the PDP evaluates the policy against the request and returns the response, including the authorization decision, to the PEP.

2.2 Mutation Testing

Mutation Testing is a technique in which syntactic faults, simulating typical programmer's mistakes, are seeded in the original program in order to produce a set of faulty programs, called mutants, each one containing one fault. The main purpose of mutation testing is to assess the adequacy of a test suite. Each test case is executed on the original program and its mutants, then outputs are collected: if the mutant's output is different from the original program's one, the fault is detected and the mutant is said to be killed. The mutation score is the ratio of the number of detected faults over the total number of seeded faults and indicates the effectiveness of the test suite. Since mutation testing was proposed in the 1970s, it has been applied to many programming languages, such as Java, Fortran, Ada, C, SQL and many mutation tools have been developed to support automated mutation analysis. We refer to [12, 21] for an extensive survey of software mutation testing.

The general process of mutation analysis consists of two steps: first, change the original program with predefined mutation operators and generate a set of mutated program, called mutants; then, the mutants are executed against a test suite, and information is collected during the execution for various purpose of analysis.

In the context of AC systems, some proposals address mutation techniques to assess the fault detection effectiveness of test sets for security policies and provide specific mutation operators. The defined mutation operators manipulate the target and condition elements of the XACML policy, in order to generate a set of faulty policies. The policy under test and the faulty policies are evaluated by the PDP against the same access requests, then the test outputs, represented by the access responses, of the original and the mutated policies are compared to get the mutation score. We refer to Sect. 5 for specific proposals of mutation testing in the context of AC systems.

3 XACML Mutation Framework

In this section we present the *XACML Mutation Framework (XMF)* useful both for testing PDP component and for assessing the test generation strategies. The framework provides three main functionalities: *(1)* test case generation, execution and assessment; *(2)* mutants generation; and *(3)* a data mart for OLAP analysis [11].

Very briefly, considering the testing of PDP, it consists on the execution of a set of access requests, derived by a specific policy on the PDP and the consequent comparison of the collected responses against the expected ones. Thus the PDP needs to be configured to use a selected policy, the requests have to be sent to the PDP under test, and the responses (permit, deny, not applicable or indeterminate) collected.

Considering instead the assessment of the test generation strategies, first it is necessary to execute the requests (test cases) on the original PDP and to collect the associated set of responses; then the PDP is replaced with one of its mutated versions, each of the test cases re-executed on this mutant, and responses are collected again; finally, the responses are analyzed and compared so as to discover the killed mutants. In the case of PDP, a mutant is considered killed when an exception is raised or when the returned response is different from the expected one. As final step, the mutation score for the whole test suite is calculated by dividing the number of killed mutants by the number of mutants.

According to the literature, a test suite is considered of high quality if it is able to reach a high mutation score, i.e., the test suite has a high fault detection capability.

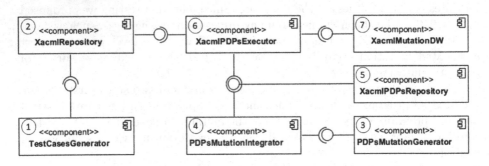

Fig. 3. The proposed XACML mutation testing framework.

Figure 3 schematizes the architecture of XMF framework which mainly consists on the following seven components:

① *TestCasesGenerator* is an automated XACML requests generator, which implements and/or integrates different testing strategies or tools so as to reduce as much as possible the time and the effort required for the test cases specification;

② *XacmlRepository* is a database that contains XACML policies, XACML requests, i.e., test cases, and XACML decisions defined by the XACML language, i.e., Permit, Deny, NotApplicable and Indeterminate. The data are organized so as to be able to associate the requests to the policies from which

they are generated and to keep track of the generator used for their generation;

③ **PDPsMutationGenerator** is a generator that automatically derives
mutated versions of the original PDP. These are generated by applying a
set of Java based mutation operators producing set of mutated java classes,
each one containing only one fault;

④ **PDPsMutationIntegrator** works in direct collaboration with the PDPsMutationGenerator for seeding the faults in the code of PDP and producing
executable mutated versions of the original PDP;

⑤ **XacmlPDPsRepository** maintains all the original PDPs and the associated mutated versions. It also contains the mutation operator applied to the
original PDP to obtain the mutated version;

⑥ **XacmlPDPsExecutor** is an automated executor of test cases on the original
PDP and the associated set of mutated PDPs;

⑦ **XacmlMutationDW** contains a data mart for storing the collected data
derived from test cases and mutants generation activities as well as the evaluation activity.

3.1   Workflow of the Testing Process

A typical testing process, shown in Fig. 4, is composed of at least four main steps:
(A) *test cases generation*; (B) *mutants generation*; (C) *test cases execution*; and
finally, (D) *results analysis*.

All these steps can be performed automatically by using a subset of components provided by the XMF framework and, as shown Fig. 4, the first two steps
(steps Ⓐ and Ⓑ) can be performed in parallel.

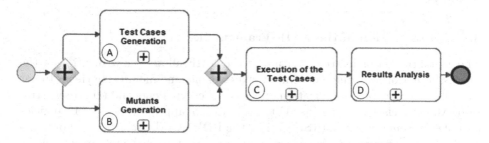

Fig. 4. Workflow of the testing process.

Generally, the first step is related to the generation of test cases (step Ⓐ),
which in our case can use the *TestCasesGenerator* component of XMF (component ① of Fig. 3) for the aim of generating a test suite starting from a given ACP.
The result of this activity can then be stored in a specific database (component
②) which contains information about the generated test cases, the policy from
which they are generated and the used generator.

The next step (Ⓑ in Fig. 4) is related to the generation of PDP mutants, which involves three components of XMF. In particular, with the help of component ③ (see Fig. 3), mutated versions of the PDP can be generated by applying a set of mutation operators; therefore, for each modified version, an executable mutated PDP can be generated by using the component ④; finally, the result of this step can be stored in a specific database (component ⑤) which, for each mutant, keeps track of: (i) the mutation operator used to create it; and (ii) the specific location of the source code affected by the mutation, e.g., the class (in case of OO programming language), method or statement.

The results of steps Ⓐ and Ⓑ are then used in the next phase (step Ⓒ in Fig. 4), which involves the XMF's component ⑥ that allows the execution of test cases on the original PDP and on its mutated versions. Finally, the result of step Ⓒ is loaded into the data warehouse (component ⑦ in Fig. 3) and used in step Ⓓ of the testing process (see Fig. 4).

The next section details how to instantiate the XMF framework and reports some analyses that can be performed.

4   Examples of Framework Application

We illustrate the application of the XMF framework through a simple scenario in which a tester wants to perform some analyses of test data. Specifically, the goal of these analyses is: (1) to compare two different test cases generation strategies in terms of the size of the generated test suites; and (2) to show the distribution of mutants of the PDP source code, considering real-world XACML policies.

To this end, the application of the XMF framework consists of two main steps: (1) instantiation of the XMF framework; and (2) illustration of some examples of analysis.

4.1   Instantiation of the XMF Framework

The instantiation or instrumentation of the XMF allows the realization of the means for performing different kinds of experiments and monitoring them. In our case, this consists of the realization of the XMF components and their orchestration. More precisely, this means (1) the selection of appropriate XACML policies and the System Under Test (SUT), i.e., the PDP; (2) the selection of appropriate mutation operators to be applied to the SUT; and (3) the integration of the considered test cases generation strategies.

XACML Repository. We populated the *XacmlRepository* component with nine real-world XACML policies taken from real contexts and European projects. As in *XACML Policy* column of Table 1, policies named *demo-5*, *demo-11* and *demo-26* have been taken from the Open Source repository software Fedora (Flexible Extensible Digital Object Repository Architecture) [1] for controlling the access to the administered digital contents; the remaining six are released by the TAS3 European project [24]. The same table reports some information about the structure of the selected policies; in particular, the columns represent the number of rules (*#Rule* column), conditions (*#Cond* column), subjects (*#Sub* column), resources (*#Res* column), actions (*#Act* column) and distinct functions (*#Funct* column) within each policy.

Table 1. XACML policies.

XACML policy	Functionality					
	#Rule	#Cond	#Sub	#Res	#Act	#Funct
2_73020419964_2	6	5	3	3	0	4
create-document-policy	3	2	1	2	1	3
demo-5	3	2	2	3	2	4
demo-11	3	2	2	3	1	5
demo-26	2	1	1	3	1	4
read-document-policy	4	3	2	4	1	3
read-informationunit-policy	2	1	0	2	1	2
read-patient-policy	4	3	2	4	1	3
Xacml-Nottingham-Policy-1	3	0	24	3	3	2

Test Cases Generator. Several testing strategies are available for XACML requests generation and can be included in the proposed testing framework. Among them, in this paper we focus on two requests derivation strategies:

- *Multiple Combinatorial* testing strategy that relies on combinatorial approaches of subject, resource, action and environment values taken from the XACML policy [5,8]. The motivation of this selection was the possibility to directly integrate in the XMF framework the tool X-CREATE [5,8] that implements the Multiple Combinatorial testing.
- *XACMET* [10] strategy, which is based on the expected behavior of an XACML-based PDP. XACMET models the expected behaviour of the evaluation of a given XACML policy as a labeled graph and guarantees the full path coverage of such graph [3,6]. The test cases generated are used only for the PDP testing purposes. This strategy has been selected because, according to its description, it can provide similar performance to the Multiple Combinatorial and can be better exploited for a fair comparison.

It is out of the scope of this paper to focus on the definition of test strategies. The framework has been voluntarily conceived to be independent from the test strategies adopted. The only mandatory constraints are that the strategies considered are based on XACML language and there exist a tool or at least a detailed specification that lets the implementation and the integration into the framework.

XACML PDPs Repository. The PDP under test we considered is the Sun PDP engine [23], which is an open source implementation of the XACML standard, written in Java. This choice was not mandatory and different PDP implementations could be considered. We decided for Sun's PDP engine because it is currently one of the most mature and widespread used engines for XACML policy evaluation, which provides complete support for all the mandatory features of XACML 2.0 and a number of optional features. This engine supports also all the standard attribute types, functions and combining algorithms and includes APIs for adding new functionalities as needed. The Sun PDP source code is broken into ten packages: seven packages include the core implementation, two packages include classes used for the configuration code, rarely used by programmers, and one package contains test code samples. In Table 2 we report for each package (column *Sun PDP Package*) the number of classes (column *# of Java Classes*) of the core implementation of Sun PDP.

Table 2. Core implementation of Sun PDP.

Sun PDP package	#Java classes
com.sun.xacml	16
com.sun.xacml.attr	24
com.sun.xacml.combine	9
com.sun.xacml.cond	34
com.sun.xacml.ctx	7
com.sun.xacml.finder	5
com.sun.xacml.finder.impl	1

PDPs Mutation Generator. In order to apply mutation analysis to the policy evaluation engine, we selected a set of mutation operators for the Java code considering the mutation operators addressed in the most commonly used object-oriented mutation tools such as μJava [15] that has been integrated within the *PDPsMutationGenerator*. Specifically, the selected mutation operators are divided into two main parts: (i) *class-level* mutation operators; and (ii) *method-level* mutation operators.

The former set of operators is specific for object-oriented languages and Java features and it can be classified in three categories based on the features of the Java language:

- *Inheritance*: the operators IHD, IHI, IOD, IPC and ISI cover the variables shadowing, the use of keyword *super*, and the constructors definition;
- *Polymorphism*: the operators OAC, OMR, PCC, PCI, PNC and PRV cover all objects references;
- *Java-Specific features*: the other operators cover other features supported in Java such as the use of keywords *this* and *static*.

The latter set of mutation operators introduces faults at the level of methods by seeding them directly into the internal code statements (e.g., *if* conditions, loops, *boolean/arithmetic* expressions *et cetera*). These operators are classified in the following categories:

- *Arithmetic* operators: the operators AODS, AODU, AOIS, AOIU, AORB, AORS and ASRS allow the deletion, insertion and replacement of both binary and unary operators;
- *Logical* operators: LOI and LOR are operators conceived for deletion and replacement of Java logical operator;
- *Conditional* operators: COD, COI and COR allow to manipulate the operators into the Java conditions that are used for expressing XACML functions and their parameters.

For a more detailed description of mutation operators we refer to [9,15].

4.2 Examples of Analysis

We performed several analysis by using the XMF framework to better understand (i) the performance of the considered XACML strategies in terms of number of test cases; (ii) the distribution of the mutations of the Sun PDP by applying the mutation operators integrated in the *PDPsMutationGenerator* component. In particular, the involved components have been *TestCasesGenerator* and *XacmlRepository* for the former analysis and *PDPsMutationGenerator*, *PDPsMutationIntegrator* and *XacmlPDPsRepository* for the latter one. Then, all test data have been stored in *XacmlMutationDW*. In the following, we report the performed analyses. Even if simple and informal, the obtained descriptive statistics let to highlight important information about the test cases generation strategies and the used mutation operators.

Size of Test Suites. Figure 5 reports, for each of the nine XACML policies, the size of test suites generated by each test strategy. Specifically, the blue bars (black in black and white printing) refer to the size of the XACMET test suites, while the orange bars (light gray in black and white printing) report the size relative to the Multiple Combinatorial test suites. As evidenced in Fig. 5, XACMET strategy produces systematically the smallest test suites. This could provide hints for an effective allocation of testing costs and efforts.

Distribution of Mutants. Considering the distribution of mutants in Sun PDP engine, Table 3 reports the cardinality of the mutants set (fourth column) and their distributions at class-level and method-level (second and third column) for each Java Package. As reported in the last row, the 76% (i.e. 6085 over 8030 mutants) of the mutants generated are derived by the application of the method-level mutation operators. Having a knowledge of mutants distribution at package level could help the tester to address the parts of the code that are more complex and could be subject to possible faults.

Distribution of the Mutations per Java Class. For each Java Class of Sun PDP, Fig. 6 shows the ordered number of the mutations applied. In particular,

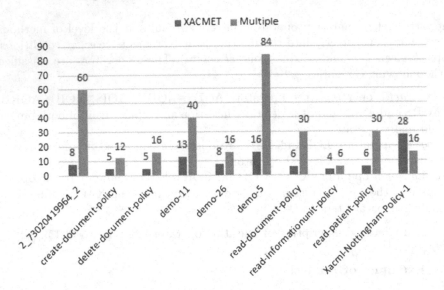

Fig. 5. Number of generated requests by policy and strategy: orange bars refer to the size of the Multiple Combinatorial test suites; blue bars refer to the size of test suites generated by XACMET strategy (Color figure online).

Table 3. Number of mutants by mutations operator level and by Java package.

Java package	Mutation operator level		All
	Class-level	Method-level	
com.sun.xacml	685	885	1570
com.sun.xacml.attr	431	2943	3374
com.sun.xacml.combine	73	277	350
com.sun.xacml.cond	344	1747	2091
com.sun.xacml.ctx	282	174	456
com.sun.xacml.finder	122	43	165
com.sun.xacml.finder.impl	8	16	24
All	1945	6085	8030

the blue bars (black in black and white printing) refer to the class-level mutation operators, while the orange bars (light gray in black and white printing) report the method-level ones. As evidenced in the figure, that shows a long-tailed distribution of all the mutations applied, most of the mutants are contained in few Java classes (the first 10 reported in the figure) and the remaining mutants are distributed in all the remaining ones. A deeper analysis of mutants distribution at class level allows the tester to focus the testing activity on the most error-prone java classes.

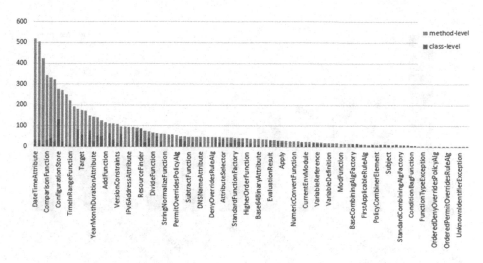

Fig. 6. Java classes ordered by number of mutations. (Color figure online)

Top 10 Mutated Java Classes. Figures 7 and 8 report a detailed extract of the top 10 mutated Java classes listed in Fig. 6. Specifically, in Fig. 7 there are the top 10 mutated Java classes ordered by the number of mutations derived by the application of mutants at class level; while in Fig. 8 there are the top 10 mutated Java classes considering the application of mutants at method level. These analyses enable to evidence the different classes of the PDP code that are most affected by *class-level* and *method-level* mutation operators. This could help the tester to focus on object-oriented features or classical features of the programming language.

5   Related Work

The work presented in this paper spans over two main research directions: mutation testing for AC systems and XACML based test generation strategies.

Mutation Testing for Access Control Systems. In the context of AC systems, many proposals rely on mutation techniques in order to evaluate testing effectiveness, namely the fault detection capabilities of testing strategies.

They leverage a set of mutation operators that is defined starting from the XACML policies, independently from any kind of implementation of the PDP in charge of evaluating the policy itself.

The authors of [16] define a fault model and a set of mutation operators that simulate syntactic faults of XACML ACPs. The work in [19] defines a generic metamodel able to express various rule-based security policy formalisms (R-BAC, OrBAC), and introduces a set of mutation operators that can be applied to all rule-based formalisms. Finally, the XACMUT tool [4] includes and enhances the mutation operators of [16] and [19] addressing specific faults of the XACML 2.0 language. It supports the automatic derivation of XACML mutation operators as well as their application to XACML policies and offers facilities to compute the mutation score of a test suite.

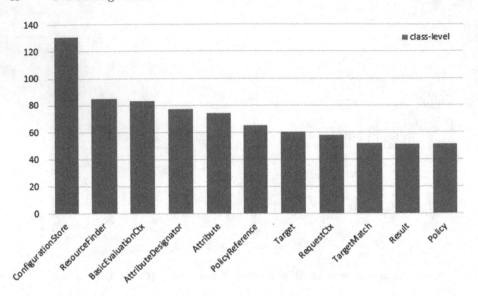

Fig. 7. Top 10 mutated Java classes ordered by number of mutations (class level).

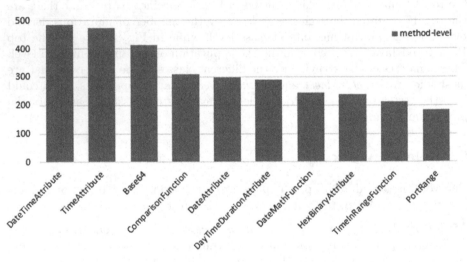

Fig. 8. Top 10 mutated Java classes ordered by number of mutations (method level).

The authors of [7] proposed a mutation-based approach to testing the PolPA based PDP. A set of mutation operators is defined according to the syntax of the PolPA policy language and mutants are created by applying mutation operators to the policy rules. The obtained faulty policies are used for generating test cases useful for assessing the PDP implementation.

Other proposals, however, exploit mutation for fault fixing and debugging of XACML policies purposes. Specifically, the approach in [25] addresses mutation-based techniques for policy repair. First, most suspicious policy elements (e.g., combining algorithm, policy target, and rules) are detected by fault localization techniques according to the execution information of test cases; then suspicious elements are modified by using well-defined mutation operators.

All the above mutation-based methodologies apply mutation analysis on ACP specification and they have been proven to be effective in the simulation of many common faults both in the policy specification and implementation [4,7,16]. However, they do not consider the specific characteristics of the PDP implementation code. To overcome these limitations, a first attempt to define specific mutation operators for PDP implementations is presented in [9]. Specifically, a set of Java based mutation operators is selected and manually applied to the code of the PDP.

The work presented in this paper includes and extends the proposal of [9] by presenting an automated testing framework for assessing the test suite effectiveness, by applying a set of classical code-based mutation operators directly on the PDP implementation. To the best of our knowledge, our approach is the first initiative that applies automated mutation analysis at the level of the policy evaluation engine, addressing specific faults of the PDP implementation language.

XACML-Based Tests Generation. Considering the automated test cases generation, solutions have been proposed for testing either the XACML policy or the PDP implementation [7,8]. Among them, the most referred ones use combinatorial approaches for test cases generation. Specifically, the X-CREATE tool [8] and the Targen tool [17] generate test inputs using combinatorial approaches of the XACML policies values and the truth values of independent clauses of policy values, respectively, whereas the work in [22] applies combinatorial analysis to the elements of the model (role names, permission names, context names) to derive test cases.

Alternatively, the Cirg approach [18] applies change impact analysis for test case generation starting from policy specification. Specifically, it provides a framework able to derive test cases as counterexamples that evidence semantic difference between two different versions of the policy under test.

Other approaches leverage existing symbolic execution techniques for generating test cases. Specifically, in [14], first the ACP under test is converted into semantically equivalent C Code Representation (CCR); then, the CCR is symbolically executed to generate test inputs.

Differently from the above approaches, authors of [6,10] propose the XACMET strategy based on the expected behaviour of an XACML-based PDP. XACMET models the expected behaviour of the evaluation of a given XACML policy as a labeled graph and guarantees the full path coverage of such graph. The test cases generated are used only for the PDP testing purposes. The main benefits of XACMET deal with the derivation of: (i) XACML requests that explicitly take into account the semantics of XACML functions as well as the policy and rule combining algorithms; and (ii) the expected verdict for each test request.

In XMF framework we integrated the X-CREATE tool, which has been proven to be more effective than Targen for the higher structural variability of the derived test inputs able to guarantee the coverage of the input domain of the XACML policy, and the XACMET strategy, that guarantees the full path coverage of graph representing the expected behaviour of the XACML-based PDP.

6   Conclusions

In this paper we presented the architecture and the behaviour of the XACML Mutation Framework (XMF), useful for assessing the XACML test suite effectiveness by means of Java code based mutation operators. XMF framework allowed the analysis of test data guaranteeing automation and replication of the experiments that are key aspects for addressing the overall testing process.

Two application examples of the framework have been provided aiming to: (i) compare two test strategies: Multiple Combinatorial *vs* XACMET approach; (ii) showing the distribution of mutants of the Sun PDP. However, it is important to remark that is out of the scope of this paper to decide which are the best test strategies. We only would like to provide an automatic testing framework that could be used for performing different analyses that provide hints to the tester for better decision-making of the testing activity.

For future work, we plan to include in XMF the XACML conformance test suite and to develop controlled experiments using also other implementations of the XACML-based PDP and other test strategies. We also would like to unify the set of mutant operators provided by the different tools and extend them in order to better target the XACML policy evaluation engine peculiarities.

Future work will also include experiments considering the last version of the XACML standard, i.e., the XACML 3.0.

References

1. Fedora commons repository software. http://fedora-commons.org/
2. Bertolino, A., Daoudagh, S., Lonetti, F., Marchetti, E.: Automatic XACML requests generation for policy testing. In: Proceedings of ICST, pp. 842–849, April 2012
3. Bertolino, A., Daoudagh, S., Lonetti, F., Marchetti, E.: Modelling and testing of XACML policies. 2012-TR-010 (2012)
4. Bertolino, A., Daoudagh, S., Lonetti, F., Marchetti., E.: XACMUT: XACML 2.0 mutants generator. In: Proceedings of the 8th International Workshop on Mutation Analysis, pp. 28–33 (2013)
5. Bertolino, A., Lonetti, F., Marchetti, E.: Systematic XACML request generation for testing purposes. In: Proceedings of the 36th EUROMICRO Conference on Software Engineering and Advanced Applications (SEAA), pp. 3–11 (2010)
6. Bertolino, A., Daoudagh, S., Lonetti, F., Marchetti, E.: An automated model-based test oracle for access control systems. In: Proceedings of the 13th International Workshop on Automation of Software Test, AST@ICSE 2018, Gothenburg, Sweden, 28–29 May 2018, pp. 2–8 (2018)

7. Bertolino, A., Daoudagh, S., Lonetti, F., Marchetti, E., Martinelli, F., Mori, P.: Testing of PolPA-based usage control systems. Softw. Qual. J. **22**(2), 241–271 (2014)
8. Bertolino, A., Daoudagh, S., Lonetti, F., Marchetti, E., Schilders, L.: Automated testing of extensible access control markup language-based access control systems. IET Softw. **7**(4), 203–212 (2013)
9. Daoudagh, S., Lonetti, F., Marchetti, E.: Assessment of access control systems using mutation testing. In: TELERISE, Florence, Italy, 18 May 2015, pp. 8–13 (2015)
10. Daoudagh, S., Lonetti, F., Marchetti, E.: XACMET: XACML modeling & testing: an automated model-based testing solution for access control systems. Softw. Qual. J. (2019, accepted)
11. Golfarelli, M., Rizzi, S.: From star schemas to big data: 20+ years of data warehouse research. In: Flesca, Sergio, Greco, Sergio, Masciari, Elio, Saccà, Domenico (eds.) A Comprehensive Guide Through the Italian Database Research Over the Last 25 Years. SBD, vol. 31, pp. 93–107. Springer, Cham (2018). https://doi.org/10.1007/978-3-319-61893-7_6
12. Jia, Y., Harman, M.: An analysis and survey of the development of mutation testing. IEEE Trans. Softw. Eng. **37**(5), 649–678 (2011)
13. Le Traon, Y., Mouelhi, T., Baudry, B.: Testing security policies: going beyond functional testing. In: Proceedings of ISSRE, pp. 93–102 (2007)
14. Li, Y., Li, Y., Wang, L., Chen, G.: Automatic XACML requests generation for testing access control policies. In: SEKE, pp. 217–222 (2014)
15. Ma, Y.S., Offutt, J., Kwon, Y.R.: MuJava: an automated class mutation system. J. Softw. Test. Verif. Reliab. **15**, 97–133 (2005)
16. Martin, E., Xie, T.: A fault model and mutation testing of access control policies. In: Proceedings of the 16th International Conference on World Wide Web, pp. 667–676 (2007)
17. Martin, E., Xie, T.: Automated test generation for access control policies. In: Supplemental Proceedings of ISSRE, November 2006
18. Martin, E., Xie, T.: Automated test generation for access control policies via change-impact analysis. In: Proceedings of SESS, pp. 5–11, May 2007
19. Mouelhi, T., Fleurey, F., Baudry, B.: A generic metamodel for security policies mutation. In: Proceedings of ICSTW, pp. 278–286 (2008)
20. OASIS: eXtensible Access Control Markup Language (XACML) Version 2.0. http://docs.oasis-open.org/xacml/2.0/access_control-xacml-2.0-core-spec-os.pdf. Accessed 10 June 2019
21. Papadakis, M., Kintis, M., Zhang, J., Jia, Y., Traon, Y.L., Harman, M.: Mutation testing advances: an analysis and survey. In: Advances in Computers, vol. 112, pp. 275–378. Elsevier (2019)
22. Pretschner, A., Mouelhi, T., Le Traon, Y.: Model-based tests for access control policies. In: Proceedings of ICST, pp. 338–347 (2008)
23. Sun Microsystems: Sun's XACML implementation (2006). http://sunxacml.sourceforge.net/
24. TAS3 project: trusted architecture for securely shared services. https://cordis.europa.eu/project/rcn/85331/factsheet/en
25. Xu, D., Peng, S.: Towards automatic repair of access control policies. In: 14th Annual Conference on Privacy, Security and Trust (PST), pp. 485–492. IEEE (2016)

The Structure and Agency Policy Language (SAPL) for Attribute Stream-Based Access Control (ASBAC)

Dominic Heutelbeck[✉]

FTK e.V. Forschungsinstitut für Telekommunikation und Kooperation,
44149 Dortmund, Germany
dheutelbeck@ftk.de
https://www.ftk.de

Abstract. Current architectures and data flow models for access control are based on request response communication. In stateful or session-based applications monitoring access rights over time this results in polling of authorization services and for Attribute-Based Access Control (ABAC) in the polling of policy information points. This introduces latency or increased load due to polling. Attribute-Stream-based Access Control (ASBAC) is an authorization model based on a publish subscribe pattern mitigating these bottlenecks. ASBAC allows the quasi real time consideration of attribute data streams for access control decisions, such as internet-of-things (IoT) sensor data. This paper introduces the Structure and Agency Policy Language (SAPL) for implementing ASBAC. In addition, the paper describes how ASBAC with SAPL can be implemented by applying a reactive programming model and describes key algorithms for evaluating SAPL policies.

Keywords: Attribute-based access control · ABAC · Attribute stream-based access control · ASBAC · Data streams · Reactive programming · IoT

1 Introduction

Attribute-based access control (ABAC) [11] has been a successful model for establishing reliable and flexible authorization infrastructures across applications in complex domains. In ABAC systems, access to resources is granted based on policies, i.e., rules and relationships which determine which behavior of a user or process (the subject) is authorized with regards to different resources. The policies themselves are encoded in a machine-readable format and the rules contained in the policies refer to traits of relevant objects, such as name, date of birth, unique identifiers, location, or security clearance level. These traits are called attributes, which may require accessing different data sources during policy evaluation to determine the outcome of the authorization process. These data sources are called *policy information points (PIPs)*. Other well-established

© Springer Nature Switzerland AG 2020
A. Saracino and P. Mori (Eds.): ETAA 2019, LNCS 11967, pp. 52–68, 2020.
https://doi.org/10.1007/978-3-030-39749-4_4

access control schemes, such as discretionary access control (DAC) [15], manda-tory access control (MAC) [15], and role-based access control (RBAC) [18] can be expressed by ABAC systems.

The two dominant ABAC control models currently in use are either based on the eXtensible Access Control Markup Language (XACML) standard [19] or on Next Generation Access Control (NGAC) [1]. The functional architectures of both XACML and NGAC share the concept of a policy enforcement point (PEP), as a functional entity which enforces access decisions made by a policy decision point (PDP). These access control models follow a request-response pattern and usually establish the access rights once prior to access and then allow the operation in question to be executed. The only way to continuously monitor access rights to a resource is to poll the PDP repeatedly. This introduces latency dependent on the poll frequency, and additional load on the infrastructure for communication and computation. Polling the PDP will also introduce load on the PIPs required for decision-making.

Since the introduction of XACML the industry has seen wide adoption of structured data serialization formats other than XML. Especially the JSON [4] format has found wide adoption for web services and IoT messages. The develop-ment of access control systems has been picking up on this and several approaches exist which use JSON for representing data or policies. E.g., the XACML JSON Profile [17] specifies a JSON representation for the authorization requests and responses in communication with a PDP. JACPoL [13,14] presents a JSON-based ABAC policy language, which proves to be less resource consuming than XACML policies. JACPoL omits the possibility to access external data sources for attributes and only uses attributes encoded in the authorization request. Both XACML and JACPoL make use of the hierarchical document structure of XML or JSON to represent rules and policies, resulting in optimization for machine processing, but are difficult to manually author by administrators since the semantics of a rule are often difficult to understand between the verbose notation in XML, and to a lesser extent, JSON. This results in an error-prone authoring process. This has been identified by commercial vendors of XACML systems, and Abbreviated Language for Authorization (ALFA) [20] has been developed as a domain-specific language (DSL) for policy authoring, which can be translated back and forth to XACML, improving the readability of policies. Other work [16] proposes to apply JSON Schema for modeling an ABAC rule language.

A common definition of attributes in ABAC [11] is: *Attributes are char-acteristics of the subject, object, or environment conditions. Attributes contain information given by a name-value pair.* The intent is to allow rules in a policy to access the domain model of the given application with regards to subject, object and environment. XACML and ALFA implement this very literally and attributes are accessed via so-called attribute designators returning the value (or a collection of values) for a given name. Further processing beyond comparisons operations is difficult, and it is explicitly not possible to use attribute values to be used as the input for further traversal intop the domain model by accessing sub-attributes of attributes. In case that the entire information required is contained in the request document, this is not a problem. As soon as the retrieval of attributes requires the access of external PIPs, required information may not be easily accessible via a simple name string, and deeper traversal of the application domain model may be necessary to get the required data. For example, when the authorization request only obtains a username, and first a tracking identifier has to be looked up to determine the current location of the user in question. This requires two PIP lookups, first lookup the tracking id by username, then lookup the location via the tracking id. XACML and ALFA does not allow this. While it may be possible to include this information apriori in the request, this would require the knowledge about the requirements made by policies (which are potentially subject to change at runtime) at the policy enforcement point during formulation of the request, which clearly is breaks separation of concerns enabled by the externalization of policy decision making which is a core motivation for the ABAC model.

In XACML and ALFA, conditions on the access of a resource can only be implemented by using obligations and advices. This requires that the PEP implements matching logic for realizing these constraints. One specific class of constraints which is commonly found in practice is the requirement to remove or transform parts of the resource data before handing it over to the client code. Examples: map birth date to an age bracket for anonymization of personal data, blacken part of a credit card number for web applications, only keep high level categorization of a medical diagnosis while removing detailed case specific symptoms, or remove classified information about the contents of shipping containers in logistics applications. The matching protection requirements may be subject to change. In this case handling these kinds of transformations within the PDP and formulating them in policies can be of advantage, providing a clear separation of concerns.

While XACML an ALFA could potentially be modified in order to support a publish-subscribe paradigm, in order to do so, a clear specification would be required on how to handle PIPs with changing values over time (streaming PIPs). Also, XACML has no notion of lazy and eager evaluation of expressions which have distinct implications for handling streaming PIPs.

The introduction of a new policy language is in major parts motivated by the limitations of XACML in expressing more complex domain model traversal while accessing PIPs, and requirements for PDP-side data transformation. However, the focus and main contribution of this paper are the description of policy evaluation approaches for PDPs supporting a publish-subscribe authorization scheme and streaming PIPs, which are also transferable to existing policy languages.

The remainder of the paper is structured as follows. Section 2 provides a brief overview of the Attribute Stream-Based Access Control (ASBAC) [8] functional model. Section 3 provides key requirements in policy language design and Sect. 4 introduces the Structure and Agency Policy Language (SAPL) and Sect. 5 discusses the implications of the streaming nature of authorization and PIPs to the

policy evaluation process and introduces the key algorithms. The paper closes
with conclusions in Sect. 6.

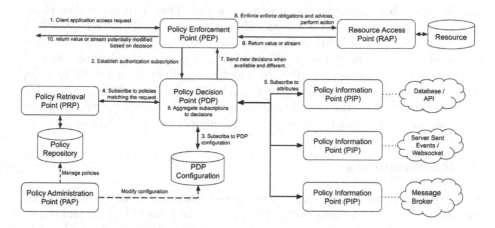

Fig. 1. ASBAC functional architecture

2   Attribute Stream-Based Access Control (ASBAC)

Attribute Stream-Based Access Control (ASBAC) [8] introduces a functional
architecture, as illustrated in Fig. 1. It is shares some key aspects with the architectures of both XACML and NGAC, with a policy decision point (PDP) in
the center, responsible for interpreting policies and making authorization decisions. The primary difference to the previously mentioned architectures is not
the structure of components, but the way they communicate. In XACML and
NGAC a single authorization request made by the PEP to the PDP results in
a number of requests and responses to and from the connected components for
accessing policies, configuration, and external attributes.

In ASBAC the authorization request is replaced by an authorization subscription to the PDP (2). The PDP in turn subscribes to the PDP configuration
(3). The configuration contains fundamental parameters for the decision making
(e.g., the default policy combining algorithm selected for the deployment) or
parameters for PIPs connected to the PDP (e.g., access tokens for message brokers or RESTful APIs). In addition, the PDP makes a subscription to the policy
retrieval point, parameterized by the authorization subscription. The PRP will
return all policies (policy sets, rules if applicable) to be evaluated for the authorization subscription, and sends a new set of matching policies if they change
due to policy management activities of the policy administration point. Each
time the PDP has a new set of configuration and matching policies, it starts
evaluating the policies. During the evaluation, when the PDP encounters references to policy information points, the PDP subscribes to them (5) as encoded

in the policies and aggregates incoming attributes from the PIPs to calculate the most recent decision (6), which is forwarded to the PEP if it differs from the most recent previous decision (7). The PEP then enforces the decision (8) and, if applicable, performs the requested action. Then it provides the client application with access to the return value, if present, of the action (9) which may be altered before being delivered to the client application (10), if this is indicated by the decision. The architecture should at every step be implemented using non-blocking asynchronous code. The functional model as presented in [8] is not specifying a policy language but covers the fundamental algorithms for stream-based PDPs and PEPs. This paper proposes a matching policy language and elaborates on implementation details to support attribute data streams.

3   Requirements

The goal is to create a lightweight, human readable policy language for ASBAC with a clean syntax avoiding boilerplate code in the form of hierarchical object structures used in policy languages expressed purely in XML or JSON. The language should be expressive enough to cover comparable scope of scenarios as XACML. For example in order to support "breaking the glass" scenarios where users may access a resource under additional constraints require policies expressing advices and obligations. These constraints usually encode additional actions to be performed on by a PEP in case of access, such as logging and notification of third parties about the occurrence of access.

The language should be extensible, i.e., it should be possible to integrate new functions on values to enable domain specific policies (such as geospatial functions for *geofencing* [12] similar to GeoXACML [5]). Geospatial policies are good candidates for attribute stream-based policies as they rely on streams of location tracking data. It should be easy to integrate new PIPs, i.e., external databases, message brokers, or location tracking services.

The policy language should support the transformation of resources. For example, granting access to medical or social science data for aggregation may require specific degradation of the original information. In this case degrading the information may require to transform the birth date in the data into an age bracket instead to avoid disclosure of the identity of patients. A second use-case may be a system storing credit card information which is accessed by a graphical frontend based on client-side JavaScript code. Here it may be indicated to only display the last four digits of a credit card number while blackening the leading digits. Policies should be able to express that the frontend only receives the blackened credit card number, while a payment backend may access the full dataset. Similarly, a logistics application may require the blackening of contents of shipping containers to certain personnel.

An appropriate data model for expressing subscriptions, authorization events and entities has to be selected. Because of its lightweight syntax and wide acceptance JSON should be basic data model of the policy language.

The policy language should support expressions that allow to query JSON values. JSONPath [7] is a popular standard for querying JSON objects and the policy language should support queries in this style.

As deployments of authorization infrastructures organically grow over time, the number of policies increases as well. Always evaluating all policies, including subscriptions to potentially required PIPs for each authorization, is not feasible and wasteful. Thus, the policy language should provide means of policy indexing, allowing for the selection of matching relevant policies for an individual subscription which does not require the full evaluation of the policy or any subscriptions to external PIPs.

As an additional structuring element, the policy language should allow for grouping of individual policies into policy sets. Policy sets have some important implications for both potential administrative models for the policies as well as for the implications for potential algorithms for resolving the occurrence of multiple different results from a number of policies for a given subscription. The policies in policy sets should ordered, allowing for additional resolution algorithms taking into account the order of decisions within a policy set.

The language should allow for deep domain model traversal allowing cascading attribute resolution.

An implementation must realize the ASBAC model.

4   The Structure and Agency Policy Language (SAPL)

This paper proposes a policy language for ASBAC, called the Structure and Agency Policy Language (SAPL). SAPL is named after the observations from social science, explaining the interdependence between social structures and the agency of individuals [2]. The following terms formalize components of the functional architecture.

Definition 1. *A* **value** *is a chunk of serialized data. All values are expressed as JSON [4] values. Then let JSON be the set of all JSON values. Let $JSON^*$:= $JSON \cup \{undefined\}$.*

Definition 2. *Data streams are composable, asynchronous sequences of values. Let S be the set of all possible streams with values in $JSON$ and S^* be the set of all possible streams with values in $JSON^*$.*

Definition 3. *A protected resource, r, is an element of R^* := $S \cup R$. Resources can be streams or in the set R of any other object depending on the domain logic or runtime environment.*

Definition 4. *Let $Subjects \subset JSON$ be the set of values describing all potential users and processes which may attempt to access any given resource $\in R^*$. Let $Resources \subset JSON$ be the set of values identifying and describing any given resource $\in R^*$. Let $Actions \subset JSON$ be the set of values describing all potentials actions to be performed by any subject $\in Subjects$ on any resource $\in R^*$.*

4.1 Subscriptions and Decisions

Definition 5. *Let sub ∈ ASub ⊂ JSON be an **authorization subscription**. ASub is the set of all objects containing the keys* subject, action, *and* resource *with matching values from Subjects, Actions, Resources. Optionally, sub may contain a key* environment *with an arbitrary JSON value.*

A *sub ∈ ASub* is used to indicate that a PEP subscribes to decisions from the PDP about the authorization of the subject to perform the action with the given resource. The three values have to unambiguously describe these objects. For JSON objects, values of keys are considered *attributes* of the object. The resource object may be a direct JSON representation of the resource, if applicable. SAPL authorization subscriptions are designed to answer authorization questions expressed similarly to XACML requests.

```
1  {
2      "subject" : { "username" : "alice", "id" : 1234321 },
3      "action"  : "SUBSCRIBE",
4      "resource": { "type": "mqtt", "topic": "track/987/location" }
5  }
```

This subscription expresses that the subject with username "alice" would like to subscribe to a topic of a MQTT message broker.

Definition 6. *An **authorization decision**, d, is an object value containing a* decision *∈ {PERMIT, DENY, INDETERMINATE, NOT_APPLICABLE}, an optional array of values for* obligations, *an optional array of values for* advices, *and an optional resource value. Let ADec ⊂ JSON be the set of all possible authorization decisions.*

The values of decision follow the same semantics as XACML [19]. An authorization decision may look as follows:

```
1  {
2      "decision"   : "PERMIT",
3      "obligations": [{ "action": "logAccess" }],
4      "advices"    : [{ "action": "sendMail", "to": "foo@bar.baz" }]
5  }
```

The authorization decision contains the decision, arrays containing obligations and advices, and an optional replacement resource. These authorization decisions can then be processed by the subscribing PEP by applying the ASBAC design patterns introduced in [8].

4.2 SAPL Documents

Policies and policy sets are organized in individual documents.

Definition 7. *A SAPL document, p ∈ SAPL, is a document containing either a policy or a policy set expressed in SAPL. A policy p **matches** sub ∈ ASub, if it does not have a target expression, or its target expression evaluates to true for sub.*

At the beginning, a SAPL document may declare imports for PIPs or function libraries enabling shorthands for potentially long attribute names or functions. After this, one document contains either exactly one policy or policy set. This paper discusses some key aspects of the full grammar of SAPL (see Appendix A) [9].

4.3   Policies

Each policy starts with the keyword policy and a policy name. Followed by the entitlement permit or deny, implying the decision indicated by the policy should it be positively evaluated. This is followed by a Boolean target expression. The target expression has the purpose to make the overall decision process more efficient, by allowing for indexing of policies and avoiding accessing external PIPs referenced by irrelevant policies. In order to support indexing, the target expression is evaluated strictly eager and no access to PIPs is allowed. Algorithms and data structures for indexing SAPL policies indexing are outside the scope of this paper and will be addressed in future publications. Target expressions may however use traversal and transformation of JSON data by using a JSONPath like syntax, comparisons, regular expression matching and application of functions. The remainder of the policy is only to be evaluated, if the target expression evaluates to *true* for a given subscription such policies are considered to *match* the subscription. If omitted, the target expression is considered to evaluate to *true* for all requests. The target expression is followed by an optional where block, consisting of a conjunction of semicolon delimited Boolean expressions. If the target expression and the where block of a policy evaluate to *true*, the policy implies the decision noted by the entitlement defined above. In the where block, or *policy body*, lazy Boolean operators are allowed and policy information points may be accessed to retrieve externally held attributes. External attributes provided by PIPs are subscribed to by angle brackets. The only two parts of a policy which are mandatory are a name String preceded by the keyword *policy* and an entitlement which is either *PERMIT* or *DENY*. A policy only consisting of these elements would match all subscriptions and always result in the given entitlement, resulting in a "permit all" or a "deny all" or policy.

After the entitlement, a target expression, where block, obligation, and advice may follow, with the semantics as outlined in the example above. The where block may contain variable declarations var name = value; assigning a value to the variable with the given name. Such a statement is considered to have evaluated to *true* for the purpose of evaluating the where block.

The final optional statement a policy can make is the *transform* statement, which is used to indicate, that the resource, as defined by the subscription, should be replaced with a different JSON value. The keyword *transform* is followed by an expression which evaluates to a JSON value.

A SAPL document with a policy matching the example subscription above may be expressed as follows:

```
1  policy "example1"
2  permit resource.type == "mqtt" & action == "SUBSCRIBE"
3  where
4    subject.id.<profile.clearanceLevel> >= 5;
5    subject.id.<physicalAccessControl.checkedIn>;
6  obligation
7    { "action": "logAccess" }
8  advice
9    { "action": "sendMail", "to": "foo@bar.baz" }
```

In this example policy, `subject.id` evaluates to the number 1234321. By appending .⟨profile.clearanceLevel⟩, the policy engine is instructed to pass the preceding result (1234321) to the PIP, or *attribute finder*, with the name "profile" to retrieve the *attribute* "clearanceLevel". The PIP in turn subscribes to the attribute. In the next line, an attribute finder subscribes to data published by the physical access control system which registers, if users have physically checked into the workplace. Thus, the policy permits access, if the subject has a sufficient security clearance and is on the company premises under physical access control. Attribute finders have to be preregistered to the PDP. If no matching PIP is present, an evaluation error occurs. In case a matching policy evaluates to *PERMIT* or *DENY*, the optional `obligation` and `advice` blocks are evaluated, which contain expressions which evaluate to arbitrary JSON values, which are then added to the authorization sent to the PEP. These events are sent to the subscribing PEP, whenever a new different authorization event occurs based on the latest PIP data.

4.4 Policy Sets

A policy set is an ordered collection of policies collected in one document. A policy set starts with the keyword *set* and a name string, followed by declaring which combining algorithms (see next section) is to be applied to the policies contained in the set for resolving potential ambiguities in the policy results. These two declarations and the presence of at least one policy below are mandatory within each policy set.

```
1  set "example2"
2  deny-unless-permit
3  for resource.type == "aType"
4  var dbUser = "admin";
5
6  policy "example2.1"
7  permit subject.function == "admin"
```

```
 8
 9  policy "example2.2"
10  permit action == "read"
11  transform resource |- filter.blacken
```

Optionally a policy set may declare a policy set target expression after the keyword for which is used in the same way as the target statement of documents containing only a policy. The policy set is only evaluated, if the policy set target-statement evaluates to *true* for a given subscription. Finally before defining the individual policies arbitrary variables may be declared to be used during evaluation of the following policies.

4.5 Combining Algorithms

SAPL foresees the following combining algorithms to resolve ambiguities when multiple policies return decisions, in the absence of transformations in the policies, these are very similar to combining algorithms found in XACML. However, the introduction of resource transformations introduces a new situation:

Definition 8. *A **transformation uncertainty** is a situation where multiple policies result in PERMIT and at least one of them has a transformation statement and it is not clear if and how a resource value should be replaced.*

Potential reactions to transformation uncertainty is to DENY access, or to return an error in the form of a INDETERMINATE result. In this way the combining algorithms ensure, that a decision event is always unambiguous with regards to a resource value replacement.

- **deny-unless-permit.** This strict algorithm is used if the decision should be DENY except for there is a PERMIT. It ensures that any decision is either DENY or PERMIT. If any policy document evaluates to PERMIT and there is no *transformation uncertainty*, the decision is PERMIT. Otherwise the decision is DENY.
- **permit-unless-deny.** This more relaxed algorithm is used if the decision should be PERMIT except for there is a DENY. It ensures that any decision is either DENY or PERMIT. If any policy document evaluates to DENY or if there is a transformation uncertainty, the decision is DENY. Otherwise the decision is PERMIT.
- **only-one-applicable.** This algorithm is used if policy sets and policies are constructed in a way that multiple policy documents with a matching target are considered an error. A PERMIT or DENY decision will only be returned if there is exactly one policy set or policy with matching target expression and if this policy document evaluates to PERMIT or DENY. If any target evaluation results in an error (INDETERMINATE) or if more than one policy documents have a matching target, the decision is INDETERMINATE. If there is no matching policy document, the decision is NOT_APPLICABLE. Otherwise, i.e., there is exactly one matching policy document, the decision is the result of evaluating this policy document.

– **deny-overrides.** This algorithm is used if a DENY decision should prevail a PERMIT without setting a default decision. If any policy document evaluates to DENY, the decision is DENY. Else, if there is any INDETERMINATE or there is a transformation uncertainty, the decision is INDETERMINATE. Else, if there is any PERMIT the decision is PERMIT. Else, the decision is NOT_APPLICABLE.
– **permit-overrides.** This algorithm is used if a PERMIT decision should prevail a DENY without setting a default decision. If any policy document evaluates to PERMIT and there is no transformation uncertainty, the decision is PERMIT. Else, if there is any INDETERMINATE or there is a transformation uncertainty, the decision is INDETERMINATE. Else, if there is any DENY the decision is DENY. Else, the decision is NOT_ APPLICABLE.
– **first-applicable.** This algorithm is exclusive for policy sets, as it assumes that the policies are ordered. It allows the policy author to manages the policy's priority by their order in a policy set. As soon as the first policy returns PERMIT, DENY or INDETERMINATE, its result is the final decision. Thus a "default" can be specified by creating a last policy without any conditions. If a decision is found, errors which might occur in later policies are ignored. Each policy is evaluated in the order specified in the policy set. If it evaluates to INDETERMINATE, the decision is INDETERMINATE. If it evaluates to PERMIT or DENY, the decision is PERMIT or DENY If it evaluates to NOT_APPLICABLE, the next policy is evaluated. If no policy with a decision different from NOT_APPLICABLE has been found, the decision of the policy set is NOT_APPLICABLE.

For all combining algorithms, the advices and obligations of the policies agreeing with the final outcome are added to the respective arrays in the decision event.

4.6   Expressions

The SAPL expression syntax contains typical operation in accessing attributes (keys) of JSON objects, arithmetic, Boolean, string and comparison operations. Due to size limitations, a full specification is out of scope of the paper, and only key features and design considerations are discussed in this section. A detailed specification is available in [9].

SAPL expressions may evaluate to any JSON value or to *undefined*. The reason for introducing the concept of undefined values is to eliminate unexpected and unwanted evaluation errors which would lead to the occurrence of policies evaluating to INDETERMINATE and thus potentially to an unintended denial of access. By introducing undefined and the matching semantics in operators, policies become easier to write and to reason about. The source for such potentially unintended behavior from the perspective of policy authors is, that policies cannot make assumptions about the contents of the values contained in a subscription. As a PDP may potentially be used by applications from different domains with individual ways of expressing subject, action, or resource in subscriptions. And also policies may be written by different individuals only aware of their own domain and what kind of subscriptions to expect from there. For example, given one policy containing a target expression `subject.username == "bob"` and another policy with the target expression `subject.age > 50` and a subscription with the subject `{ "username" : "bob" }`. The first target expression evaluates to *true*, while for the second target expression the subject object does not contain the key `age` and without the possibility of evaluating to *undefined* the expression would result in an error causing the policy to error and evaluate to INDETERMINATE as a whole with the implied results based on the applied combining algorithm. With *undefined*, the comparison can evaluate to *false* and the evaluation is only resulting in a policy that does not match, or is not applicable if such cases occur in the where block of a policy.

Expressions may contain function calls `library.function(expression)`. Functions may return a JSON value or *undefined*. The PDP may have arbitrary function libraries installed, such as libraries for processing geographical information.

Expressions may contain access to attribute data streams provided by policy information points. Accessing a PIP is expressed by angled brackets: `subject.id.<tracker.location>`. Such an expression is turned into a subscription to the attribute `tracker.location` with the value of `subject.id` as a parameter. The PDP may have arbitrary attribute finders installed each providing a set of attributes to subscribe to. Attribute finders may include time-based attributes returning the current time as a data stream in regular intervals. The implications of subscribing to attribute streams for evaluating expressions and policies will be examined in the implementation section.

Expressions may contain JSONPath style queries on values. For example given an array `persons` containing JSON objects describing persons including their age, the expression `persons[?(@.age >= 50)]` will return a new array only containing the persons with age 50 and up. Other queries include wildcards, recursive search for keys, and array slicing.

A unique feature of JSON processing in SAPL is the ability to apply filters to JSON values. SAPL provides two default filters `remove`, which removes a key from an object, and `blacken` which operates on strings and overwrites a substring with a provided character (e.g., overwrite the leading digits of a credit card number with asterisks). Filters are expressed by using the filter operator `|-`. For example, `resource |- { @.credit_card : blacken }` overwrites the characters in the string containing the credit card information. Additionally, filters can be applied to all elements in an array by preceeding the expression with the keyword `each`.

5 Implementation of an Attribute Stream-Based Policy Evaluation

The general algorithm for implementing an attribute stream based PDP were previously described in [8]. The algorithm was described without taking a specific policy language into account. This section examines how to implement the evaluation of SAPL policies with access to attribute streams.

5.1   Reactive Programming

In the following, this paper presents a number of asynchronous algorithms for policy evaluation where asynchronous information can change the evaluation result over time. A publish-subscribe design is applied, similar to the observer pattern [6]. The principles of reactive programming as proposed by the Reactive Manifesto [3] are applied, which also addresses requirements regarding responsiveness, resilience, elasticity and message-driven systems. A notable difference to the original observer pattern is the introduction of functionality for handling back-pressure, i.e., for informing upstream data sources about bottlenecks in downstream processing and allowing for elastic adjustment of data transfer. To be able to express algorithms following this paradigm, this paper uses a simplified notation for reactive algorithms. This notation mostly ignores error handling and only introduces a few required asynchronous operations on data streams.

Definition 9. *For a stream, $s \in S^*$, $s.first()$ returns a stream only containing the first element of the stream s.*

Definition 10. *Let $combineLatest : [S_1, \ldots, S_n] \to S^*$, $n \in \mathbb{N}$ be a function returning a stream which, starting from the time all input streams have emitted at least one value, emits an array of the most recent values for each input stream whenever a new value is emitted by any input stream.*

Definition 11. *For a stream, $s \in S^*$, $s.map(fun|fun : JSON^* \to JSON^*)$ returns a stream, where for each value $v \in s$, $s.map(fun)$ contains $fun(v)$.*

Definition 12. *For a stream, $s \in S^*$, $s.switchMap(fun|fun : JSON^* \to S^*)$ returns a new stream s', where the each time a new value from s is emitted, a new stream $fun(s)$ is generated, and until the next value from s arrives, all values from $fun(s)$ are emitted by s' as they occur.*

Definition 13. *$just(v) \in S^*, v \in JSON^*$ is the stream only containing v.*

5.2   Reactive Policy Document Evaluation

Passing a SAPL policy p into a SAPL parser will generate an in-memory abstract syntax tree (AST) representing the document, containing nodes for the different syntactical elements and their respective children as defined by the SAPL grammar [9].

Definition 14. *Each node n in the abstract syntax tree of a SAPL document implements a function $eval_n : ASub \to S^*$, returning a data stream.*

Determining if any given policy document matches a subscription is does not need to take data streams into account. The check for a match is to be implemented as a blocking synchronous function. Even, in the context of an otherwise primarily asynchronous implementation of a policy engine this is the right thing to do, as the function an be immediately be evaluated based on the subscription and AST alone without accessing external resources and blocking IO operations. The limitations of the paper do not allow to specify the evaluation algorithms for all node types in a SAPL AST. The following example expression contains a few key constructs that allow explain how attribute streams are handled when evaluating SAPL policies.

```
1    subject.<physicalAccessControl.checkedIn>
2    && (   subject.<profile.clearanceLevel> >= 5
3        || environment.<threatLevel> < 2 )
```

This expression subscribes up to three attribute streams. The result depends on the subject to be registered on company premises and one of the two next conditions must be met. The subject has either a security clearance level greater or equal of five or the estimated threat level of the environment is below 2. SAPL differentiates between eager and lazy operations. Operators like arithmetic, string concatenation, and comparisons are always evaluated eagerly. This means that a node in the AST constructs the output data stream by subscribing to its parameter data streams and applying the operator when the data streams emit new values. The *eval* function of each AST node for eager operators construct the result data stream by applying Algorithm 1 for a matching operator function *op*.

Algorithm 1. Eager Evaluation

Given : $left, right \in S^*, op : JSON^* \to JSON^*$
$combineLatest(left, right).map([l, r] \mapsto op(l, r))$

In the case of Boolean operations, policy evaluation may not always need to look at both values in order to determine the outcome. In most programming languages, the expression left of a Boolean operation is evaluated first and the right expression is not evaluated at all, if the outcome is clear at this point. This allows for both conditional evaluation and reduces computation cost. In the case of the SAPL expression above, the evaluation can stop end return *false* if the subject.<physicalAccessControl.checkedIn> returns false. Ideally, the policy evaluation should not only not look at the other values, but also not subscribe to the PIPs on the right side of the conjuction as long as the latest value of the left data stream is *false*. This behavior is realized by Algorithm 2. Here, if the left data stream returns *false* just a false value is emitted. However if it was true, the evaluation subscribes to the right data steam and returns its values, and unsubscribes as soon as the left side becomes *false* again. SAPL operators can be implemented on following variants of these two basic algorithms, while adding checks for typing.

Algorithm 2. Lazy Conjunction Evaluation

Given: $left, right \in S^*$, where $\forall v \in left, right : v \in \{true, false\}$
$left.switchMap(l \mapsto \{$
  if (l)
    return $right$;
  else
    return $just(false)$;
$\})$

---

6 Conclusions

This paper presented the fundamentals of a new policy language for attribute stream-based access control (ASBAC) solving a number of issues occurring with existing ABAC systems in scenarios where access rights may change during access and polling the authorization infrastructure is not an acceptable solution. The proposed reactive implementation strategy together with the algorithms presented in [8] illustrates how to implement an ASBAC engine supporting SAPL. An authorization infrastructure following the proposed patters is a natural fit for applications following the reactive programming model and allows for quasi-real time publish-subscribe authorization in stateful applications. The syntax of SAPL has been designed to be both expressive and also easily readable by humans to reduce errors in policy auditing. SAPL has built in support for JSON queries, filtering and transformation. A complete reference implementation of the ASBAC architecture has been implemented and is publicly available as open source under the Apache 2.0 license at [9], including a full implementation of SAPL. A number of case studies based on medical scenarios and geographic access control are available [10]. The proposed solution addresses a number of shortcomings of existing XACML-based (domain navigation, transformations, readability) and its unique feature is the support of publish-subscribe patterns for all architecture components (incl. PEP, PDP, PRP, PIP). This paper could not cover all evaluation steps required for a full implementation, aspects such as combining algorithms and variable handling have been omitted due to space limitations. While the presented algorithms are simple, they demonstrate a significant paradigm shift im policy handling compared to existing ABAC approaches and implementations and that adding data stream processing to authorization infrastructure is feasible. A quantitative performance evaluation of ASBAC and data structures for policy indexing will be covered in future publications. Further work will examine how to apply ASBAC in collaborative IoT applications, where ASBAC will first be applied in message brokers due to the hardware limitations at sensor level. ASBAC is not defining an administrative model, which should be investigated.

A   SAPL Grammar

```
sapl = { import },( policy-set | policy ) ;
import = "import", ID, { ".", ID }, ".",
  ( ID | "*" ) | "import", { ID, "." },
  ID, "as", ID ;
policy-set = "set", STRING,
  combining-algorithm,
  [ "for", target-expression ],
  { value-definition, ";" },
  policy, { policy } ;
combining-algorithm =
    "deny-overrides"|"permit-overrides"
  |"first-applicable"|"only-one-applicable"
  |"deny-unless-permit"|"permit-unless-deny";
target-expression = expression ;
value-definition = "val", ID, ":=",expression ;
policy = "policy", STRING, entitlement,
  [ target-expression ],
  [ "where", policy-body ],
  [ "obligation", expression ],
  [ "advice", expression ],
  [ "transform" expression ] ;
entitlement = "permit" | "deny" ;
policy-body = statement, ";", {statement,";"};
statement = value-definition | expression ;
expression = addition ;
addition = multiplication, { ( "+" | "-"
  | "&&" | "&" ), multiplication } ;
multiplication = comparison, { ( "*" | "/"
  | "||" | "|"), comparison } ;
comparison = prefixed, [ ( "==" | "=~" | "<"
  | "<=" | ">=" | ">" | "in" ), prefixed ] ;
prefixed = [ ( "-" | "!" ) ],basic-expression;
basic-expression = ( value | "@" | ID
  | function-call | ( "(", expression, ")" ) ),
  { selection-step },
  [ ("|-", filter) | ( "::", value ) ] ;
function-call = ID, { ".", ID }, "(",
  [ expression, {",", expression } ], ")" ;
selection-step = key-step | index-step
  | wildcard-step | rec-descent-step
  | rec-wildcard-step | slicing-step
  | expression-step | condition-step
  | union-step | attr-finder-step ;
key-step = ".", ID | "[", STRING, "]" ;
index-step = "[", NUMBER, "]" ;
wildcard-step = ".", "*" | "[", "*", "]" ;
rec-descent-step = "..", ID | "..",
  "[", STRING, "]" | "..",
  "[", NUMBER, "]" ;
rec-wildcard-step = "..", "*" | "..",
  "[", "*", "]" ;
slicing-step = "[", [ NUMBER ], ":",
  [[ NUMBER ], [":",[ NUMBER ]]], "]" ;
expression-step = "[","(",expression,")","]";
condition-step = "[", "?", "(", expression,
  ")", "]" ;
union-step = "[", NUMBER, ",", NUMBER,
  { ",", NUMBER }, "]"
  | "[", ID, ",", ID, { ",", ID }, "]" ;
attr-finder-step = ".", "<", ID, { ".",
  ID }, ">" ;
filter = [ "each" ], filter-function |
  "{", filter-statement, { ",",
  filter-statement }, "}" ;
filter-statement = [ "each" ], "@",
  {selection-step}, ":", filter-function ;
filter-function = ID, { ".", ID }, [ "(",
  [ expression, {",",expression}],")" ] ;
value = object | array | NUMBER | STRING
  | "true" | "false" | "null" | "undefined";
object = "{", [ STRING, ":", expression,
  { ",", STRING, ":", expression } ], "}" ;
array = "[", [ expression, { ",", expression}
  ], "]" ;
ID = ( LETTER | "_" | "$" ),{ LETTER | DIGIT
  | "_" | "$" } ;
LETTER = "A"|"B"|... |"Z"|"a"|"b"|...|"z" ;
DIGIT="0"|"1"|"2"|"3"|"4"|"5"|"6"|"7"|"8"|"9";
STRING='"',? any character except " ?,
  '"'|"'", ? any character except ' ?, "'" ;
NUMBER = ? JavaScript number definition ? ;
```

References

1. American National Standards Institute: INCITS 499–2018: Information technology - next generation access control - functional architecture. Technical report, American National Standards Institute (2018)
2. Barker, C.: Cultural Studies: Theory and Practice. Sage, Thousand Oaks (2003)
3. Bonér, J., et al.: The reactive manifesto (2014). https://www.reactivemanifesto.org/. Accessed 15 May 2019
4. Bray, T.: The JavaScript Object Notation (JSON) Data Interchange Format. RFC 7159, March 2014. https://doi.org/10.17487/RFC7159, https://rfc-editor.org/rfc/rfc7159.txt
5. Open Geospatial Consortium: Geospatial extensible access control markup language (GeoXACML). Technical report, Open Geospatial Consortium (2011). https://www.opengeospatial.org/standards/geoxacml

6. Gamma, E., Helm, R., Johnson, R., Vlissides, J.: Design Patterns: Elements of Reusable Object-oriented Software. Addison-Wesley Longman Publishing Co., Inc., Boston (1995)
7. Gossner, S.: JSONPath - XPath for JSON (2006). https://goessner.net/articles/JsonPath/. Accessed 14 June 2019
8. Heutelbeck, D.: Attribute stream-based access control (ASBAC) - functional architecture and patterns. In: Proceedings of the 2019 International Conference of Security and Management (SAM 2019) (2019)
9. Heutelbeck, D.: SAPL policy engine (2019). https://github.com/heutelbeck/sapl-policy-engine. Accessed 10 May 2019
10. Heutelbeck, D.: SAPL policy engine demos (2019). https://github.com/heutelbeck/sapl-demos. Accessed 10 May 2019
11. Hu, V.C., et al.: Guide to attribute based access control (ABAC) definition and considerations. Technical report, National Institute of Standards and Technology, January 2014. https://doi.org/10.6028/nist.sp.800-162
12. Ijeh, A.C., Brimicombe, A.J., Preston, D.S., Imafidon, C.O.: Geofencing in a security strategy model. In: Jahankhani, H., Hessami, A.G., Hsu, F. (eds.) ICGS3 2009. CCIS, vol. 45, pp. 104–111. Springer, Heidelberg (2009). https://doi.org/10.1007/978-3-642-04062-7_11
13. Jiang, H., Bouabdallah, A.: JACPoL: a simple but expressive JSON-based access control policy language. In: Hancke, G.P., Damiani, E. (eds.) WISTP 2017. LNCS, vol. 10741, pp. 56–72. Springer, Cham (2018). https://doi.org/10.1007/978-3-319-93524-9_4
14. Jiang, H., Bouabdallah, A.: Towards a JSON-based fast policy evaluation framework. In: Panetto, H., et al. (eds.) OTM 2017. LNCS, vol. 10574, pp. 22–30. Springer, Cham (2017). https://doi.org/10.1007/978-3-319-69459-7_2
15. Latham, D.C.: Department of defense trusted computer system evaluation criteria. Department of Defense (1986)
16. Linklater, G., Smith, C., Connan, J., Herbert, A., Irwin, B.V.: JSON schema for attribute-based access control for network resource security. In: Proceedings of Southern Africa Telecommunication Networks and Applications Conference (SATNAC 2017). (2017)
17. Lockhart, H., Parducci, B.: JSON profile of XACML 3.0 version 1.0 (2017). http://docs.oasis-open.org/xacml/xacml-json-http/v1.0/xacml-json-http-v1.0.html. Accessed 10 May 2019
18. Sandhu, R.S.: Role-based access control. In: Advances in Computers, vol. 46, pp. 237–286. Elsevier (1998)
19. XACML 3.0 Committee: extensible access control markup language (XACML) version 3.0 (2013). http://docs.oasis-open.org/xacml/3.0/xacml-3.0-core-spec-os-en.html. Accessed 10 May 2019
20. XACML 3.0 Committee: Abbreviated language for authorization version 1.0 (2015). https://www.oasis-open.org/committees/download.php/55228/alfa-for-xacml-v1.0-wd01.doc. Accessed 10 May 2019

NoCry: No More Secure Encryption Keys for Cryptographic Ransomware

Ziya Alper Genç[✉], Gabriele Lenzini, and Peter Y. A. Ryan

Interdisciplinary Centre for Security, Reliability and Trust (SnT),
University of Luxembourg, Luxembourg City, Luxembourg
{ziya.genc,gabriele.lenzini,peter.ryan}@uni.lu

Abstract. Since the appearance of ransomware in the cyber crime scene, researchers and anti-malware companies have been offering solutions to mitigate the threat. Anti-malware solutions differ on the specific strategy they implement, and all have pros and cons. However, three requirements concern them all: their implementation must be secure, be effective, and be efficient. Recently, Genç *et al.* proposed to stop a specific class of ransomware, the cryptographically strong one, by blocking *unauthorized* calls to cryptographically secure pseudo-random number generators, which are required to build strong encryption keys. Here, in adherence to the requirements, we discuss an implementation of that solution that is more secure (with components that are not vulnerable to known attacks), more effective (with less false negatives in the class of ransomware addressed) and more efficient (with minimal false positive rate and negligible overhead) than the original, bringing its security and technological readiness to a higher level.

Keywords: Ransomware · Malware · Cryptovirus · CSPRNG

1 Introduction

Cryptographic ransomware reached the peak of its fame after WannaCry's worldwide attack, in May 2017. On victim's machine, it encrypts files, asking for a ransom (hence the name) to release the cryptographic key the victim needs to decrypt the files and re-access them. Unsurprisingly, according to a recent survey [6], 50.6% of the victims did not get any key in return, after the payment, irremediably losing the data and money.

Encryption is a strong instrument in the hands of criminals. If properly implemented, its impact is irreversible: without knowing the decryption key, recovering the contents of an encrypted file is computationally unfeasible, a very disruptive fact for the victims. However, implementing cryptography flawlessly is a difficult task, and coders of ransomware are challenged by the same issues that have been troubling security engineers in charge of implementing cryptographic applications. One of the most relevant is to generate (cryptographically secure) encryption keys and keep them safe. Failing in this makes the encryption weak

© Springer Nature Switzerland AG 2020
A. Saracino and P. Mori (Eds.): ETAA 2019, LNCS 11967, pp. 69–85, 2020.
https://doi.org/10.1007/978-3-030-39749-4_5

in the sense that it becomes likely to reproduce or retrieve the decryption keys, which would jeopardize the ransomware business model. In this issue, there is hope as same defence and some anti-ransomware solutions (see Sect. 6) indeed offer to recover files counting on ransomware engineering's being naïve in implementing strong cryptography.

Unfortunately, modern ransomware programs are coded more professionally than those in the past. Such professional variants (and attack relying on them are increasing and demanding higher ransom, contrarily the general trend that sees the number of ransomware attacks dropping, see [7]) are quite sophisticated, well designed, and properly implemented. Among them, there are variants of WannaCry, and variants of other ransomware families such as Petya, NotPetya, and GoldenEye, CryptoLocker, Crysis, Cerber, and RAA. They all pose serious threats. Bajpai *et al.* [2], who propose for ransomware a scale similar to the Saffir-Simpson for hurricanes, classify them as having severity categories 5 and 6.

Are then they unstoppable? Genç *et al.* discuss a strategy in [8], called USHALLNOTPASS. The core idea is to impede them to call cryptographically secure pseudo-random number generators (CSPRNGs). These functions offered by the operating system return the essential ingredients required to build cryptographically secure encryption keys: "good" pseudo-random numbers. The solution described in [8] has a sufficiently accurate detection rate (*i.e.,* 94%), but it is not yet an effective and efficient solution. What it needs is an access control system that guarantees at least three important requirements: (1) to rely on architectural components that are not vulnerable against known or arguable targeted attacks; (2) to have lower false positive rate; (3) to impose a negligible performance overhead.

Contribution. We discuss improvements to the solution proposed in [8] that satisfies requirements (1)–(3). It meets (1) by avoiding interprocess communication (IPC), a choice that is potentially vulnerable to named pipes hijacking (Sect. 4.1). It meets (2) by bootstrapping and maintaining a *Whitelist DB* of honest applications that also call CSPRNG (Sect. 4.2). It meets (3) by showing that, when run in respect to vanilla system, our implementation has a negligible overhead (Sect. 5) over applications that use CSPRNGs, with a relative improvement of roughly two orders of magnitude with respect the prototype presented in [8]. We also re-test the implementation against 747 active real-world ransomware samples, and measure the false negative rate.

To appreciate fully this paper's contribution, we recall USHALLNOTPASS's in Sect. 2, security model and assumptions in Sect. 3, and the state of the art in anti-ransomware in Sect. 6. We discuss and test our implementation in Sect. 4 and in Sect. 5, arguing that our version of USHALLNOTPASS, which we call NOCRY, in antithesis to the infamous WannaCry, has potential to become the best defense against ransomware at the time of writing (June 2019).

2   Recalling USHALLNOTPASS: No Random, No Ransom

USHALLNOTPASS [8] has been proposed as a solution to stop cryptographically strong ransomware attacks. It intercepts calls made to application programming interfaces (APIs) of cryptographically secure pseudo-random number generators (CSPRNGs) and allows only authorized applications to get through, blocking and terminating all the others.

On modern operating systems (OSs), CSPRNG APIs are the only reliable source of cryptographically secure pseudo-random numbers that are necessary to build (cryptographically strong) encryption keys, which are the instruments that a crypto-ransomware needs to be certain that it is unfeasible for a victim to reverse the damage without paying the ransom.

Genç et al. showed that a proof-of-concept implementation, proving they are able to neutralize even NotPetya, and collect evidence that the concept works against a very large class of about five hundreds real-word active cryptographically strong ransomware samples including WannaCry, and other ransomware families such as Petya and GoldenEye, CryptoLocker, Crysis, Cerber, and RAA.

The goal of [8] is to prove that by controlling access to CSPRNG, ransomware can be blocked before any damage occurs. However, how the authorization is decided has not been detailed, but claimed relying on a *Whitelist* database (DB) accessible only with admin privileges and upon an undefined security policy. It suggests however two optional mechanisms for authorization: (i) digitally signed executables can call CSPRNG; and (ii) not digitally signed executables can also call CSPRNG, if the administrator decides so at run time.

The architecture of USHALLNOTPASS and the workflow is depicted in Fig. 1. It has two separate components: Interceptor, and Controller. Interceptor captures the calls made to CryptGenRandom API (a CSPRNG offered by Windows OS) and dispatches the process ID to the Controller, which searches the Whitelist DB to decide whether to allow or deny access. No parameters or outputs are logged. The overhead which the proof-of-concept prototype of USHALLNOTPASS brings to the clean system is significant. Details and benchmarks can be found in [8].

3   Security Assumptions

USHALLNOTPASS [8] works under two assumptions, which remain valid in our implementation of the concept, NoCry: (i) at the moment in which the anti-ransomware is installed on a target system and before it becomes active and operational, the system is non-compromised; (ii) the host machine can run anti-virus software to detect, stop and neutralize common malicious actions such as keystroke logging, process injection, etc.

We also stress one key point once more. The original concept, and thus NoCry, has been conceived to work against cryptographically strong ransomware *only*. At least in the ransomware samples that we have analyzed, those are the ransomware programs that access secure random number sources.

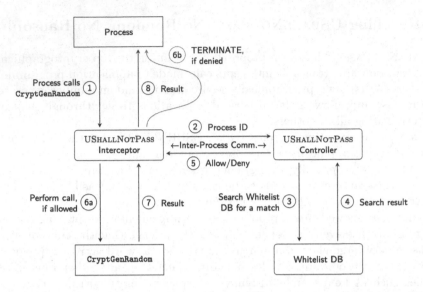

Fig. 1. Architectural view of USHALLNOTPASS [8]. When `CryptGenRandom` API is called, Interceptor identifies the caller and dispatches the process ID to Controller. If the application is authorized, the call is executed and the result is returned to the caller. Otherwise, the call is blocked and the caller process is terminated.

NoCRY does not stop ransomware that does not follow secure development standards and, for instance, derives keys from a *non-cryptographic* pseudo-random number generators (PRNGs), like `rand` function in C runtime library or `System.Random` class provided by .NET framework. In Sect. 5.3, we argue that such ransomware variants are weak, cannot achieve success in the long term, or can be stopped otherwise. Therefore, NoCRY is not all-in-one defence but meant to work side-by-side with (or even, integrated into) traditional anti-malware solutions or in combination with other anti-ransomware systems.

4   NoCRY: Requirements, Design and Implementation

We believe that an anti-ransomware application should be effective and non-invasive in at least the following meanings:

Robust Architecture. The execution and operation of the defense system should rely on architectural choices that minimize the attack surface and have no vulnerabilities against known and arguable targeted attacks. In our case, the authorization mechanism be robust against targeted attacks.

Low False Positive Rate and Minimal User Intervention. While providing the security, the defense system must also ensure (arguably and measurably) a low rate of false positive. The challenge regards our Whitelist DB. The list needs to be safely bootstrapped, and software updates should be reflected in the Whitelist DB with no interruption, inconsistency, or possibility of intrusions.

Optimized Decision Procedure. The performance impact of running an anti-ransomware should be negligible and must be imperceptible by the user. In NoCry, the overhead is due to the interception of calls to CSPRNG APIs and the time required by the access control decision procedure.

We discuss the NoCry in the reminder of the section. We refer to Windows systems, as they have been the target of most of the ransomware attacks known at today. What we discuss applies to other platforms as well.

4.1 Robust Architecture

As described in Sect. 2, USHALLNOTPASS consists of two components: Interceptor detects the calls made to CSPRNG APIs and Controller makes authorization decisions for the caller processes. This architecture needs an active communication channel between Interceptor and Controller components. In order to fulfill this need, USHALLNOTPASS employs *named pipes*.

A named pipe is an interprocess communication (IPC) mechanism which enables processes to communicate to each other using a client-server architecture [17]. In this model, the *pipe server* is the application which creates the named pipe. Once the pipe is created, *pipe clients* – the applications that connects to the pipe server – can start sending/receiving messages to/from the pipe server. In the access control system of USHALLNOTPASS, Interceptor creates two simplex named pipes, one for dispatching the process ID to Controller and another for getting the authorization result.

That said, named pipes in Windows platform are infamous with their security issues [3]. Among them, one particular issue constitutes a critical vulnerability for USHALLNOTPASS. Namely, a malicious application can attempt to create a named pipe before the legitimate application does, and act like the pipe server. The pipe name of USHALLNOTPASS is static and therefore a ransomware can hijack the pipe by creating the pipe instance more quickly than Controller of USHALLNOTPASS. This would make the attacker owner of the named pipe object, allowing the ransomware to impersonate the Controller and authorize itself.

Observing this vulnerability, NoCry is designed to be IPC-free. In this new architecture, Interceptor and Controller are moved into Unified Agent, a single module which intercepts and controls CSPRNG calls. The architectural view of NoCry is illustrated in Fig. 2. The capability of direct data exchange between Interceptor and Controller renders NoCry immune to the potential targeted attacks. Consequently, we conclude that NoCry is a more robust protection system.

4.2 Low False Positive Rate and Minimal User Intervention

We introduce two methods that NoCry offers in order to increase the usability.

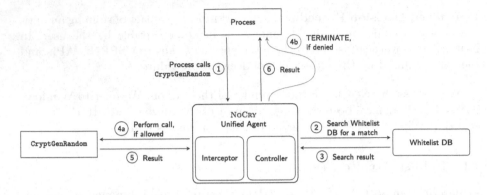

Fig. 2. Architectural view of NoCry. Interceptor and Controller reside in the same module, Unified Agent. This new construction enables robust and efficient information exchange between Interceptor and Controller for making an authorization decision.

Bootstrapping Whitelist DB. USHALLNOTPASS does not come with a pre-determined whitelist of benign applications. The list, presumably, is initially empty and if access control over CSPRNG APIs were applied immediately after USHALLNOTPASS is installed, every cryptographic application invoking these functions would be stopped: this is surely not what the authors mean to happen. Thus, benign cryptographic applications should be whitelisted before USHALL-NOTPASS is launched. To make this task as much automatic as possible we suggest in NoCry a *Training Mode*. It starts immediately after installation: the Interceptor listens the calls made to CSPRNG APIs without blocking any. Under our assumptions (Sect. 3), all access requests to CSPRNG APIs should come from honest processes. The hash of the binary executables are added to the Whitelist DB. Training Mode can only be activated once and just after the setup.

What if, against our assumption, Training Mode is run on a system that is infected by some strains of silent ransomware [13]? Some strains in fact infect computers but stay inactive until being activated by command and con-quer (C&C) servers or simply await until a certain time has passed. This way, ransomware attempts to look like a benign application and evade behavioral analysis-based detection systems. It is unlikely that such ransomware bypass NoCry: the ransomware executable would not call CSPRNG APIs in the sleeping phase and therefore they will not be whitelisted, unless the training phase coincides with the awakening of ransomware. This may be a remote possibility, but raises our assumption of making mandatory running our Training Mode in a clean system a must, as it is usually the case for any anti-malware.

Handling Software Updates. Whitelist DB can change. Programs that access CSPRNG APIs but are installed after the Training Mode has ended, must have their hashes be added to it. OS components are updated for various reasons, including patching security vulnerabilities, fixing bugs and adding new functionalities and since the update process involves replacing the existing executables with new ones, their hash values in the Whitelist DB have to be updated consequently. User applications also regularly check for new updates and install them in the background. The hashes of these updated executables should also be reflected to the Whitelist DB.

In environments where this could potentially lead to delays, *e.g.,* due to slow human reaction, we suggest that NoCry can be configured to defer access control to keep the system stable and workflow uninterrupted. We call this *Deferred Mode.*

When working in Deferred Mode, NoCry does not immediately block calls to CSPRNG APIs coming from unknown processes. Instead, the parameters and outputs of these calls are securely logged in a protected location until administrator takes an action. Here, administrator can find the software benign, thus add the hash of the executable to Whitelist DB and dispose the logs associated with that process. Otherwise, the process is suspended and, if necessary, recovery procedure is initiated. The logging, and when necessary, recovery procedures are similar to the approach of PayBreak [14] which we discuss in Sect. 6. However, there are two notable differences in NoCry:

(i) logging is applied per unidentified process, not system-wide; and
(ii) once the administrator makes a positive decision, the logs are disposed.

The rationale of the variations above is to reduce the potential impact of logging the outputs of CSPRNG. In our approach, random numbers obtained by whitelisted processes are not logged. This eliminates the security risks which could arise due to the persistence of the generated random numbers which are potentially used for cryptographic purposes.

4.3   Optimized Decision Procedure

In UShallNotPass, the access control over CSPRNG APIs requires to make an authorization decision which cause a significant delay. Mainly, the delay is due to two factors:(i) time spent for establishing IPC; and (ii) time spent by Controller for authorization.

As discussed in [8], the IPC is the main bottleneck of the authorization procedure and causes an overhead on CSPRNG APIs calls with a factor ranging from 62 to 125. In addition to the improved the security, eliminating the IPC from access control system is another motive which led us to unify Controller and Interceptor in a new module Unified Agent in NoCry. This way, both interception and authorization tasks are carried out in one place, without needing to consume time for IPC which enables to decide and act faster.

Furthermore, in UShallNotPass, the subsequent calls from the same process are authorized independently. While this approach would provide the highest level of time-granularity in access control, it might be an overkill for the security goals and a waste of resources for many systems. It is reported in [8] that the security checks performed in Controller causes an overhead up to a factor of

5.52. NoCry, therefore, holds an authorization to be valid for the lifetime of a process.

It is reasonable to expect that the two optimizations above would bring a significant performance improvement, which we assess in the next section.

5 Methods, Experiments and Results

On NoCry, we have run a series of experiments aiming at to measure the performance overhead, and *false positive* & *false negative* rates. For each experiment we describe the methodology, then we report and discuss the result.

5.1 Performance

Methodology. We measure the time that a benchmark program spends invoking `CryptGenRandom` API repetitively for 100 000 times. We run the benchmark program first on a clean system, then on a system with NoCry. We made this experiment on Windows 7 32-bit OS , running on a VM with 2 CPU cores clocked at 2.7 GHz. Overall, this is the same setting used in [8].

Results and Discussion. Table 1 shows the results of our measurements. It also reports the result from [8], obtained using the exact same methodology.

Table 1. Time benchmarks of 100 000 iterative calls to `CryptGenRandom` API. Performance gain is calculated as $(old - new) \setminus old \times 100$. Measurements of UShallNotPass are recalculated.

Measurement mode	Random number length (bits)			
	128	256	1024	2048
Clean System (sec)	0.13	0.14	0.18	0.24
UShallNotPass (sec)	15.59	15.80	15.84	16.91
UShallNotPass Overhead	11992 %	11285 %	8800 %	7024 %
NoCry (sec)	0.17	0.18	0.22	0.29
NoCry Overhead	30 %	22 %	18 %	20 %
Performance Gain	**98.9×**	**98.9×**	**98.6×**	**98.3×**

Our analysis shows that NoCry brings drastically lower overhead in terms of time for getting the output of `CryptGenRandom` API. This improvement is due to the unification of Interceptor and Controller components of UShallNotPass which enables interception and control actions to be managed by a single component, Unified Agent, and thereby removing IPC. This result is not surprising after our improvements in Sect. 4.3 and confirms our hypothesis.

Another cause of the performance increase is the use of cache mechanism during authorization. In UShallNotPass, iterative calls from the same process are authorized individually, causing a significant overhead, as much as a factor of 5.52 [8]. With NoCRY, process authorizations are valid for the lifetime of a process. That is, accessing to the Whitelist DB is performed once after the first invocation of CSPRNG API. This allows eliminating the need for accessing the Whitelist DB for authorizing subsequent calls.

Lastly, the architecture of USHALLNOTPASS limited the maximum number of iterative calls to `CryptGenRandom` API to the order of 100 000 as the system becomes unstable beyond this point [8]. Since NoCRY is IPC-free, it was able to handle a significantly larger number of requests. This makes it a better candidate for a protection system where CSPRNGs are heavily consumed.

5.2 Evaluation of False Positives

In the domain of NoCRY, *false positive* describes the condition that a legitimate process calls a CSPRNG API and is stopped by NoCRY.

Methodology. We have collected the Top 20 Installed Programs according to Avast PC Trends Report 2019 [1], and we look at whether they have digital signatures, the criterion which NoCRY can use for authorization.

Results and Discussion. Table 2 presents the results of our findings. Among the Top 20, the only unsigned application is `7-Zip`. Being `7-Zip` is an open source software, system administrators can obtain the source code, compile themselves, and add it to the NoCRY whitelist.

It is reasonable to expect that digital signatures of applications and source code availability of open source software together help system administrators maintain Whitelist DB and therefore lower the number of false positives. In the lights of these circumstances, we perceive that the false positive rate of NoCRY will be at a non-invasive level.

5.3 Evaluation of False Negatives

Modern ransomware employs hybrid cryptosystems for scalability and efficiency reasons. Consequently, managing the encryption keys in a secure manner is critical for a successful ransomware campaign, as a flaw in the transport, usage or storage of the keys might allow security professionals to build a decryptor. In particular, if the victims can obtain the keys used to encrypt files, decrypting the files without paying a ransom would be feasible. This is obviously against the goals of ransomware authors so they try to obtain encryption keys securely. The analyses in previous works [2,10] recognizes the following three strategies to obtain the encryption keys:(i) using embedded keys in the binary file; (ii) generating keys on the victim's machine; and (iii) downloading keys from a certain network location.

The security analyses of key generation in ransomware are found in [2,10]. Here, we resume it. If a ransomware follows (i), keys can be extracted from the ransomware binary, and the encrypted files can be recovered. Most of the

Table 2. Top 20 Installed Programs according to [1]. All applications in the table calls one or more CSPRNG APIs. NoCry will allow these calls automatically since the applications are digitally signed, except for 7-Zip, which is an open source software.

Rank	Program	Calls CSPRNG APIs	Digitally Signed	Source Code Open
1	Google Chrome	✓	✓	
2	Acrobat Reader	✓	✓	
3	WinRAR	✓	✓	
4	MS Office	✓	✓	
5	Mozilla Firefox	✓	✓	✓
6	VLC Media Player	✓	✓	✓
7	Skype	✓	✓	
8	CCleaner	✓	✓	
9	iTunes	✓	✓	
10	TeamViewer	✓	✓	
11	Windows Live Essentials	✓	✓	
12	7-Zip	✓		✓
13	Stream	✓	✓	
14	Dropbox	✓	✓	
15	Opera	✓	✓	
16	CyberLink PowerDVD	✓	✓	
17	CyberLink PowerDirector	✓	✓	
18	HP Photo Creations	✓	✓	
19	CyberLink YouCam	✓	✓	
20	CyberLink Power2Go	✓	✓	

ransomware prefer to generate the keys on victim's machine. In this case, there are two options: to use the CSPRNG, which produces high entropy random values; or to use a non-cryptographic PRNG. The first has been largely discussed already. The second is a weak choice: PRNGs are designed to be reproducible thus their outputs are guessable. If the ransomware uses a non-cryptographic PRNG, like `rand` function in C runtime library or `System.Random` class provided by .NET framework, decryption is feasible. If ransomware fetches keys from a remote server (iii) then blocking the malicious IPs inhibits the ransomware, which forces ransomware developers to fallback to (i) or (ii). The only option for current ransomware to get good encryption keys is therefore to use a CSPRNG.

In order to support our argument that CSPRNG is vital for the success of a ransomware, we designed experiments: the first, (**A1**), aims at to find out how common it is to use CSPRNG among current ransomware families. Indirectly, we also measure the false negative rate of NoCry. The second, (**A2**), aims at to check if there exists a publicly available decryptor for those samples that did not call any CSPRNG APIs.

Methodology. Following the previous research [8], we (1) obtain malware corpus from VirusTotal[1]; (2) pick potential ransomware among them; (3) rebuilt the same test environment, using Cuckoo Sandbox[2] to identify the active ransomware samples; and, (4) classify the families using AVCLASS [22] tool; (5) run NoCry against them; (6) (if any) discover the reason for false negative.

Results and Discussion. We identified 747 active samples from 56 cryptographic ransomware families. Next, we installed NoCry on the test machines and run the executables against NoCry. Table 3 shows the results: 97.1% of the samples have been stopped by NoCry before any user file is damaged, *i.e.,* encrypted by the ransomware program. They were the samples that attempted to call CSPRNG during the attacks, and were terminated by NoCry as they were not present in the Whitelist DB.

Among the 2.9% of samples that cause false negative, there may be ransomware executables that either circumvented NoCry's access control, or ransomware process did not call CSPRNG APIs. To discover the exact reason behind the false negatives, we picked random samples from the families we missed, and manually analyzed the API call tree. The missing samples from `Cryptxxx` and `Dalexis` did call `CryptGenRandom` API, however, said API could not be hooked by NoCry. We believe this is due to a problem of our implementation. The missing samples from `Carberp`, `Cryakl`, `Crysis`, `Gator`, `Neoreklami` and `Sigma` families did not call any CSPRNG APIs. Among them, we found decryptors for `Cryakl`, `Crysis` and `Sigma` on ID Ransomware[3] platform.

6   State of the Art in Ransomware Defense

There have been several proposals from the community of information security to mitigate the cryptographic ransomware threat. NoCry falls into the *access control* class, as Genç *et al.*'s USHALLNOTPASS [8]. We can categorize other defense systems, based on their main strategies, into three groups: *behavioral analysis*, *key escrow* and *deceptive protection*.

Behavioral Analysis. A common anti-malware strategy is to monitor the processes and terminate the ones with a suspicious behavior. The monitored behaviors include file system I/O, network connections and interaction with the OS. Among these, the fundamental characteristic of the ransomware is its aggressively encrypting victim's data, causing an unusual file system activity. Using this fact, several defense systems are proposed. One of them, Scaife *et al.*'s CRYPTODROP [21] monitors file type changes by looking file headers, compares sdhash [20] outputs and measures the Shannon Entropy before and after file-write operations. Another one, SHIELDFS [4] by Continella *et al.* tracks the low-level file system operations and collects the following features: folder listing,

---

[1] VirusTotal Threat Intelligence, https://virustotal.com.
[2] Cuckoo Sandbox – Automated Malware Analysis, https://cuckoosandbox.org/.
[3] ID Ransomware, https://id-ransomware.malwarehunterteam.com/.

Table 3. List of active ransomware samples tested against NoCry. The notation x/y means that *x samples out of y could be successfully stopped.*

Family	Samples (%)	Family	Samples (%)
Barys	1/1 (100%)	Occamy	4/4 (100%)
Birele	1/1 (100%)	OpenCandy	2/2 (100%)
Bitman	152/152 (100%)	Petya	2/2 (100%)
Browserio	2/2 (100%)	QQPass	1/1 (100%)
Bzub	1/1 (100%)	Razy	6/6 (100%)
Carberp	0/1 (0%)	SageCrypt	1/1 (100%)
Cerber	60/60 (100%)	Saturn	1/1 (100%)
Cryakl	0/1 (0%)	Scar	3/3 (100%)
Cryptxxx	0/2 (0%)	Scatter	2/2 (100%)
Crysis	2/3 (66%)	Shade	2/2 (100%)
Dalexis	1/3 (33%)	ShadowBrokers	1/1 (100%)
Daws	5/5 (100%)	Shiz	17/17 (100%)
Delete	1/1 (100%)	Sigma	0/1 (0%)
Deshacop	1/1 (100%)	Sivis	3/7 (42%)
Dlhelper	1/1 (100%)	Spigot	2/2 (100%)
Enestaller	1/1 (100%)	Spora	2/2 (100%)
Enestedel	1/1 (100%)	Striked	0/1 (0%)
Expiro	1/1 (100%)	Swisyn	0/1 (0%)
Gamarue	2/2 (100%)	Tescrypt	5/5 (100%)
GandCrab	1/1 (100%)	TeslaCrypt	316/316 (100%)
Gator	1/2 (50%)	Tpyn	1/1 (100%)
GlobeImposter	1/1 (100%)	Upatre	2/7 (28%)
Godzilla	1/1 (100%)	Ursnif	1/1 (100%)
Jaff	1/1 (100%)	Vobfus	1/1 (100%)
Lethic	4/4 (100%)	Wowlik	1/1 (100%)
Locky	47/47 (100%)	Wyhymyz	1/1 (100%)
Midie	1/1 (100%)	Zerber	52/52 (100%)
Neoreklami	0/1 (0%)	Zusy	7/7 (100%)
		Total:	726/747 (97.1%)

file-read/write/rename operations, file extension and average entropy of file-write operations. Comparing these characteristics with that of benign applications allows the detection of ransomware. In addition to detection, SHIELDFS creates a copy for each file before a file-write operation, eliminating the potential damage of ransomware. Moreover, Kharraz *et al.* proposed REDEMPTION [11] that also uses the similar metrics for identifying a ransomware activity. However, in contrast to SHIELDFS, REDEMPTION redirects file-write operations to sparse files, rather than creating a full copy of each written file. Differently, *Data Aware Defense* (DAD) by Palisse *et al.* [18] uses chi-square test to determine if the written data is close to random distribution which is indicates that the file is being encrypted. DAD computes the sliding median of this indicator on the last fifty file-write operations and suspends the corresponding process that exceeds a predetermined threshold.

Key Escrow. Key-escrow based defense allows the ransomware to complete its attack. This approach is based on the idea that the files encrypted by ransomware can be recovered if the encryption keys can be retrieved after the attack. For this aim, logging the keys used by ransomware is first appeared in the literature by Palisse *et al.* [19] and independently by Lee *et al.* [15]. The first public implementation of this idea PAYBREAK, with extending the idea to cover the third party crypto libraries was given by Kolondenker *et al.* [14]. In this system, all known cryptographic API are hooked, cryptographic materials are extracted and securely stored in a key vault. In the case of a ransomware attack, the encrypted files are tried by brute-forcing to be decrypted by retrieving the keys and other necessary parameters from the key vault. A slightly different method, *Deterministic Random Bits Generator* (DRBG) is proposed by Kim *et al.* [12] to retrieve the random numbers that ransomware used after an attack. DRBG replaces the CSPRNG of the system with a back-doored PRNG. The trapdoor is known only by the user and is preferably stored in the user's mobile device. After a ransomware incident, this trapdoor is retrieved and given to the PRNG to generate the same outputs that ransomware used. Using these outputs, ransomware's operations are reverted and files are recovered.

Deceptive Protection. In this strategy, carefully-crafted files are placed as a *decoy* in the file system with the user's files. These decoys are not supposed to be modified/deleted by the user, so any write request to the decoy files are treated as an indicator of ransomware activity. RWGUARD, a recently proposed system by Mehnaz *et al.* [16] uses this technique – in addition to behavioral analysis – to mitigate ransomware threat in real time.

7   Critical Discussion and Conclusions

Cryptographic ransomware is a modern global crime and a large amount of public and private institutions have been attacked already. The problem is that encryption is a powerful tool in the hands of criminals, hard to fight. By encrypting critical files on the victim's machine, ransomware blocks access to information and compromises critical services, wreaking an economical and social havoc because, unless victims pay the demanded ransom to receive the correct decryption key, they might not be able to recover their files if no backup is available. Computational complexity results ensure that a properly implemented encryption is irreversible, but to realize this theoretical result in practice, ransomware has to use cryptographically secure encryption keys. Many variants choose weaker alternatives: although there could be a theoretical solution to reverse their encryption at affordable costs, such *scareware* succeed in persuading victims to pay. Other variants, implement a theoretically weak but good-enough encryption to make decryption-without-the-key sufficiently painful to convince that paying the ransom is the lesser of two evils.

But in the restricted niche of ransomware that want their damage to be computationally irreversible, one finds the most disruptive variants, for instance, `WannaCry`, `Petya`, `GoldenEye`, `CryptoLocker`, `Crysis`, `Cerber`, `RAA`, and `NotPetya`. These ransomware families need a good source of random numbers and all of them find it in the CSPRNG available on a victim's system. Today, such functions are indeed reliable and *de facto* source of cryptographic randomness available on a computer.

To contain the threat coming from ransomware in this cryptographically strong niche, Genç *et al.* proposed in [8] to control access to CSPRNG APIs. They proved the concept by stopping a very large class of real active ransomware from doing any damage to any file—remarkably including `NotPetya`, which was till that moment believed unstoppable. But a concept, as much as promising can be, is not yet a fully-fledged application. Discussing how to implement it into an effective anti-ransomware defense, herein called NoCry, is what we have done in this paper. We solved several critical security and design issues: how to ensure that the attack surface of the architecture is reduced; how to bootstrap the Whitelist DB, honest cryptographic applications calling CSPRNG APIs and maintain it with a minimal user intervention, arguably resulting in a very low false positive rate; how to reduce the overhead that the access control imposes on the systems performance to a negligible amount. By not relying on any IPC, we removed any know-to-be-vulnerable elements from the architecture, so addressing the first issue; we addressed the last, by a better decision making that drastically improves the overhead. With respect to the previous proof-of-concept, reducing it from several thousands percent down to about 20%: quantified, the overhead is now a few *hundredth of a second*.

These are quite evident improvements, but the solution we proposed to address the second issue *i.e.,* how to manage the Whitelist DB, needs further discussion. In a system assumed uncorrupted, we bootstrap the list in *Training mode* by feeding in honest applications that call CSPRNG. In *Deferred mode* we update the list when a new version of a whitelisted application is available; we temporarily grant it the right to call CSPRNG but retaining critical data that can help recovering files in rare case where the upgrade hides a ransomware. Despite looking reasonable to us, one can still challenge our choices. For instance, one can ask why managing a Whitelist DB of applications that call CSPRNG in the first place? In fact Windows OS already offers a protection, `AppLocker`, that enables to deny non-whitelisted apps (*e.g.,* malware) from running. Cannot be ransomware dismissed as any other malware? First, we observe, this practice seems not have slowed down ransomware so we conclude that it needs more time and maturity to be widely accepted. Second, the problem with the whitelists is that they may not be complete, generating fastidious false positives. This issue, of course, affects also NoCry, but differently from a system which offers protection against generic *harmful* apps (a term that may have different interpretation). NoCRY targets and operate against a very specific situation. If we imagine to defer to the user the decision about whether a potential false positive is indeed so, NoCRY can precisely state that a certain application is trying to call critical functions, potentially to create strong encryption keys and unless the application is meant to encrypt data, it is better to let NoCRY kill it. We fail to imagine instead stating a similar precise claim to warn about a generic harmful application. The best could be a warning message sounding like "something insecure may happen", alert that users have learned to ignore [5]. A precise claim like that, enabled by NoCRY, will help users take more informed decisions, arguably reducing the number of false positives, and we intend to test this hypothesis in a future work.

Another critic can be that by only guarding access to CSPRNG, we miss to stop ransomware that generate encryption keys using different strategies. If this critics were well founded, this would count as a serious deficiency for NoCRY because would lead to false negatives. To this critic we answer first by observing that NoCRY was neither designed to stop other ransomware than those calling CSPRNG APIs nor conceived to work in isolation from other anti-ransomware. Indeed, we think, the full potential of NoCRY will emerge only in integration with an anti-malware that provably can reverse the damage done by ransomware that make use of the encryption keys obtained not by calling CSPRNG. Theoretical solutions exist that have the potential ability to reduce the cost of reversing encryption to a feasible time complexity and a few solutions are actually implemented [23]. These seems, indirectly, to support the argument that by not calling CSPRNG APIs, ransomware can realize only cryptographically-weak encryption. It is then by uniting different methods that we imagine a good anti-ransomware can reliably combat this crypto-crime. How to do it properly is an open problem but considering the improvements that we have herein discussed, we believe this union is possible and practical.

There is a further observation to reinforce our rebutting to the critic. We are aware that there is no silver bullet for ransomware mitigation. Each defense system has pros and cons, and NoCRY may well find its beater in some next generation ransomware. As discussed in [9], ransomware applications can find other ways than calling CSPRNG to get random numbers *e.g.,* by relying on non-cryptographic sources of randomness, but we believe that the alternative choices have weak points. The fact is that all the samples and variants of ransomware in the cryptographically-hard niche that we have analyzed so far, do call CSPRNG APIs. Thus, today, these functions are the most reliable source of randomness for application in search to build cryptographically strong encryption keys. And if in the future other functions will available for the same task, the fundamental question that remains to be solved is how many of these functions are, and whether by controlling access to these APIs, we can still implement a targeted strategy as the one in NoCRY that enables a decision making with an arguably low false positive rate. Investigating such research questions requires time and we leave it as future work.

Other future work still needs to be done. The argument that we have a reduced false positive rate has to be supported by experimental evidence. This means to run stress tests while running a generous number of various benign cryptographic applications under different conditions. Beyond having measured the overhead in terms of loss of performance, we still need to assess the user experience (UX) of NoCry running on different kinds of computers, included on battery powered mobile devices, to verify whether the overhead is imperceptible, as we claim, by users in their daily activities.

Acknowledgements. This work was partially funded by Luxembourg National Research Fund (FNR) under the grant agreement PoC18/13234766-NoCry PoC.

References

1. Avast: PC Trends Report 2019, April 2019. https://blog.avast.com/pc-trends-reports. Accessed 1 June 2019
2. Bajpai, P., Sood, A.K., Enbody, R.: A key-management-based taxonomy for ransomware. In: 2018 APWG Symposium on Electronic Crime Research (eCrime), pp. 1–12, May 2018
3. Bui, T., Rao, S.P., Antikainen, M., Bojan, V.M., Aura, T.: Man-in-the-machine: exploiting ill-secured communication inside the computer. In: 27th USENIX Security Symposium, pp. 1511–1525. USENIX Association, Baltimore (2018)
4. Continella, A., et al.: Shieldfs: a self-healing, ransomware-aware filesystem. In: Proceedings of the 32nd A Conference on Computer Security Applications, pp. 336–347. ACM, New York (2016)
5. Cormac, H.: So long, and no thanks for the externalities: the rational rejection of security advice by users. In: Proceedings of the 2009 New Security Paradigm Workshop (NSPW), 8–11 September 2009, Oxford, United Kingdom, pp. 133–144. ACM (2009)
6. CyberEdge: 2018 Cyberthreat Defense Report, March 2018. https://cyber-edge.com/wp-content/uploads/2018/03/CyberEdge-2018-CDR.pdf. Accessed 3 June 2019
7. Gammons, B.: 4 surprising backup failure statistics that justify additional protection (2017). https://blog.barkly.com/backup-failure-statistics. Accessed 3 June 2019
8. Genç, Z.A., Lenzini, G., Ryan, P.Y.A.: No random, no ransom: a key to stop cryptographic ransomware. In: Giuffrida, C., Bardin, S., Blanc, G. (eds.) DIMVA 2018. LNCS, vol. 10885, pp. 234–255. Springer, Cham (2018). https://doi.org/10.1007/978-3-319-93411-2_11
9. Genç, Z.A., Lenzini, G., Ryan, P.Y.A.: Next generation cryptographic ransomware. In: Gruschka, N. (ed.) NordSec 2018. LNCS, vol. 11252, pp. 385–401. Springer, Cham (2018). https://doi.org/10.1007/978-3-030-03638-6_24
10. Genç, Z.A., Lenzini, G., Ryan, P.Y.A.: Security analysis of key acquiring strategies used by cryptographic ransomware. In: Proceedings of the Central European Cybersecurity Conference 2018, CECC 2018, pp. 7:1–7:6. ACM, New York (2018)
11. Kharraz, A., Kirda, E.: Redemption: real-time protection against ransomware at end-hosts. In: Dacier, M., Bailey, M., Polychronakis, M., Antonakakis, M. (eds.) RAID 2017. LNCS, vol. 10453, pp. 98–119. Springer, Cham (2017). https://doi.org/10.1007/978-3-319-66332-6_5

12. Kim, H., Yoo, D., Kang, J.S., Yeom, Y.: Dynamic ransomware protection using deterministic random bit generator. In: 2017 IEEE Conference on Application, Information and Network Security (AINS), pp. 64–68, November 2017

13. KnowBe4: KnowBe4 alert: new strain of sleeper ransomware, May 2015. https://www.knowbe4.com/press/knowbe4-alert-new-strain-of-sleeper-ransomware. Accessed 1 June 2019

14. Kolodenker, E., Koch, W., Stringhini, G., Egele, M.: Paybreak: defense against cryptographic ransomware. In: Proceedings of the 2017 ACM on Asia Conference on Computer and Communications Security, pp. 599–611. ACM, New York (2017)

15. Lee, K., Oh, I., Yim, K.: Ransomware-prevention technique using key backup. In: Jung, J.J., Kim, P. (eds.) BDTA 2016. LNICST, vol. 194, pp. 105–114. Springer, Heidelberg (2017). https://doi.org/10.1007/978-3-319-58967-1_12

16. Mehnaz, S., Mudgerikar, A., Bertino, E.: RWGuard: a real-time detection system against cryptographic ransomware. In: Bailey, M., Holz, T., Stamatogiannakis, M., Ioannidis, S. (eds.) RAID 2018. LNCS, vol. 11050, pp. 114–136. Springer, Cham (2018). https://doi.org/10.1007/978-3-030-00470-5_6

17. Microsoft: Named Pipes, May 2018. https://docs.microsoft.com/en-us/windows/desktop/ipc/named-pipes. Accessed 3 June 2019

18. Palisse, A., Durand, A., Le Bouder, H., Le Guernic, C., Lanet, J.-L.: Data aware defense (DaD): towards a generic and practical ransomware countermeasure. In: Lipmaa, H., Mitrokotsa, A., Matulevičius, R. (eds.) NordSec 2017. LNCS, vol. 10674, pp. 192–208. Springer, Cham (2017). https://doi.org/10.1007/978-3-319-70290-2_12

19. Palisse, A., Le Bouder, H., Lanet, J.-L., Le Guernic, C., Legay, A.: Ransomware and the legacy crypto API. In: Cuppens, F., Cuppens, N., Lanet, J.-L., Legay, A. (eds.) CRiSIS 2016. LNCS, vol. 10158, pp. 11–28. Springer, Cham (2017). https://doi.org/10.1007/978-3-319-54876-0_2

20. Roussev, V.: Data Fingerprinting with Similarity Digests. In: Chow, K.-P., Shenoi, S. (eds.) DigitalForensics 2010. IAICT, vol. 337, pp. 207–226. Springer, Heidelberg (2010). https://doi.org/10.1007/978-3-642-15506-2_15

21. Scaife, N., Carter, H., Traynor, P., Butler, K.R.B.: Cryptolock (and drop it): stopping ransomware attacks on user data. In: 2016 IEEE 36th International Conference on Distributed Computing Systems (ICDCS), pp. 303–312, June 2016

22. Sebastián, M., Rivera, R., Kotzias, P., Caballero, J.: AVCLASS: a tool for massive malware labeling. In: Monrose, F., Dacier, M., Blanc, G., Garcia-Alfaro, J. (eds.) RAID 2016. LNCS, vol. 9854, pp. 230–253. Springer, Cham (2016). https://doi.org/10.1007/978-3-319-45719-2_11

23. Young, M., Zisk, R.: Decrypting the negozi ransomware (2017). https://yrz.io/decrypting-the-negozi-ransomware. Accessed 1 June 2019

Security Requirements
for Store-on-Client and Verify-on-Server
Secure Biometric Authentication

Haruna Higo[1], Toshiyuki Isshiki[1], Masahiro Nara[1], Satoshi Obana[2],
Toshihiko Okamura[1], and Hiroto Tamiya[1]([⊠])

[1] NEC Corporation, Kawasaki, Japan
{h-higo-aj,toshiyuki-isshiki,naramasahiro,t_okamura,htamiya}@nec.com
[2] Hosei University, Tokyo, Japan
obana@hosei.ac.jp

Abstract. The Fast IDentity Online Universal Authentication Framework (FIDO UAF) is an online two-step authentication framework designed to prevent biometric information breaches from servers. In FIDO UAF, biometric authentication is firstly executed inside a user's device, and then online device authentication follows. While there is no chance of biometric information leakage from the servers, risks remain when users' devices are compromised. In addition, it may be possible to impersonate the user by skipping the biometric authentication step.

To design more secure schemes, this paper defines Store-on-Client and Verify-on-Server Secure Biometric Authentication (SCVS-SBA). Store-on-client means that the biometric information is stored in the devices as required for FIDO UAF, while verify-on-server is different from FIDO UAF, which implies that the result of biometric authentication is determined by the server. We formalize security requirements for SCVS-SBA into three definitions. The definitions guarantee resistance to impersonation attacks and credential guessing attacks, which are standard security requirements for authentication schemes. We consider different types of attackers according to the knowledge on the internal information.

We propose a practical concrete scheme toward SCVS-SBA, where normalized cross-correlation is used as the similarity measure for the biometric features. Experimental results show that a single authentication process takes only tens of milliseconds, which means that it is fast enough for practical use.

Keywords: Biometric authentication · Privacy · FIDO · Normalized cross-correlation

1 Introduction

User authentication is one of the most important security issues in many IT systems. Biometric authentication can achieve higher usability than password authentication because it does not require users to consciously remember or

© Springer Nature Switzerland AG 2020
A. Saracino and P. Mori (Eds.): ETAA 2019, LNCS 11967, pp. 86–103, 2020.
https://doi.org/10.1007/978-3-030-39749-4_6

possess anything as credentials. Thanks to the spread of mobile devices such as smartphones and tablets with cameras or fingerprint sensors, we are now able to use biometric authentication for many services.

In a simple online authentication scheme, a credential (e.g., a password and biometric feature) of the user is stored in the server of the service provider. On an authentication trial, a credential that is newly obtained through a user's device (hereafter known as the client) by the user is sent to the server and compared with the stored one.

Such a simple scheme is susceptible to large-scale data breaches from the server. Importantly, biometric authentication potentially induces the reuse problem because biometric features cannot be changed, and special care needs to be taken. Even if encrypted, biometric features are defined as personal data by the EU General Data Protection Regulation (GDPR) and by laws in some other countries and regions. Therefore, especially for biometric authentication, means that are more robust to data breaches are needed.

Fast IDentity Online (FIDO) [2] is a set of online authentication specifications defined on the assumption that users possess their own mobile devices or tokens. Among the protocols, the Universal Authentication Framework (UAF) offers passwordless authentication using clients with biometric sensors. In FIDO UAF, biometric authentication is firstly executed inside a client, and only if it is successful, online device authentication follows as the second step by a challenge-response manner using digital signature. The important advantage of FIDO UAF is that the credentials, the biometric feature and the secret key, never leave the client. Therefore, even if the server suffers from a data breach, any secret information for authentication is not leaked. In other words, service providers using FIDO UAF do not need to manage the users' credentials by themselves.

On the other hand, client security is crucial in FIDO UAF, while it is under severe threats of both physical and cyber attacks. Although FIDO provides security guidelines, the following attack vectors still remain:

1. **Steal or forge the biometric feature.** Attackers have chances to learn raw biometric features by stealing the raw ones while they are decrypted for authentication or the encrypted ones with the decryption keys stored also in the client. Moreover, if an attacker replaces the stored biometric feature with his or hers, the authentication will be successful.
2. **Manipulate the result of the biometric authentication.** By manipulating the result of the biometric authentication to be successful, attackers succeed in the whole authentication. That is, the first step is skipped, and the authentication flow is no longer two-step.

Secure hardware-based modules such as trusted execution environment (TEE) are candidates of the strong countermeasures, but software-based cryptographic methods are attractive because not only can they be deployed widely as applications, but also their security can be ensured theoretically.

Our Contributions. The main reason why above attacks may be possible is that the server is not able to confirm the result of the biometric authentication step. In

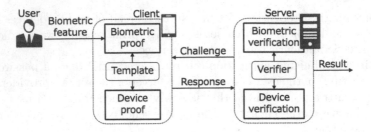

Fig. 1. Authentication flow of SCVS-SBA schemes.

general, two-factor authentication mechanism can prevent the attacks, because the server verifies on both factors, and the client only learns the overall authentication result. As sketched in Fig. 1, it is a combinatorial method for biometric authentication and device authentication. All credentials are stored in the client as the template, and the server determines the authentication result. We call this model store-on-client and verify-on-server secure biometric authentication (SCVS-SBA).

In this paper, we define the model of SCVS-SBA and formalize security requirements for SCVS-SBA into three definitions. One is, like FIDO UAF, to avoid having the server deal with the biometric features. The others are resistance to impersonation attacks and credential guessing attacks, which are standard security requirements for authentication schemes. We define each of them with a security game, which is a standard cryptographic technique. In the games, we consider several types of attackers according to the knowledge of the internal information. Moreover, the scheme should prevent attacks with forged templates.

We propose a scheme in which normalized cross-correlation (NCC) is used as the similarity measure for the biometric features. NCC is traditionally and widely used in the field of pattern matching including biometric authentication [9,14,17,25]. The proposed scheme is based on Schnorr's identification protocol. For similar reasons as the security of Schnorr's protocol, the proposed scheme have resistance to attacks by attackers except for one type. Although the scheme is susceptible to attacks from a type of attackers, such attacks can be mitigated with some practically used methods. The proposed scheme has low computational complexity and is fast enough for practical use as the experimental results show that a single authentication process takes only tens of milliseconds.

2 Definitions of Store-on-Client Verify-on-Server Secure Biometric Authentication (SCVS-SBA)

In this section, we define the components and security of SCVS-SBA. Store-on-client means that the credentials are only stored in the client, and verify-on-server implies that the authentication result is determined by the server. We define three security requirements to guarantee these two features and other requirements for secure authentication schemes. The security definitions take into account multi clients.

To define the correctness and security of SCVS-SBA, the fuzziness of biometric features needs to be formalized. Biometric features extracted from the identical biometric characteristic do not match exactly because of some conditions. For the model of biometric features, we use the universal error model defined by Takahashi et al. [18] in which the error distribution is assumed to be the same for every user. Below, a model of biometric features is denoted as $\mathcal{F} = (X, \text{Similarity}, \text{Decide}, \mathcal{X}, \Phi)$ of which components are defined as follows.

X: A domain space of biometric features.

$\sigma \leftarrow \text{Similarity}(x, y)$: A function to calculate a similarity score σ between two biometric features x and y.

$result \leftarrow \text{Decide}(\sigma)$: A function to determine an authentication result $result \in \{accept, reject\}$ from a similarity score σ.

$\mathcal{X}$: A distribution of extracted biometric features.

Φ: An error distribution according to extracted biometric features. (If a biometric feature x is extracted from a biometric characteristic at the first extraction, biometric features extracted from the same biometric characteristic after that follows the distribution $\{e \leftarrow_u \Phi : x + e\}$.)

Note that even with most state-of-the-art techniques, extracted biometric features do not have high entropy compared with cryptographic requirements. Therefore, biometric features are susceptible to brute-force attacks [16]. That is, for a secret biometric feature $x \in X$, it is able to find a biometric feature that is sufficiently similar to (sufficient to be accepted against) x within practical time. We denote by $\delta_{\mathcal{F},\tau}$ the probability of the successful finding of a target biometric feature with τ trials.

To mitigate such attacks in practice, the number of accesses to this oracle for the same ID should be limited by a parameter determined with respect to the biometric feature model. This kind of limitation is called rate limiting [15]. Also, it is helpful for prevention of such attacks to use sound client modules which check if the input is in the biometric feature space or allow input only from trusted biometric sensors. For example, with the Android Fingerprint API [1], both fingerprint capturing and feature extraction are done inside a trusted environment.

2.1 Components

An SCVS-SBA scheme for a biometric feature model $\mathcal{F}$ consists of the five algorithms $\text{Setup}_{\mathcal{F}}$, Join, Issue, Prove, and Verify described as follows.

$pp \leftarrow \text{Setup}_{\mathcal{F}}(1^{\lambda}, param)$: The setup algorithm Setup takes a security parameter λ and a tuple of parameters $param$ as input and outputs a public parameter pp (if it is clear from the context, we omit writing it).

($temp, verif$) ← ⟨Join(pp, x), Issue(pp)⟩: The registration protocol (Fig. 2) is executed between the two interactive algorithms Join and Issue. The client's
algorithm Join takes as input a public parameter pp and a biometric feature
x, and the server's Issue takes a public parameter pp. As a result, Join and
Issue output a template $temp$ and a verifier $verif$, respectively.

($\perp, result$) ← ⟨Prove($pp, y, temp$), Verify($pp, verif$)⟩: The authentication protocol
(Fig. 3) is executed between the two interactive algorithms Prove and Verify.
The client's algorithm Prove takes as input a public parameter pp, a biometric
feature y, and a template $temp$, and the server's Verify takes a public parameter pp and a verifier $verif$. As a result, only Verify outputs an authentication
result $result \in \{accept, reject\}$.

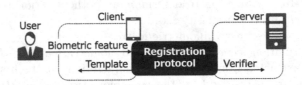

Fig. 2. Input and output of the registration protocol of SCVS-SBA schemes.

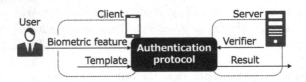

Fig. 3. Input and output of the authentication protocol of SCVS-SBA schemes.

An SCVS-SBA scheme is said to be correct if the two authentication results,
i.e., the one decided through the similarity function Similarity and the decision
function Decide and the other through the SCVS-SBA scheme, are identical
except for negligible errors. The formal definition is as follows.

Definition 1. *For a model of biometric features $\mathcal{F} = (X, \text{Similarity}, \text{Decide}, \mathcal{X},$
$\Phi)$, we say an SCVS-SBA scheme $\Pi = (\text{Setup}_{\mathcal{F}}, \text{Join}, \text{Issue}, \text{Prove}, \text{Verify})$ is correct if we have the following for any $\lambda \in \mathbb{N}$ and $x, y \in X$:*

$$\text{Pr}\left[\begin{array}{l} pp \leftarrow \text{Setup}_{\mathcal{F}}(1^{\lambda}, param); \\ (temp, verif) \leftarrow \langle \text{Join}(pp, x), \text{Issue}(pp)\rangle; \\ (\perp, result) \leftarrow \langle \text{Prove}(pp, y, temp), \text{Verify}(pp, verif)\rangle; \\ result' \leftarrow \text{Decide}(\text{Similarity}(x, y)) : \\ result = result' \end{array}\right] \geq 1 - negl(\lambda).$$

2.2 Security

In this section, we formalize three security requirements for SCVS-SBA. The first one is about secrecy of biometric features against the servers. In SCVS-SBA, the verifier stored in the server is required not to include even partial information on the biometric features. The other two requirements are standard ones for authentication schemes: infeasibility of impersonation attacks and biometric feature guessing attacks, which are called unforgeability and irreversibility, respectively. We define these requirements through security games in which multiple clients and adaptive attackers are considered. Before the games, we describe the oracles commonly used in the two games.

Below, we denote by $\Pi = (\mathsf{Setup}_{\mathcal{F}}, \mathsf{Join}, \mathsf{Issue}, \mathsf{Prove}, \mathsf{Verify})$ an SCVS-SBA scheme for a biometric feature model $\mathcal{F} = (X, \mathsf{Similarity}, \mathsf{Decide}, \mathcal{X}, \Phi)$.

Server's Ignorance on Biometric Features. The verifier is required not to leak any information on the registered biometric feature. We define this requirement by perfect secrecy [22] as follows.

Definition 2. *An SCVS-SBA scheme Π for a biometric feature model $\mathcal{F}$ is said to satisfy the* server's ignorance on biometric features *if for any public parameter $pp \leftarrow \mathsf{Setup}_{\mathcal{F}}(1^{\lambda})$, $x' \in X$, and verif' it holds that*

$$\Pr\left[x \leftarrow \mathcal{X} : x = x' | verif = verif'\right] = \Pr\left[x \leftarrow \mathcal{X} : x = x'\right],$$

where x is a biometric feature chosen according to $\mathcal{X}$, and verif is a verifier that is generated by the registration protocol $(temp, verif) \leftarrow \langle \mathsf{Join}(pp, x), \mathsf{Issue}(pp) \rangle$.

For example, this requirement is satisfied if the verifier is generated independently from the biometric feature, or the verifier is XOR of a uniformly random value and the biometric feature. However, as is the case in many schemes in the store-on-server models (described in Sect. 4), the schemes in which the server stores ciphertexts of biometric features using public key encryption schemes cannot satisfy this requirement.

Oracles for Unforgeability and Irreversibility Games. The second and the third requirements are defined through security games in which an attacker and a challenger execute an SCVS-SBA scheme.

We consider attackers who are able to compromise some clients or the server and eavesdrop on communication. To illustrate such attackers, we provide seven oracles. The first three, named **AddUser**, **RegServer**, and **RegClient**, are related to the registration protocol, the second three, **AuthServer**, **AuthClient**, and **Eavesdrop**, are related to the authentication protocol, and the last one, **LeakData** leaks information to the attacker. We denote by $\mathcal{O}$ the set of the seven oracles. To deal with multiple users, a unique ID is assigned and notified to the attacker on each execution of the registration oracles, and the attacker designates the IDs on each execution of the authentication oracles.

The challenger possesses 2 tables to remember data that it learns. For each user with ID i, the first table T stores the biometric feature, template, and verifier of the user at $T[i].x$, $T[i].t$, and $T[i].v$, respectively. Each item is set to be $\perp$ at first. After each execution of the registration oracles, the challenger stores to T the items specified in Table 1. T is referred to when the challenger answers queries to the authentication and leakage oracles.

The second table L stores flags to indicate the attacker's knowledge of the user's biometric feature, template, and verifier at $L[i].x$, $L[i].t$, and $L[i].v$, respectively. The default flag is 0, and it is switched to 1 if the corresponding item is leaked to, chosen by, or learned by the attacker through the registration and leakage oracles as in Table 2.

Table 1. Items stored with each registration oracle.

	$T[i].x$	$T[i].t$	$T[i].v$
AddUser	✓	✓	✓
RegServer		✓	
RegClient	✓	✓	

Table 2. Flags switched with each registration oracle.

	$L[i].x$	$L[i].t$	$L[i].v$
AddUser($x = \perp$)	0	0	0
AddUser($x \neq \perp$)	1	0	0
RegServer	1	1	0
RegClient	0	0	1

We here describe the behaviors of the oracles. Below, pp denotes the public parameter predetermined by $pp \leftarrow \mathsf{Setup}_{\mathcal{F}}(1^\lambda)$.

AddUser: This oracle handles registration of a new user. First, the oracle is given $x \in X \cup \{\perp\}$ and chooses a new ID i. If $x \neq \perp$, the oracle sets $L[i].x = 1$, and otherwise chooses x according to the distribution $\mathcal{X}$. Then the oracle executes $(temp, verif) \leftarrow \langle \mathsf{Join}(pp, x), \mathsf{Issue}(pp) \rangle$ and stores x, $temp$, and $verif$ at $T[i].x$, $T[i].t$, and $T[i].v$, respectively. Finally, i is replied to $\mathcal{A}$.

RegServer: This oracle acts as a server and deals with registration requests from $\mathcal{A}$. First, the oracle chooses a new ID i. Then the oracle executes $\mathsf{Issue}(pp)$ to interact with $\mathcal{A}$ and stores the resulting $verif$ into $T[i].v$ (note that $T[i].x$ and $T[i].t$ are still set to be $\perp$). Also, $L[i].x$ and $L[i].t$ are switched into 1. Finally, i is replied to $\mathcal{A}$.

RegClient: This oracle plays the client's role in the registration protocol. First, the oracle chooses a new ID i and a biometric feature $x \leftarrow \mathcal{X}$. Then the oracle executes $\mathsf{Join}(pp, x)$ to interact with $\mathcal{A}$. The chosen x and the resulting $temp$ are stored at $T[i].x$ and $T[i].t$, and $L[i].v$ is switched into 1. Finally, i is replied to $\mathcal{A}$.

AuthServer: This oracle acts as the server and deals with authentication requests from $\mathcal{A}$. First, the oracle is given an ID i from $\mathcal{A}$. If a verifier of i is not stored (i.e., $T[i].v = \perp$), the oracle outputs $\perp$ and aborts. Otherwise, the oracle executes $\mathsf{Verify}(pp, T[i].v)$ to interact with $\mathcal{A}$. Finally, the authentication result $result$ is sent to $\mathcal{A}$.

AuthClient: This oracle plays the client's role in the authentication protocol. First, the oracle is given two IDs i and j from $\mathcal{A}$. If either $T[i].x$ or $T[j].t$ is $\perp$, the oracle outputs $\perp$ and aborts. Otherwise, the oracle chooses a fuzziness $e \leftarrow \Phi$ and executes $\mathsf{Prove}(pp, T[i].x + e, T[j].t)$ to interact with $\mathcal{A}$.

Eavesdrop: This oracle simulates eavesdropping attackers. First, the oracle is given three IDs i, j, and k from $\mathcal{A}$. If any of $T[i].x$, $T[j].t$, or $T[k].v$ is $\perp$, the oracle outputs $\perp$ and aborts. Otherwise, the oracle chooses a fuzziness $e \leftarrow \Phi$ and executes $(\perp, result) \leftarrow \langle \mathsf{Prove}(pp, T[i].x + e, T[j].t), \mathsf{Verify}(pp, T[k].v) \rangle$. Finally, the transcript (i.e., the set of messages exchanged) is provided to $\mathcal{A}$.

LeakData: This oracle leaks data to $\mathcal{A}$. First, $\mathcal{A}$ designates an ID i and an index $e \in \{x, t, v\}$. If $T[i].e = \perp$, the oracle outputs $\perp$ and aborts. Otherwise, the oracle switches $L[i].e$ to 1 and replies with $T[i].e$ to $\mathcal{A}$.

Unforgeability. In the unforgeability game, the attacker first makes an arbitrary number of queries to the seven oracles introduced above in an arbitrary order to adaptively select an ID of a user as a target. Then, the challenger executes the authentication protocol with the attacker for the target and finally obtains an authentication result. The attacker is considered to succeed if the authentication result is *accept*.

We categorize the attackers according to the knowledge as listed in Table 3. Among the eight rows, we eliminate three types of trivial attackers. Because the knowledge of the target's biometric feature and template is equivalent to that of the target, the attackers in the first and second rows are able to successfully impersonate the target. Also, the attacker in the fifth row who has the template and the verifier is able to find a biometric feature of the target through brute force testing without accessing the challenger (i.e., offline). Therefore, we only consider the remaining five types.

Type-1: Attackers who do not know the template of the target (i.e., who may have the biometric feature and the verifier of the target).

Type-2: Attackers who do not know either the template or verifier of the target (i.e., who may have the biometric feature of the target).

Type-3: Attackers who do not know either the biometric feature or verifier of the target (i.e., who may have the template of the target).

Type-4: Attackers who do not know either the biometric feature or template of the target (i.e., who may have the verifier of the target).

Type-5: Attackers who do not know any of the biometric feature, template, or verifier of the target.

We say an attacker wins the unforgeability game if the final authentication result is *accept* while satisfying the above requirements on the knowledge. The unforgeability game outputs 1 if the attacker wins. Table 3 describes the unforgeability game $\mathbf{Exp}_{\Pi,\mathcal{F},(\mathcal{A}_1,\mathcal{A}_2)}^{\mathrm{UNF},j}(\lambda)$ played by a type-j attacker $(\mathcal{A}_1, \mathcal{A}_2)$.

Table 3. Knowledge and types of attackers for unforgeability game (left) and unforgeability game $\mathbf{Exp}_{\Pi,\mathcal{F},(\mathcal{A}_1,\mathcal{A}_2)}^{\mathrm{UNF},j}(\lambda)$ (right).

Knowlege on target			
Bio. feat.	Template	Verifier	Type
✓	✓	✓	—
✓	✓		—
✓		✓	Type-1
✓			Type-2
	✓	✓	—
	✓		Type-3
		✓	Type-4
			Type-5

1: $pp \leftarrow \mathsf{Setup}_\mathcal{F}(1^\lambda, param)$
2: $(i^*, st) \leftarrow \mathcal{A}_1^\mathcal{O}(pp)$
3: **if** $\mathrm{T}[i^*].v = \bot$ **return** 0
4: $(\cdot, result) \leftarrow \langle \mathcal{A}_2^\mathcal{O}(st), \mathsf{Verify}(pp, \mathrm{T}[i^*].v) \rangle$
5: **return** 1 **if** $result = accept$ **and**
6: $\quad \cdot j = 1$: $\mathrm{L}[i^*].t = 0$
7: $\quad \cdot j = 2$: $\mathrm{L}[i^*].t = \mathrm{L}[i^*].v = 0$
8: $\quad \cdot j = 3$: $\mathrm{L}[i^*].x = \mathrm{L}[i^*].v = 0$
9: $\quad \cdot j = 4$: $\mathrm{L}[i^*].x = \mathrm{L}[i^*].t = 0$
10: $\quad \cdot j = 5$: $\mathrm{L}[i^*].x = \mathrm{L}[i^*].t = \mathrm{L}[i^*].v = 0$
11: **return** 0

An SCVS-SBA scheme is said to be unforgeable if the probability of any PPT attacker's winning is small enough. In particular, type-3 attackers are able to check if a chosen biometric feature y matches the target's biometric feature with a query to the **AuthServer** oracle by honestly running $\mathsf{Prove}(pp, y, t)$ where t is the target's template. Therefore, the probability of type-3 attackers' winning is lower bounded by the probability of successfully guessing the target's biometric feature $\delta_{\mathcal{F},\tau}$ where τ is the number of queries to the **AuthServer** oracle for the target's ID.

Definition 3. *Let Π be an SCVS-SBA scheme for a biometric feature model $\mathcal{F}$, $j \in \{1, 2, 4, 5\}$ and ϵ a function. We say Π satisfies ϵ-unforgeability against type-j attackers if for any $\lambda \in \mathbb{N}$ and PPT attacker $\mathcal{A} = (\mathcal{A}_1, \mathcal{A}_2)$, it holds that $\Pr\left[1 \leftarrow \mathbf{Exp}_{\Pi,\mathcal{F},\mathcal{A}}^{\mathrm{UNF},j}(\lambda)\right] \leq \epsilon$. We say Π satisfies ϵ-unforgeability against type-3 attackers if for any $\lambda \in \mathbb{N}$ and PPT attacker $\mathcal{A} = (\mathcal{A}_1, \mathcal{A}_2)$, it holds that $\Pr\left[1 \leftarrow \mathbf{Exp}_{\Pi,\mathcal{F},\mathcal{A}}^{\mathrm{UNF},3}(\lambda)\right] - \delta_{\mathcal{F},\tau} \leq \epsilon$, where τ is the number of queries to the* **AuthServer** *oracle for the target's ID.*

Irreversibility. Compared with the unforgeability game, the irreversibility game differs only in the final protocol execution step. That is, after querying to the oracles and selecting the target's ID, the attacker outputs a biometric feature as its guess of the target's one. If the guessed one is in X and similar enough to the stored one, it is considered that the attacker succeeds in guessing the user's biometric feature.

The attackers are categorized in Table 4. The attackers from the first to fourth rows are trivial because they know the biometric feature of the target. Also, the fifth attacker is able to find a biometric feature of the target through brute force testing without accessing the challenger. Therefore, we only consider the remaining three types of attackers that are labeled type-3, 4, and 5 for the unforgeability game.

Table 4. Knowledge and types of attackers for irreversibility game (left) and irreversibility game $\mathbf{Exp}_{\Pi,\mathcal{F},\mathcal{A}}^{\mathrm{IRR},j}(\lambda)$ (right).

Knowledge on target			
Bio. feat.	Template	Verifier	Type
✓	✓	✓	—
✓	✓		—
✓		✓	—
✓			—
	✓	✓	—
	✓		Type-3
		✓	Type-4
			Type-5

```
1: pp ← Setup_F(1^λ, param)
2: (i*, y*) ← A_1^O(pp)
3: if T[i*].x = ⊥ return 0
4: if y* ∉ X return 0
5: result = Decide(Similarity(T[i*].x, y*))
6: return 1 if result = accept and
7:  · j = 3: L[i*].x = L[i*].t = 0
8:  · j = 4: L[i*].x = L[i*].v = 0
9:  · j = 5: L[i*].x = L[i*].t = L[i*].v = 0
10: return 0
```

We say an attacker wins the irreversibility game if the attacker succeeds in guessing the biometric feature of the target while satisfying the above requirements on the knowledge. The irreversibility game outputs 1 if the attacker wins. Table 4 describes the irreversibility game $\mathbf{Exp}_{\Pi,\mathcal{F},\mathcal{A}}^{\mathrm{IRR},j}(\lambda)$ played by a type-j attacker $\mathcal{A}$.

We say an SCVS-SBA scheme is irreversible if the probability of any PPT attacker's winning is small enough. Similar to the discussion for the unforgeability, the winning probability of type-3 attackers is lower bounded by $\delta_{\mathcal{F},\tau+1}$, where $+1$ counts the final output.

Definition 4. *Let Π be an SCVS-SBA scheme for a biometric feature model $\mathcal{F}$, $j \in \{4,5\}$ and ϵ a function. We say Π satisfies ϵ-irreversibility against type-3 attackers if for any $\lambda \in \mathbb{N}$ and PPT attacker $\mathcal{A}$, it holds that $\Pr\left[1 \leftarrow \mathbf{Exp}_{\Pi,\mathcal{F},\mathcal{A}}^{\mathrm{IRR},3}(\lambda)\right] - \delta_{\mathcal{F},\tau+1} \leq \epsilon$, where τ is the number of queries to the* **AuthServer** *oracle for the target's ID. We say Π satisfies ϵ-irreversibility against type-j attackers if for any $\lambda \in \mathbb{N}$ and PPT attacker $\mathcal{A}$, it holds that $\Pr\left[1 \leftarrow \mathbf{Exp}_{\Pi,\mathcal{F},\mathcal{A}}^{\mathrm{IRR},j}(\lambda)\right] \leq \epsilon$.*

Remark 1. One may think that the unforgeability implies the irreversibility; however, it is not always the case. Even if some Type-4 and 5 attackers successfully guess the biometric feature, the attackers may not be able to break the unforgeability because the attackers do not possess the target's template that is necessary for the client's authentication algorithm Prove. Moreover, the two games set different restrictions on the attackers' knowledge. That is, the attackers in the unforgeability game are required not to have the target's verifier, while the irreversibility game accepts attackers who know it.

3   Proposed Scheme and Its Analysis

We propose a scheme that deals with biometric features of which similarity is measured by normalized cross-correlation (NCC). NCC-based methods have many applications such as face and fingerprint recognitions [9,14,17,25]. The proposed scheme utilizes group operations of which discrete logarithm problem is hard to solve. Although the scheme is shown to be secure against attackers except for type-3 ones, the attacks can be prevented by using sound modules or mitigated with the practically used technique as rate limiting. The scheme is also shown to run fast enough for practical use.

One may think that a fuzzy extractor [7] with a digital signature scheme is a good candidate for an SCVS-SBA scheme (see also Sect. 4). However, as far as we know, schemes are considered for simpler similarity measures such as Hamming distance or L_∞-distance, and good schemes do not exist for complex similarity measures such as Euclidian distance and NCC.

3.1 Preliminaries

In the proposed scheme, we use a group on an elliptic curve E in which solving the elliptic curve discrete logarithm problem is hard. An algorithm to select an elliptic curve E and a base point G of which order q is a λ-bit prime is denoted by $\mathsf{GGen}(1^\lambda)$. For an integer s and a point G on E, a scalar multiplication is denoted by $[s]G$. We note that the group can be substituted for other groups of which discrete logarithm problem is hard to solve.

We denote by $x = (x_i)_{i=1}^n$ the vector $(x_1, x_2, \ldots, x_n)$ below. NCC of two vectors is the inner product divided by the product of the sizes, that is, for vectors x and y, the NCC of them is $\langle x, y \rangle / \sqrt{\sum(x_i)^2}\sqrt{\sum(y_i)^2}$. For the sake of simplicity, the proposed scheme deals with biometric features that are pre-normalized and calculates inner vectors as the similarity. Let z be a biometric feature of which size $\sqrt{\sum(z_i)^2}$ equals A and S a constant. Then $(S/A)z$ is a normalized vector that has a constant size S and is in $[-S, S]^n$. Obviously, the inner products of the normalized vectors are the NCCs multiplied by S^2. For group operations, we further round down the elements into integers. For $L = \lceil \log(S+1) \rceil + 1$, the resulting vectors are in $[-2^{L-1}, \ldots, 0, 1, \ldots, 2^{L-1} - 1]^n$. In formal, we use the biometric feature model $\mathcal{F} = (X, \mathsf{Similarity}, \mathsf{Decide}, \mathcal{X}, \Phi)$ detailed as follows.

- $X = \{x \mid x \in [-2^{L-1}, \ldots, 0, 1, \ldots, 2^{L-1} - 1]^n \wedge \sum_{i=1}^n (x_i)^2 \approx S^2\}$.
- $\mathsf{Similarity}((x_1, \ldots, x_n), (y_1, \ldots, y_n)) = \sum_{i=1}^n x_i \cdot y_i$.
- For a predetermined acceptance range θ, $\mathsf{Decide}(\sigma) = accept$ if $\sigma \in \theta$, otherwise $\mathsf{Decide}(\sigma) = reject$.

3.2 Construction

Before the detailed construction, we provide a brief introduction. The registration protocol linearly masks a biometric feature $x = (x_i)_{i=1}^n$ with $n + 2$ fresh random values $s_1, s_2, t_1, \ldots, t_n \in \mathbb{Z}_q$. The masked biometric feature $r = (s_1 x_i - s_2 t_i \bmod q)_{i=1}^n$ is stored in the client as the template.

The authentication protocol is based on the Schnorr's identification protocol [21]. Recall that the Schnorr's protocol is to prove the prover P's knowledge of s corresponding to a public data $H = [s]G$ to the verifier V as follows.

1. P randomly chooses $r \in \mathbb{Z}_q$ and sends $A = [r]G$ to V.
2. V randomly chooses $e \in \mathbb{Z}_q$ and sends it to P.
3. P computes $z = es - r \bmod q$ and sends it to V.
4. V confirms that it holds that $[e]H = [z]G + A$.

In the proposed scheme, the client is to prove that the two biometric features $\boldsymbol{x}$ and $\boldsymbol{y}$ are similar enough. Since the client only possesses the masked biometric feature $\boldsymbol{r}$, the client proves the inner product $\langle \boldsymbol{x}, \boldsymbol{y} \rangle$ is in $\boldsymbol{\theta}$ with $\langle \boldsymbol{r}, \boldsymbol{y} \rangle = s_1 \langle \boldsymbol{x}, \boldsymbol{y} \rangle - s_2 \langle \boldsymbol{t}, \boldsymbol{y} \rangle$. We view this value as s in the Schnorr's protocol in the proposed scheme. From a different point of view, s is secretly shared between the user and client.

Therefore, the final step checks if it holds that $[e]H = [z]G + A + [es_2 \langle \boldsymbol{t}, \boldsymbol{y} \rangle]G$ for some $H \in \{[s_1\theta]G \mid \theta \in \boldsymbol{\theta}\}$. To compute this equation, the server possesses s_1, s_2, and $\boldsymbol{T} = ([t_i]G)_{i=1}^n$ as the verifier. That is, H in the Schnorr's protocol is secretly shared among the user, client, and server.

Here we describe the proposed SCVS-SBA scheme $\Pi = (\mathsf{Setup}_{\mathcal{F}}, \mathsf{Join}, \mathsf{Issue}, \mathsf{Prove}, \mathsf{Verify})$ for the biometric feature model $\mathcal{F}$ as follows.

The setup algorithm $\mathsf{Setup}_{\mathcal{F}}(1^\lambda, \boldsymbol{\theta})$**:**
  1. $\mathsf{Setup}_{\mathcal{F}}$ executes $(E, G, q) \leftarrow \mathsf{GGen}(1^\lambda)$, computes $\boldsymbol{\Theta} = \{[\theta_j]G \mid \theta_j \in \boldsymbol{\theta}\}$, and outputs a public parameter $pp = (E, G, q, \boldsymbol{\Theta})$.

The registration protocol $\langle \mathsf{Join}(pp, \boldsymbol{x}), \mathsf{Issue}(pp) \rangle$**:**
  1. Join chooses $n + 2$ random values $s_1, s_2, t_1, \ldots, t_n \in \mathbb{Z}_q$, computes $\boldsymbol{r} = (s_1 x_i - s_2 t_i \bmod q)_{i=1}^n$ and $\boldsymbol{T} = ([t_i]G)_{i=1}^n$, sends s_1, s_2, and $\boldsymbol{T}$ to Issue, and outputs $temp = \boldsymbol{r}$.
  2. Issue outputs $verif = (s_1, s_2, \boldsymbol{T})$.

The authentication protocol $\langle \mathsf{Prove}(pp, \boldsymbol{y}, temp), \mathsf{Verify}(pp, verif) \rangle$**:**
  1. Prove chooses a random value $r \in \mathbb{Z}_q$, computes $A = [r]G$, and sends A to Verify.
  2. Verify chooses two random values $e, b \in \mathbb{Z}_q$, computes $\boldsymbol{B} = ([b]T_i)_{i=1}^n$, and sends e and $\boldsymbol{B}$ to Prove.
  3. Prove computes $z = e\langle \boldsymbol{r}, \boldsymbol{y} \rangle - r \bmod q$ and $C = \sum[y_i]B_i$, and sends z and C to Verify.
  4. Verify outputs $reject$ if $C = 0$, computes $V = [1/s_1]([1/e]([z]G + A) + [s_2/b]C)$, and outputs $accept$ if $V \in \boldsymbol{\Theta}$ holds; otherwise it outputs $reject$.

When the algorithms run correctly, the value V is computed to be $[\langle \boldsymbol{x}, \boldsymbol{y} \rangle]G$. Therefore, the authentication result is determined according to whether $\mathsf{Similarity}(\boldsymbol{x}, \boldsymbol{y}) = \langle \boldsymbol{x}, \boldsymbol{y} \rangle \in \boldsymbol{\theta}$ holds or not. That is, the proposed scheme satisfies the correctness.

3.3 Security Analysis

We analyze the security of the proposed scheme in this section. The proposed scheme is designed to handle multiple clients (i.e., multiple users). The random values and the key pairs are generated independently for each registration. Namely, if the attacker obtains some data or transcripts according to some clients, it is not useful in attacking the other clients. Without loss of generality, we only consider single-client cases in the security analysis below.

Server's Ignorance on Biometric Features. The verifier consists of random values chosen independently from the biometric features. Therefore, it is clear that the following theorem holds.

Theorem 1. *The SCVS-SBA scheme Π satisfies the server's ignorance on biometric features.*

Unforgeability. Next, we discuss the unforgeability of the proposed scheme. The scheme is unforgeable against type-1, 2, 4, and 5 attackers.

Theorem 2. *The SCVS-SBA scheme Π satisfies $negl(\lambda)$-unforgeability against type-1, 2, 4, and 5 attackers if the success probability of solving the elliptic curve discrete logarithm of the underlying group is bounded by $negl(\lambda)$.*

For a successful attack, the attackers need to compute z and $C \neq 0$ that satisfies $[z]G + [es_2/b]C = [es_1\theta - r]G$ for some $\theta \in \boldsymbol{\theta}$, the chosen value r, and the given values e and $\boldsymbol{B} = ([bt_i]G)_i$. Based on the discrete logarithm assumption, it is impossible even for the strongest type of type-1 attackers who know the target's biometric feature and verifier $(s_1, s_2, ([t_i]G)_i)$ except for a negligible probability. Formal proof is based on a similar discussion with that of the Schnorr's protocol, which is omitted because of space limitations.

Irreversibility. Irreversibility against type-4 and 5 attackers is satisfied based on the difficulty of solving the elliptic curve discrete logarithm problem of the underlying group.

Theorem 3. *The SCVS-SBA scheme Π satisfies $negl(\lambda)$-irreversibility against type-4, and 5 attackers if the success probability of solving the elliptic curve discrete logarithm of the underlying group is bounded by $negl(\lambda)$.*

Even if the attackers query to the authentication oracles, the attackers only learns inner products of the target's biometric feature and randomly chosen biometric features. The information is not helpful in guessing the target's one. Formal proof is omitted because of space limitations.

Unforgeability and Irreversibility Against Type-3 Attackers. The scheme is susceptible to attacks by type-3 attackers who have the target's template. This is because the authentication protocol cannot detect if an illegal input $\boldsymbol{y} \notin X$ is used as the input to Prove, and then the type-3 attackers are possibly able to exploit the **AuthServer** oracle with Prove($pp, \boldsymbol{y}, t$) where $\boldsymbol{y} \notin X$ and t is the target's template.

If we can add a functionality in the authentication protocol to verify that the input biometric feature $\boldsymbol{y}$ is in the biometric space, the proposed scheme will satisfy all the security requirements. To develop a practical scheme that is secure against all types of attackers is an interesting future work. In reality, we are able to mitigate the threats with extra restrictions such as rate-limiting.

3.4   Implementation Results

We used two machines for the measurements: the server's is an Intel Xeon Silver 4114 @ 2.2 GHz CPU with 96 GByte memory running Ubuntu 18.04, and the client's is a Qualcomm Snapdragon 450 @ 1.8 GHz with 4 GByte memory running Android 8.1. We implemented the programs in C using OpenSSL 1.1.1 [20] for multi-precision arithmetic and elliptic curve cryptography. For the server, the programs were compiled with gcc 7.4.0, and for the client, we used clang 8.0.2 (Android NDK 19.2.5345600) to compile and the Java Native Interface (JNI) to call the C libraries.

For the elliptic curve, we used P-256 defined in NIST FIPS PUB 186-4 [19], where the size of a scalar is 256 bits, and each point is compressed to be 257 bits. In this evaluation, we used 2% of the range of inner products of the biometric features as the size $|\theta|$ of acceptance range.

Execution Time. Table 5 shows execution times of each algorithm of the proposed scheme. Both registration and authentication processes take only tens of milliseconds for the slowest case, which seems to have little burden on users.

Recall that the last step of Verify checks if the value V is in Θ. In the implementation, we utilized binary search in the verification step with the elements of Θ sorted in Setup. We evaluated the worst case time in which V is not in the range as shown in Table 5.

Table 5. Parameters and execution time of each algorithm. (n is the dimension of a biometric feature. L is the bit length of each element of the biometric feature.)

n	L	$|\theta|$	Setup	Registration		Authentication	
			Setup[s]	Join[ms]	Issue[ms]	Prove[ms]	Verify[ms]
			@Server	@Client	@Server	@Client	@Server
16	8	10,444	1.47	1.22	0.01	0.86	1.62
	10	167,608	31.5	1.09	0.01	1.02	1.63
	12	2,683,699	636	1.10	0.01	1.21	1.66
64	8	41,779	6.73	4.27	0.02	3.04	4.35
	10	670,433	145	4.36	0.02	3.81	4.39
	12	10,734,796	2,943	4.29	0.02	4.62	4.48
256	8	167,116	32.4	17.1	0.06	12.0	15.1
	10	2,681,733	652	17.1	0.06	15.1	15.8
	12	42,939,187	13,231	17.1	0.06	18.2	15.9

Data Size. The server stores the public parameter pp and the verifier $verif$ and the client stores the template $temp$.

The public parameter pp includes Θ which consists of $|\theta|$ points of the elliptic curve. From Table 5, the size of pp is about 1GByte in the largest case of $n = 256$ and $L = 12$.

Table 6 shows the sizes of *temp* and *verif* and the sizes of messages transmitted in the registration and the authentication protocols. The sizes of *temp* and *verif* are proportional to n. They are around 8KByte in the largest case $n = 256$. The message sizes are also around 8KByte in both registration and authentication protocols. This would suggest that the proposed scheme does not require either large storage or bandwidth.

Table 6. Storage and message sizes for each user.

n	Storage [Byte]		Message [Byte]	
	temp	*verif*	Registration	Authentication
16	512	578	578	644
64	2048	2120	2120	2186
256	8192	8288	8288	8354

4   Related Work

There is a line of work [4,7,10,13,18] that designs and constructs schemes for securely executing online biometric authentication. Most of the work concentrates on developing a way to enhance security while ensuring a similar usability level compared with that of the non-secured online biometric authentication. Because of this concept, the users are not allowed to possess their own devices or remember their passwords and are assumed to use shared biometric sensors such as those equipped at ATMs. To store the templates on the server (i.e., store-on-server model), the templates are ciphertexts of the biometric features and are never decrypted. The matching of the registered and the queried biometric features are computed without decryption by utilizing linear codes [3,7,12,13,23], homomorphic encryption [3,4,10,11,24], homomorphic signatures [18], and some other secure computation tools [6].

Even if the template is the ciphertexts of the biometric features, it may not be sufficient to protect privacy information from data breaches. As for what FIDO uses, service providers are recommended not to possess any information generated from biometric features.

There seems to be a potential for securely applying the store-on-server schemes into SCVS-SBA by changing the entity who manages the template. However, it is not correct because there is another chance of impersonation attack in the proposed model. That is, because the clients are able to compute templates related to any arbitrary biometric feature, the attacker is able to forge templates to be used in impersonation. To prevent this attack, the schemes require rejection of the use of illegal templates that are not generated in the honest execution of the registration protocol.

The fuzzy extractor [7], which is a technique to extract a random string from a fuzzy data source, in combination with the digital signature may be regarded as a candidate of a SCVS-SBA scheme. In the authenticate phase of the scheme, the client uses a reproduction algorithm with a biometric feature and the helper data to obtain the signature key, and a signature generated with the key will prove the legitimacy of the user. However, its security depends on a concrete scheme and must be examined well. For example, the fuzzy extractor is not generally sufficient for achieving correctness because there is no guarantee on the reproduced random string when the input is from another source. For practicality, as far as we know, existing fuzzy extractor schemes cannot afford complex similarity metrics such as NCC. Moreover, though the errors of some biometric features are known to be very large, constructing a fuzzy extractor that deals with high error rate sources has proved to be impossible [8].

With respect to password authentication, a FIDO-style model has been proposed by Bringer et al. [5]. In the model, a token generated from a password is stored by the client. While the entity model is similar to that of this work, passwords are not fuzzy and are not as sensitive as biometric information. Therefore, the model is not sufficient for dealing with biometric authentication instead of password authentication.

5   Conclusion

We introduced a model of store-on-client and verify-on-server secure biometric authentication (SCVS-SBA) as a security enhancement of FIDO UAF. SCVS-SBA is a combinatorial method for biometric authentication and device authentication in which all credentials are stored in the client and the server determines the authentication result. We took into account the possible attack vectors in the FIDO UAF authentication flow and formalized security requirements that guarantee both confidentiality of biometric features and resistance against impersonation.

As a first step for SCVS-SBA schemes, this paper also proposed a scheme that is shown to run practically fast. The scheme is susceptible to attacks that exploit the target's template in the defined model. To develop a practical scheme that is secure against all types of attackers is one of interesting future work.

References

1. Android keystore system. https://developer.android.com/training/articles/key store
2. FIDO Alliance. https://fidoalliance.org/
3. Bringer, J., Chabanne, H.: An authentication protocol with encrypted biometric data. In: Vaudenay, S. (ed.) AFRICACRYPT 2008. LNCS, vol. 5023, pp. 109–124. Springer, Heidelberg (2008). https://doi.org/10.1007/978-3-540-68164-9_8

4. Bringer, J., Chabanne, H., Izabachène, M., Pointcheval, D., Tang, Q., Zimmer, S.: An application of the Goldwasser-Micali cryptosystem to biometric authentication. In: Pieprzyk, J., Ghodosi, H., Dawson, E. (eds.) ACISP 2007. LNCS, vol. 4586, pp. 96–106. Springer, Heidelberg (2007). https://doi.org/10.1007/978-3-540-73458-1_8

5. Bringer, J., Chabanne, H., Lescuyer, R.: Software-only two-factor authentication secure against active servers. In: Pointcheval, D., Nitaj, A., Rachidi, T. (eds.) AFRICACRYPT 2016. LNCS, vol. 9646, pp. 285–303. Springer, Cham (2016). https://doi.org/10.1007/978-3-319-31517-1_15

6. Bringer, J., Chabanne, H., Patey, A.: Privacy-preserving biometric identification using secure multiparty computation: an overview and recent trends. Signal Process. Mag. **30**(2), 42–52 (2013)

7. Dodis, Y., Ostrovsky, R., Reyzin, L., Smith, A.: Fuzzy extractors: how to generate strong keys from biometrics and other noisy data. SIAM J. Comput. **38**(1), 97–139 (2008)

8. Fuller, B., Reyzin, L., Smith, A.: When are fuzzy extractors possible? In: Cheon, J.H., Takagi, T. (eds.) ASIACRYPT 2016. LNCS, vol. 10031, pp. 277–306. Springer, Heidelberg (2016). https://doi.org/10.1007/978-3-662-53887-6_10

9. Hassner, T., et al.: Pooling faces: template based face recognition with pooled face images. In: The IEEE Conference on Computer Vision and Pattern Recognition (CVPR) Workshops, June 2016

10. Higo, H., Isshiki, T., Mori, K., Obana, S.: Privacy-preserving fingerprint authentication resistant to hill-climbing attacks. IEICE Trans. Fundam. Electron. Commun. Comput. Sci. **E101.A**(1), 138–148 (2018)

11. Hirano, T., Hattori, M., Ito, T., Matsuda, N.: Cryptographically-secure and efficient remote cancelable biometrics based on public-key homomorphic encryption. In: Sakiyama, K., Terada, M. (eds.) IWSEC 2013. LNCS, vol. 8231, pp. 183–200. Springer, Heidelberg (2013). https://doi.org/10.1007/978-3-642-41383-4_12

12. Isshiki, T., Araki, T., Mori, K., Obana, S., Ohki, T., Sakamoto, S.: New security definitions for biometric authentication with template protection: toward covering more threats against authentication systems. In: International Conference of the Biometrics Special Interest Group (BIOSIG), pp. 1–12 (2013)

13. Juels, A., Wattenberg, M.: A fuzzy commitment scheme. In: Proceedings of the 6th ACM Conference on Computer and Communications Security, pp. 28–36. ACM, New York (1999)

14. Karna, D.K., Agarwal, S., Nikam, S.: Normalized cross-correlation based fingerprint matching. In: 2008 Fifth International Conference on Computer Graphics, Imaging and Visualisation, pp. 229–232, August 2008

15. Lai, R.W.F., Egger, C., Reinert, M., Chow, S.S.M., Maffei, M., Schröder, D.: Simple password-hardened encryption services. In: 27th USENIX Security Symposium (USENIX Security 2018), pp. 1405–1421. USENIX Association, Baltimore (2018)

16. Martinez-Diaz, M., Fierrez-Aguilar, J., Alonso-Fernandez, F., Ortega-Garcia, J., Siguenza, J.: Hill-climbing and brute-force attacks on biometric systems: a case study in match-on-card fingerprint verification. In: 40th Annual IEEE International Carnahan Conferences Security Technology, ICCST 2006, pp. 151–159, October 2006

17. Masi, I., Trãn, A.T., Hassner, T., Leksut, J.T., Medioni, G.: Do we really need to collect millions of faces for effective face recognition? In: Leibe, B., Matas, J., Sebe, N., Welling, M. (eds.) ECCV 2016. LNCS, vol. 9909, pp. 579–596. Springer, Cham (2016). https://doi.org/10.1007/978-3-319-46454-1_35

18. Matsuda, T., Takahashi, K., Murakami, T., Hanaoka, G.: Fuzzy signatures: relaxing requirements and a new construction. In: Manulis, M., Sadeghi, A.-R., Schneider, S. (eds.) ACNS 2016. LNCS, vol. 9696, pp. 97–116. Springer, Cham (2016). https://doi.org/10.1007/978-3-319-39555-5_6
19. National Institute of Standards and Technology (NIST): FIPS PUB 186-4: Digital Signature Standard (DSS) (2013)
20. OpenSSL Software Foundation: OpenSSL. https://www.openssl.org/
21. Schnorr, C.P.: Efficient identification and signatures for smart cards. In: Brassard, G. (ed.) CRYPTO 1989. LNCS, vol. 435, pp. 239–252. Springer, New York (1990). https://doi.org/10.1007/0-387-34805-0_22
22. Shannon, C.E.: Communication theory of secrecy systems. Bell Syst. Tech. J. $28(4)$, 656–715 (1949)
23. Tuyls, P., Akkermans, A.H.M., Kevenaar, T.A.M., Schrijen, G.-J., Bazen, A.M., Veldhuis, R.N.J.: Practical biometric authentication with template protection. In: Kanade, T., Jain, A., Ratha, N.K. (eds.) AVBPA 2005. LNCS, vol. 3546, pp. 436–446. Springer, Heidelberg (2005). https://doi.org/10.1007/11527923_45
24. Yasuda, M., Shimoyama, T., Kogure, J., Yokoyama, K., Koshiba, T.: New packing method in somewhat homomorphic encryption and its applications. Secur. Commun. Netw. $8(13)$, 2194–2213 (2015)
25. Yoo, J.C., Han, T.H.: Fast normalized cross-correlation. Circ. Syst. Signal Process. $28(6)$, 819 (2009)

Reflexive Memory Authenticator: A Proposal for Effortless Renewable Biometrics

Nikola K. Blanchard[1]([⊠]), Siargey Kachanovich[2], Ted Selker[3],
and Florentin Waligorski[4]

[1] Digitrust, Loria, Université de Lorraine, Nancy, France
Nikola.K.Blanchard@gmail.com
[2] Université Côte d'Azur, Inria Sophia-Antipolis, Nice, France
[3] University of Maryland, Baltimore County, Palo Alto, CA, USA
[4] Observatoire de Paris, Paris, France
http://www.koliaza.com/

Abstract. Today's biometric authentication systems are still struggling with replay attacks and irrevocable stolen credentials. This paper introduces a biometric protocol that addresses such vulnerabilities. The approach prevents identity theft by being based on memory creation biometrics. It takes inspiration from two different authentication methods, eye biometrics and challenge systems, as well as a novel biometric feature: the pupil memory effect. The approach can be adjusted for arbitrary levels of security, and credentials can be revoked at any point with no loss to the user. The paper includes an analysis of its security and performance, and shows how it could be deployed and improved.

Keywords: Eye biometrics · Authentication · Adaptive systems

1 Introduction

Until recently, biometric authenticators seemed to be the holy grail for access security. Improved sensor technology made available new alternatives such as iris and eye muscle signature, with the most accurate approaches reaching error rates below 0.01%. Unfortunately, even these top biometric solutions suffer from two important problems. The first is that an adversary can record and replicate the iris or even simulate eye muscle motions to present as a user. The second problem is that each person requires independent security for a large array of services, such that compromising one does not affect the others. Aggregating the authentication would necessitate some independent trusted reliable intermediary service. Such a service then becomes a single point of failure, which easily exposes users to access failure and other related problems. An ideal approach would allow a person to create new authentication mechanisms if old ones get compromised or to independently access services without compromising other services' access methods, which is unfeasible with most biometric authentication systems. This

© Springer Nature Switzerland AG 2020
A. Saracino and P. Mori (Eds.): ETAA 2019, LNCS 11967, pp. 104–121, 2020.
https://doi.org/10.1007/978-3-030-39749-4_7

paper works to demonstrate a new kind of biometric approach that could allow ongoing creation and cancellation under attacks, by using unconscious memory as a biometric feature.

Contributions. We propose a resettable reflexive biometric authentication system that does not suffer from credential theft and re-use, with arbitrary security due to a time-security trade-off. We analyse its security against multiple standard attacks, and the principal obstacles to its implementation in practice. This proposal is presented to motivate development, and although the system could be used today, empirical tests will be needed to validate and optimise its performance.

This paper is structured as follows: Sects. 2 and 3 go over the related work for the two main authentication methods on which the protocol is based. Section 4 introduces the specific biometric mechanism used, and Sect. 5 goes over the details of the protocol. Section 6 analyses the resistance of the protocol to multiple kinds of attacks. Finally, extensions of this protocol to different use-cases, vulnerabilities, and potential improvements are discussed in Sect. 7.

2 Challenge-Based Authentication

2.1 Text Challenges

Typical challenge-based authentication uses text questions: requesting answers to a series of questions or the completion of a list of tasks. Such approaches can achieve a relatively high level of security, with a higher promised level of usability than common passwords. This idea has been around since at least the early 1990s, initially as a list of personal questions [53].

This kind of system suffers from multiple issues:

- It is vulnerable to targeted attacks when answers are findable online [22].
- Free-form answers can lead to high error rates and frustration as people tend to misremember the exact spelling they used [45].
- To achieve high entropy, a potentially long sequence of challenges is needed. This requires more time and effort from the user and increases the system complexity [22].
- A large set of potential challenges is needed to avoid repetition of challenges between different services. User-provided challenges are also riddled with usability and security issues [23].

As such, text challenges have mostly been superseded by different systems, based on intrinsic human visual pattern recognition abilities.

2.2 Graphical Challenges

The main alternative to text challenges is visual—or graphic—passwords, where the user is confronted with a sequence of images and has to react, for example, by identifying known pictures [21], especially pictures of faces [7]. An alternative is to click on certain zones in a sequence of pictures, which can either come from an image corpus or be automatically generated [8,52]. Some research has also looked at mixing different methods and mnemonics, such as storytelling plus visuals [39] or sound-augmented visual passwords [50].

Graphical challenges do not solve all the problems mentioned:

- They still require either more complex challenges or a long sequence of challenges.
- Any system used by multiple service providers encounters the same risk of challenge re-use.
- Depending on the structure of the interaction, the systems are generally quite vulnerable to another person or camera recording the visual challenge by "shoulder-surfing" [29].
- Attempts at limiting shoulder-surfing impose strong constraints on the image set sizes, which lowers entropy [1].

Techniques inspired by these challenges are still present in the forms of CAPTCHAs, often in conjunction with passwords systems to frustrate automated attacks through rate-limiting [19,25]. While they are present in multiple popular commercial solutions, such systems have not solved the central issue of authentication. We now turn to biometric authentication, which has been considered as a lower-effort security approach and plausibly an ultimate alternative to passwords.

3   Biometric Authentication Methods

For the purpose of authentication, a wide array of biometrics features has been used, going from hand shape to fingerprint, voice print, or typing patterns. These methods have been used for decades, initially with limited uses in specific high-security sectors, such as banking or the military in the 1970s [31]. Their prevalence has increased dramatically in recent years, with more than 40% of users unlocking their phones through fingerprints or face recognition in 2018 [18]. A central issue to biometric authentication is the possibility to steal biometric information and to use it later in what is called a *replay attack*. A large amount of work has been done to solve this, going from storing data in a way that is not directly re-usable [9,30,35] to using parallel systems to make sure that the sensor is not being fooled by a previously captured video in a process called *liveness detection* [28,42]. Alas, these techniques are not entirely secure yet [34,49].

3.1   Error Rates

Comparing biometric features and authentication systems requires a common metric. The most frequently used metric depends on two error rates: false rejection rate (FRR) and false acceptance rate (FAR). The false rejections, although not being a critical security issue, are a source of frustration for the users. The false acceptances, on the other hand, are a security failure. The two error rates are related: the stricter the system is, the lower the FRR and the higher the FAR become. Hence, we generally use the equal error rate (EER), the tolerance level for which FAR and FRR are equal. These rates are generally within 1% and 6–7% for any kind of authentication except for the iris-based ones, which have 0.01% EER but—like most classical biometrics—are not renewable and are vulnerable to theft. Even multimodal biometrics—where one uses multiple sources and biometric features for liveness detection and improved error rates [43]— rarely improve below 0.2% EER [9,17,44]. Making the strong assumption that the user data are quite well-distributed—which is far from guaranteed—this corresponds to a min-entropy below 7 bits, on par with typical password systems. Moreover, most of the EER mentioned in papers on biometrics are against non-optimised adversaries: for a given set of user patterns, they check which proportion would be accepted as sufficiently similar to another user. An adversary that can compute an optimal distribution of fake patterns to cover the space of user data points more efficiently might get a success rate high enough to impersonate more than 10% of users despite a three-strike policy[1].

3.2   Eye and Reflexive Biometrics

After problems were discovered in fingerprint-based authentication, focus shifted to eye biometrics, with more than a hundred papers published on the subject in the last decade. Most of the research has been on iris recognition [5], where the unique patterns present in the iris allows for a much lower EER. More recently, eye movements have received a lot of interest, as muscular performance is quite distinctive [3,17,26]. Despite the much improved EER, the unchangeability of the underlying biometric pattern stays an intrinsic problem for nearly all biometric authentication systems.

As such, some of the proposed systems have been inspired by challenge systems. Notably, multiple systems were developed based on gaze analysis, which concentrates on how the eye moves when faced with specific images [13,16]. In 2016, Sluganovic *et al.* proposed a challenge-based eye movement system [51], in which the server creates challenges in the form of a single dot quickly moving on a screen. As the point's location is random, it prevents replay attacks. The speed and patterns in the eye's movement are characteristic of the user's muscle function and allow them to authenticate them. This uses the user's unconscious reflexes, which means that it is quite low-effort to the user. However, the system still depends on a hidden model of the user's muscles. As such, it is vulnerable to an adversary that can compute a sufficiently accurate model of the user. Once this model is computed, it is impossible to reset the stimulus pattern. This means that the user cannot safely use that biometric on this service, or any other service, potentially compromising dozens of accounts.

To this date, there seems to be only one type of biometric authentication systems that are based on partially unconscious actions while being *resettable*.

---

[1] Meaning that the person trying to authenticate is blocked after three failed attempts.

That is, where the stimulus and the reaction pattern can instantly be changed if they become compromised, just as one resets their password. These systems are all based on electro-encephalography (EEG), and tend to give an arbitrary task to the user before recording their electrical brain patterns—which are not consciously controllable—while they concentrate on the task [2,11,33]. Alas, they suffer from common EEG drawbacks [12]:

- they tend to have high EER;
- they are costly and require specialised equipment that is hard to set up;
- they require an extended time to capture and process the signals;
- they are not entirely stable over extended time periods.

Our idea is to create reflexive challenge biometrics that rely on a different biometric feature that has not been used previously for this purpose. Results on this feature from the psychological literature are presented in the next section.

4   The Pupil Memory Reflex

The interactions between memory and eye behaviour have been studied for more than half a century [36,38,41] and are still a subject of ongoing research [10,14, 24]. In 1967, Roger N. Shepard showed that recognition memory for pictures vastly exceeded recognition memory for words. A week after having been shown a set of 600 pictures, users who were shown two pictures and were asked to select the ones they had seen previously were correct 87.0% of the time. Even after four months without being shown the pictures, they still managed to be right 57.7% of the time [36]. 5 years later, Loftus showed that pupil patterns could predict how well remembered an image would be [32]. Part of this memorisation is conscious, but some unconscious processing is also involved [20].

The feature central to the Reflexive Memory Authenticator protocol is quite simple: when presented with a stimulus, the pupil contraction reflex indicates how *new* the stimulus is to the user. More precisely, the pupil starts contracting between 200 ms and 300 ms after the stimulus starts. After this contraction and depending on whether the stimulus is still present, the pupil dilates back to its baseline over the course of a few seconds.

The contraction effect tends to be faster with novel stimuli, in which case it also takes more time to get back to the baseline. This is directly influenced by how familiar the image is. This effect has been shown through both declarative experiments—where the user states whether the image is familiar—and free viewing—where the already-seen images are recorded. In experiments performed by Naber, Frässle, Rutishauser, and Einhäuser [37], 48 participants were shown a list of pictures to memorise, and were later shown some of those pictures or new pictures randomly, while their pupil behaviour was recorded. Figure 1 shows the evolution of pupil size during retrieval on the right. Two main curves show this effect—depending on whether the user judged the picture familiar or not—and confidence intervals, which start diverging while the image is still shown (before the 1s mark). Figure 2 (top) shows the curve slopes.

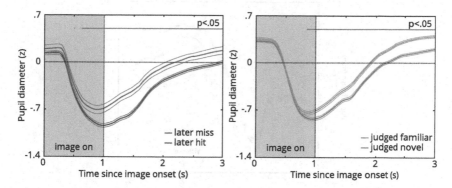

Fig. 1. Figures redrawn from [37, Fig. 3A (left) and 4A (right), Experiment 1], showing the evolution of the pupil size during the memorisation phase (left) and retrieval phase (right). The red curve corresponds to an image that the user later forgets, and the blue one to a picture that is remembered. The green curve corresponds to a image that the user remembers, and the yellow one to a image that is perceived as novel. The grey area corresponds to when the images are on screen. (Color figure online)

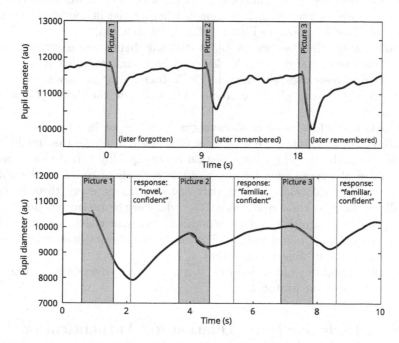

Fig. 2. Figure redrawn from [37, Fig. 1B (top) and 1C (bottom)], showing the evolution of the pupil size during the memorisation and retrieval phase. On the top graph, the slopes vary depending on whether the image will later be judged as novel. The bottom graph shows the slopes varying with whether the image is being judged as novel and how confident the user is in that judgement (not shown here). The grey areas correspond to when the images are on screen.

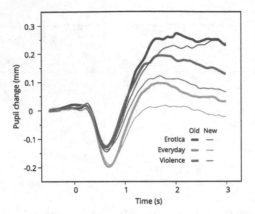

Fig. 3. Figure redrawn from [6, Fig. 1], showing the evolution of pupil size as a function of time, novelty of stimulus, and emotional content. The image is shown for 3 s starting from 0 (the baseline is shown for 1 s before the stimulus).

A second effect also shown in the same study was that, during memorisation, pupil size can also serve as an indicator of whether the image would later be remembered. This is shown on Figs. 1 (left) and 2 (bottom).

An interesting effect, shown in [6], is that this behaviour is strongly modulated by the emotional content. Violent and erotic images elicit stronger and slightly different responses, as shown in Fig. 3. Image content as well as uniqueness will affect the protocol, and care has to be taken on the choice of images in the database.

Without user effort beyond observing a sequence of images, this method can reliably decide whether the user is familiar with an image that might have previously been shown. The main question is how quickly this decision can be made, with most experiments leaving multiple seconds of rest for the pupil to return to baseline dilation, showing only one new image every three seconds, which allows them to know quite accurately whether the image was novel. This delay depends on cognitive and perceptual phenomena which are affected by factors including sleep, mood and intoxication. More experimentation may reveal further constraints on image recognition.

With all the building blocks in place, it is now time to introduce the Reflexive Memory Authenticator protocol.

5   Using Reflexive Pupil Dilation for Authentication

The protocol has two different modes of functioning: when the user registers for the first time, and when they try to authenticate afterwards.

5.1 Basic Protocol

Registration. At the registration phase, the user provides their username, and the system selects a set of images (say, 30) and records that they correspond to the user. The server tells the user to look attentively at the following pictures and shows them one by one for 1.5 s each[2].

Authentication. Each time the user tries to authenticate, the protocol works as follows:

- The system computes two lists of images. The first comes from the set of known images (based on the ones recorded in the registration phase), and the other comes from a database of never-seen-before images.
- In a series of rounds, an image is selected from one of the two lists, with probability 1/2 for each.
- The image is shown to the user for a recognition period of 1 s. The screen then becomes blank for 1 s to allow the user to return to their baseline.
- The system evaluates if dilation of the user's pupil corresponds to whether the shown image is known or unknown to the user.
- The system estimates the probability that the person who is trying to authenticate is indeed the user.
- If the probability exceeds a certain threshold, the system logs the user in.
- If more than a reasonable number of images (e.g. 50) have been shown or the probability is below a second threshold (indicating a high probability of spoofing attempt), the system requires a CAPTCHA and warns the user of the authentication attempt (e.g. by email).
- Otherwise, the system chooses another image to show to the user from one of the two lists at random.
- If the user manages to get authenticated but had at least one false positive, the one with the strongest reaction is added to the list of known images.

In practice, many explicit and implicit parameters affect the performance of the Reflexive Memory Authenticator, which are covered below.

5.2 Implementation Constraints and Parameters

Before implementing this protocol in practice, here are the questions we must ask:

- Which images should be considered?
- How long should each image be shown, and how long should the resting period between images be?
- How do we ensure that the protocol eliminates noise coming from pupil size variability due to environmental conditions (such as glasses, camera characteristics, lighting variations)?

---

[2] This is enough for the users to have high memory performance as in [37], while still being faster than nearly all password composition policies [46].

- Should known and unknown images be shown with the same probability?
- Which thresholds should govern acceptance, rejection, and continued testing?
- How can targeted attacks be prevented?
- What should be the protocol for retiring images from the known set?
- How should the system keep track of which images are treated as known?

The first three questions are addressed here, and the last four in Sect. 6.

Image Types and Sources. Natural scenes—for example, pictures of mountains, flowers or clouds— have been used in multiple studies [6,24,37] and form a common baseline. However, emotionally loaded images elicit strong reactions in both directions [6]. As this increases noise, emotionally loaded images should probably be avoided. ·

The system requires many unseen images for each login attempt. It then requires appropriately large databases to avoid the user seeing an image twice and being too familiar with it. For example, consider 20 authentication attempts per day, each with 20 novel images. Assuming that an image can be reused after six months, this would require 72000 images to be drawn without repetition. It could easily be done with the multiple online databases numbering in the millions of public domain images—such as Wikimedia Commons (https://commons.wikimedia.org), Snappygoat (https://snappygoat.com) or Free-images (https://free-images.com).

For the images to be drawn at random with little to no repetition, we would have to avoid random collisions [27]. This would require close to 4 billion images, so the server needs to store at least partial information on the images seen. Subsection 6.6 expands on how to do this.

Time Parameters. A parameter with a direct linear impact on usability is the delay per image. For example, each image can be shown for 1 s, with a rest period of 2 s, as has been done in previous psychological studies [37]. This means that to show 20 images—a lower bound to get the equivalent of 20 bits of security— a whole minute of authentication would be required. To keep a high level of usability, making the authentication process no-effort is not enough—it should also be quite fast, to avoid disturbing the user's workflow. The problem is that the shorter the time allowed for both presentation and rest, the harder it becomes to discriminate between the two contraction modes corresponding to a known or unknown image.

A lowered accuracy could still improve security by showing images at an increased rate. For example, instead of a 95% classification accuracy in 3 s, a system with 75% accuracy in 0.5 s could take much less time to authenticate a user, depending on the actual number of errors. Based on previous work, a reasonable upper bound on the frequency, assuming no resting period, would be around 3 images per second [37], leading to a time cost of less than ten seconds to exceed median password security [4]. This kind of frequency brings two problems, however. First, it provides less data on an earlier time frame, which shows a less marked pupil memory effect. Second, it means that there is an interference because of the lack of resting period. This requires much more advanced statistical models to handle. One image per 3 s is doable today but finding optimal parameters would require additional empirical studies.

Handling Environmental Variability. One common issue with eye biometrics is that capturing software has to accommodate for a large variability in real data. For example, pupil sizes react to cognitive load [14], but also to ambient light, alcohol and drug use, and mood. Because of this, most experiments control the luminance levels and try to keep them constant across all stimuli [20,40]. One way to handle this in our context is to show a grey screen for a few seconds before authentication (or measure pupil sizes while the user types their login). Alternatively, we could show two or four initial images—half of them known, the others unknown—and use the reactions as a baseline for the rest of the authentication process.

6   Error Tolerance and Security Considerations

6.1   Kinds of Errors

The protocol that we described in Sect. 5 is prone to various errors, which can be classified into four types:

- *User false negatives*, where the user is not recognising an image that had previously been shown.
- *User false positive*, where the user recognises an image that is supposed to be unknown, as the image has been seen before by coincidence (for example, on someone else's screen).
- *System misclassification*, in which the pupil dilation is badly interpreted.
- *Sensor or environmental error*, where the hardware has a bug or something prevents the capture (e.g. due to the user suddenly turning their head).

Probabilistic Formalism. To be formal, we can integrate the previous errors into probabilities that the user is correct or not, depending on what is shown on the screen.

The probabilities that we take into account are the following:

- The base probability p_u of being the user. We use the value $p_u = 0.5$ in the calculations in the following (which is not far from real world data [48]).
- The probability p_s of the user successfully classifying an image. Unless stated otherwise, we assume that this probability is 0.95. The analogous probability for the adversary considered here is fixed to be 0.5 throughout this section.
- The probabilities p_x and $p_y = 1 - p_x$ of being shown an unknown (respectively known) image.
- The probabilities p_{x_0} and $p_{x_1} = 1 - p_{x_0}$ that the user does not recognise (respectively recognises) an unknown image.
- The probabilities p_{y_0} and $p_{y_1} = 1 - p_{y_0}$ that the user does not recognise (respectively recognises) an already known image.

We start by investigating the question whether p_x should be equal to p_y.

6.2 Showing More Unknown or Known Images

Let us now consider a model in which the two probabilities p_x and p_y are not necessarily equal, and the adversary classifies any image as "unknown" with a probability x and as "known" with probability $1 - x$. We then get the following result:

Lemma 1. *The optimal strategy for the adversary is to classify every image as "unknown" if $p_x > p_y$, and as "known" if $p_y > p_x$.*

Proof. Without loss of generality, let us assume that $p_x > p_y$. This implies in particular that $p_x > 0.5$. In this case, the probability for the adversary to successfully authenticate after being shown n images is:

$$p'_s(x) = p_x x + (1 - p_x)(1 - x) = (1 - p_x) + (2p_x - 1)x.$$

Because $p_x > 0.5$, the function p'_s increases when x increases. Therefore, the optimal strategy for the adversary is to set $x = 1$.

With the optimal strategy, the probability for the adversary to succeed the authentication after being shown n images is $\max(p_x, p_y)^n$. As such, we have an interest in setting $p_y = p_x = 0.5$, which minimises this probability.

6.3 Handling the Probability of an Error

In our first model, we assume that $p_x = p_y = 0.5$. In addition, the adversary in this model randomly guesses whether an image is known or unknown to the user with probability 0.5.

We are interested in comparing the probabilities of successful authentication for the user and the adversary. These probabilities depend on two parameters: the number n of shown images and the number e of errors tolerated by the system. The general formulae for the probability of the successful authentication for the user and the adversary are:

$$\sum_{i=0}^{e} \binom{n}{i} (1 - p_s)^i p_s^{n-i} \text{ and } \sum_{i=0}^{e} \binom{n}{i} (0.5)^n \text{ respectively.}$$

Figure 4 plots the success probabilities for $e = 0, 1, 2$ and $p_{x_0} = p_{y_1} = 0.95$.

6.4 Adaptive Error Probability

As seen on Fig. 4, even by tolerating two errors, we eventually deny access to some users. As such, it is better to use an adaptive system where the probability of being the adversary is computed after each round.

The probability of being the adversary after n shown images with at most e errors can be found using Bayes' theorem:

$$\frac{\sum_{i=0}^{e} \binom{n}{i} (0.5)^n (1 - p_u)}{\sum_{i=0}^{e} \binom{n}{i} (1 - p_s)^i p_s^{n-i} p_u + \sum_{i=0}^{e} \binom{n}{i} (0.5)^n (1 - p_u)}.$$

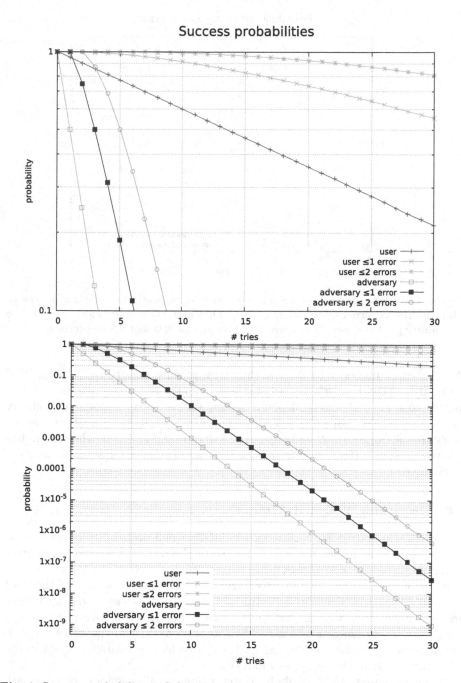

Fig. 4. Success probabilities of the user and the adversary trying to authenticate in the system, where different curves correspond to the number of errors tolerated by the system. Note that the probability axis is log-scaled. The same curve are shown again on the bottom with a larger logarithmic scale.

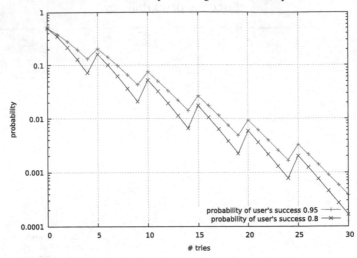

Fig. 5. The probability of the person who tries to authenticate being an adversary after an error occurred after each 5 images. The curve above and below take as base probability p_s of the user to be correct to be equal to 0.95 and 0.8 respectively.

We ran exact numbers for a user that tries to authenticate but misclassified every fifth image. Figure 5 shows how the probability of being a real user evolves in this context, and that it depends weakly on the server's stored probability that a user is misclassified. Even in a scenario where the user makes a mistake every five pictures—much higher than real data would indicate—the system has a lower error rate than all current biometric authentication systems in at most 27 challenges.

6.5   Preventing Targeted Attacks

A brute-forcing adversary has an exponentially small probability of success, as long as they do not remember which images have been shown. However, a smarter adversary could memorise previously shown images. Let us denote by N' the number of images seen by the adversary, and by N the total size of the pool of known images, which can be estimated. Once an adversary sees an image, necessarily this image is known to the user. Therefore, the adversary always classifies such an image as "known" if it appears again. On the other hand, if the adversary has not seen an image before, we fix a probability $\frac{N'}{N}$ that the adversary classifies the image as unknown.

We can compute the probability of successful classification for the adversary separately for images that are known and unknown to the user, which are:

$$\frac{N'}{N} + \left(1 - \frac{N'}{N}\right)^2 \text{ and } \frac{N'}{N} \text{ respectively.}$$

From these formulae, the adversary has at least 75% of success on each single image if $N'/N \geq 0.75$. We will denote this ratio as ε. We can estimate the expected number A of attempts by the adversary to know at least a proportion ε of the whole number N of images. This problem is related to the so-called *coupon collector's problem*. From the formula in [15, Sect. 2.1], we get:

$$A = N \sum_{i=\varepsilon N}^{N} \frac{1}{i} \sim N \ln \left(\frac{1}{1-\varepsilon} \right) \approx 1.39N.$$

We should then stop the adversary from obtaining too many images. If new images are added at every login, we get that N should quickly be in the hundreds. This means that a targeted attack would require many login attempts. This would get detected by the system which could create a lock-out. An alternative would be to increase $P(x)$ when many errors are detected and re-using old pictures, making brute-force easier but targeted attacks harder.

6.6 Constraint on a Generalised Use

To be sure that the protocol is scalable, having many different accounts with different services should not create any problem. Getting some seen images list stolen should also not affect it, as it is possible to reset the protocol by removing all the stolen images from the set and memorising new ones. One issue comes from the re-use of similar image databases. It is quite related to the problem of not showing the same images again by keeping track of which ones were seen, with the problem that there is no common database.

One improvement over the naive method of randomly selecting images is to select sets of 10 to 20 images. This lowers the probability of getting a familiar set, at the cost of obtaining all positives when a known set is used (in which case it is quite easy for the server to notice and cancel that set). Still, if all services apply this method with the same categorisation of images into sets, the probability of collision gets divided by 10.

This also means that less information has to be stored about which images have been seen. Depending on future empirical research on the performance of generated and composite images, a database of 10^{10} artificial images could be used naively for improved performance. This is just one of many potential improvements to the Reflexive Memory Authenticator, and we will now discuss a few other options.

7 Extensions and Discussion

7.1 Potential Extensions

Besides the potential optimisations already mentioned, we want to mention three ways to extend and improve this protocol. The first would be to reduce the waiting time. This could be done by using loading times as an opportunity to show some images. The background images while the user waits or types their information could also be used as a way to create a baseline.

A second possibility would be to use this kind of protocol for continuous authentication, with an image being shown periodically, especially after extended pauses to make sure that the person using the device is the correct one. Such approaches would add security in the most critical times. As this interruption can be costly to the user, care has to be taken to ensure that it does not disrupt the workflow. This could be improved by using ideas from the field of considerate computing [47]. As such, the image challenges should not be shown while the user is typing, talking, making selections, or being presented with a complex decision or action. Instead, it would be better to issue a challenge as they are about to change task: closing a file or a tab, for example.

Finally, there is still a controversy about how much the brain really reacts to images shown for very brief durations (e.g. 30 ms). An effect can be seen in certain cases, especially when it comes to pupil behaviour, where it can prime the user for faster reaction [20]. If that could be controlled, inserting test images within a short video could make a longer authentication process more bearable. However, this might bother some users conceptually, and it would require better models of pupil contraction.

This method could also be used in a more worrisome way, as it could allow an adversary to identify users without their knowledge or consent, by showing discreet images and studying their pupil reactions. It would be possible to counter this by making some mental computations, which affect pupil size, but this counter requires being aware that the test is ongoing. Even without going as far as identifying users, pupil biometrics also have the potential to be used to expose the emotional state of the user—as well as whether they are intoxicated.

7.2 Testing Reflexive Pupil Biometrics

One central outcome of this paper is that we need specific empirical studies on pupil sizes in memory effects, especially in the context of classification. Such efforts would not just improve the performance and understanding of the Reflexive Memory Authenticator, but also answer some fundamental questions. Many are still open:

- How fast can the system accurately discriminate between a familiar and a new image?
- What interactions need to be considered when using a resting period or when presenting many stimuli in a row, and can the interference be compensated?
- We currently try to get a single bit, but how much information can be reliably obtained by the dilation response? This could be done by allowing the classification to estimate the strength of recall instead of simply checking whether the image is familiar.
- How does the pupil react to images that are closely related to ones that are known or were recently shown?
- How is the pupil reaction affected by the use of synthetic or composite images?

– How usable would showing this stream of images be, and how would users react to it, especially for high frequencies? Could ocular fatigue be a problem?

Acknowledgements. We'd like to thank Leila Gabasova for their help with the figures. This work was supported partly by the french PIA project "Lorraine Université d'Excellence", reference ANR-15-IDEX-04-LUE.

References

1. Asghar, H.J., Li, S., Pieprzyk, J., Wang, H.: Cryptanalysis of the convex hull click human identification protocol. Int. J. Inf. Secur. **12**(2), 83–96 (2013)
2. Ashby, C., Bhatia, A., Tenore, F., Vogelstein, J.: Low-cost electroencephalogram (EEG) based authentication. In: 5th International IEEE/EMBS Conference on Neural Engineering - NER, pp. 442–445. IEEE (2011)
3. Bednarik, R., Kinnunen, T., Mihaila, A., Fränti, P.: Eye-movements as a biometric. In: Kalviainen, H., Parkkinen, J., Kaarna, A. (eds.) SCIA 2005. LNCS, vol. 3540, pp. 780–789. Springer, Heidelberg (2005). https://doi.org/10.1007/11499145_79
4. Bonneau, J.: The science of guessing: analyzing an anonymized corpus of 70 million passwords. In: IEEE Symposium on Security and Privacy, pp. 538–552 (5 2012). https://doi.org/10.1109/SP.2012.49
5. Bowyer, K.W., Hollingsworth, K., Flynn, P.J.: Image understanding for iris biometrics: a survey. Comput. Vis. Image Underst. **110**(2), 281–307 (2008)
6. Bradley, M.M., Lang, P.J.: Memory, emotion, and pupil diameter: repetition of natural scenes. Psychophysiology **52**(9), 1186–1193 (2015)
7. Brostoff, S., Sasse, M.A.: Are passfaces more usable than passwords? A field trial investigation. In: McDonald, S., Waern, Y., Cockton, G. (eds.) People and Computers XIV – Usability or Else!: Proceedings of HCI, pp. 405–424. Springer, London (2000). https://doi.org/10.1007/978-1-4471-0515-2_27
8. Chiasson, S., Biddle, R., van Oorschot, P.C.: A second look at the usability of click-based graphical passwords. In: Proceedings of the 3rd Symposium on Usable Privacy and Security, SOUPS 2007, pp. 1–12. ACM, New York (2007)
9. Choudhury, B., Then, P., Issac, B., Raman, V., Haldar, M.: A survey on biometrics and cancelable biometrics systems. Int. J. Image Graph. **18**, 1850006 (2018)
10. Cody, S.: Do Only The Eyes Have It? Predicting subsequent memory with simultaneous neural and pupillometry data. Master's thesis, The Ohio State University (2015)
11. Curran, M.T., Yang, J., Merrill, N., Chuang, J.: Passthoughts authentication with low cost EarEEG. In: IEEE 38th Annual International Conference of the Engineering in Medicine and Biology Society - EMBC, pp. 1979–1982. IEEE (2016)
12. Das, R., Maiorana, E., Campisi, P.: EEG biometrics using visual stimuli: a longitudinal study. IEEE Signal Process. Lett. **23**(3), 341–345 (2016)
13. Deravi, F., Guness, S.P.: Gaze trajectory as a biometric modality. In: Biosignals, pp. 335–341 (2011)
14. Einhäuser, W.: The pupil as marker of cognitive processes. In: Zhao, Q. (ed.) Computational and Cognitive Neuroscience of Vision. CST, pp. 141–169. Springer, Singapore (2017). https://doi.org/10.1007/978-981-10-0213-7_7
15. Ferrante, M., Saltalamacchia, M.: The coupon collector's problem. Materials Matemàtics 0001–35 (2014)

16. Galdi, C., Nappi, M., Riccio, D., Cantoni, V., Porta, M.: A new gaze analysis based soft-biometric. In: Carrasco-Ochoa, J.A., Martínez-Trinidad, J.F., Rodríguez, J.S., di Baja, G.S. (eds.) MCPR 2013. LNCS, vol. 7914, pp. 136–144. Springer, Heidelberg (2013). https://doi.org/10.1007/978-3-642-38989-4_14
17. Galdi, C., Nappi, M., Riccio, D., Wechsler, H.: Eye movement analysis for human authentication: a critical survey. Pattern Recogn. Lett. **84**, 272–283 (2016)
18. German, R.L., Barber, K.S.: Consumer attitudes about biometric authentication. Technical report, University of Texas at Austin Center for Identity (2018)
19. Golla, M., Schnitzler, T., Dürmuth, M.: Will any password do? Exploring rate-limiting on the web. In: Who Are You ?! Adventures in Authentication (2016)
20. Gomes, C.A., Montaldi, D., Mayes, A.: The pupil as an indicator of unconscious memory: introducing the pupil priming effect. Psychophysiology **52**(6), 754–769 (2015)
21. Jensen, W., Gavrila, S., Korolev, V., et al.: Picture password: a visual login technique for mobile devices. Technical report, National Institute of Standards and Technology (2003)
22. Just, M., Aspinall, D.: Personal choice and challenge questions: a security and usability assessment. In: Proceedings of the 5th Symposium on Usable Privacy and Security, p. 8. ACM (2009)
23. Just, M., Aspinall, D.: Challenging challenge questions: an experimental analysis of authentication technologies and user behaviour. Policy Internet **2**(1), 99–115 (2010)
24. Kafkas, A., Montaldi, D.: Recognition memory strength is predicted by pupillary responses at encoding while fixation patterns distinguish recollection from familiarity. Q. J. Exp. Psychol. **64**(10), 1971–1989 (2011)
25. Karthika, S., Devaki, P.: An efficient user authentication using captcha and graphical passwords - a survey. Int. J. Sci. Res. **3**(11), 123 (2014)
26. Kasprowski, P., Komogortsev, O.V., Karpov, A.: First eye movement verification and identification competition at BTAS 2012. In: IEEE 5th International Conference on Biometrics: Theory, Applications and Systems - BTAS, pp. 195–202. IEEE (2012)
27. Klamkin, M.S., Newman, D.J.: Extensions of the birthday surprise. J. Comb. Theory **3**(3), 279–282 (1967)
28. Kollreider, K., Fronthaler, H., Bigun, J.: Evaluating liveness by face images and the structure tensor. In: IEEE 4th Workshop on Automatic Identification Advanced Technologies - AutoID, pp. 75–80, October 2005
29. Lashkari, A.H., Farmand, S., Zakaria, O.B., Saleh, R.: Shoulder surfing attack in graphical password authentication. Int. J. Comput. Sci. Inf. Secur. - IJCSIS **6**(2) (2009). http://arxiv.org/abs/0912.0951
30. Lee, C., Kim, J.: Cancelable fingerprint templates using minutiae-based bit-strings. J. Netw. Comput. Appl. **33**(3), 236–246 (2010)
31. de Leeuw, K.M.M., Bergstra, J.: The History of Information Security: A Comprehensive Handbook. Elsevier, Amsterdam (2007)
32. Loftus, G.R.: Eye fixations and recognition memory for pictures. Cogn. Psychol. **3**(4), 525–551 (1972)
33. Marcel, S., Millán, J.R.: Person authentication using brainwaves (EEG) and maximum a posteriori model adaptation. IEEE Trans. Pattern Anal. Mach. Intell. **29**(4), 743–752 (2007)
34. McCulley, S., Roussev, V.: Latent typing biometrics in online collaboration services. In: Proceedings of the 34th Annual Computer Security Applications Confer-

ence, ACSAC 2018, pp. 66–76. ACM, New York (2018). https://doi.org/10.1145/3274694.3274754

35. Moon, D., Yoo, J.H., Lee, M.K.: Improved cancelable fingerprint templates using minutiae-based functional transform. Secur. Commun. Netw. **7**(10), 1543–1551 (2014). https://doi.org/10.1002/sec.788

36. Shepard, R.N.: Recognition memory for words, sentences, and pictures. J. Verbal Learn. Verbal Behav. **6**, 156–163 (1967). https://doi.org/10.1016/S0022-5371(67)80067-7

37. Naber, M., Frässle, S., Rutishauser, U., Einhäuser, W.: Pupil size signals novelty and predicts later retrieval success for declarative memories of natural scenes. J. Vis. **13**(2), 11–11 (2013)

38. Noton, D., Stark, L.: Scanpaths in saccadic eye movements while viewing and recognizing patterns. Vis. Res. **11**(9), 929–942 (1971)

39. Phetmak, N., Liwlompaisan, W., Boonma, P.: Travel password: a secure and memorable password scheme. In: Nguyen, N.T., Attachoo, B., Trawiński, B., Somboonviwat, K. (eds.) ACIIDS 2014. LNCS (LNAI), vol. 8397, pp. 402–411. Springer, Cham (2014). https://doi.org/10.1007/978-3-319-05476-6_41

40. Rajan, R., Selker, T., Lane, I.: Task load estimation and mediation using psychophysiological measures. In: Proceedings of the 21st International Conference on Intelligent User Interfaces, pp. 48–59. ACM (2016)

41. Rayner, K.: Eye movement latencies for parafoveally presented words. Bull. Psychon. Soc. **11**(1), 13–16 (1978)

42. Reddy, P.V., Kumar, A., Rahman, S., Mundra, T.S.: A new antispoofing approach for biometric devices. IEEE Trans. Biomed. Circ. Syst. **2**(4), 328–37 (2008)

43. Rigas, I., Abdulin, E., Komogortsev, O.: Towards a multi-source fusion approach for eye movement-driven recognition. Inf. Fusion **32**, 13–25 (2016)

44. Roberts, C.: Biometric attack vectors and defences. Comput. Secur. **26**(1), 14–25 (2007)

45. Schechter, S., Brush, A.J.B., Egelman, S.: It's no secret. Measuring the security and reliability of authentication via "secret" questions. In: 30th IEEE Symposium on Security and Privacy, pp. 375–390. IEEE (2009)

46. Segreti, S.M., et al.: Diversify to survive: making passwords stronger with adaptive policies. In: 13th Symposium on Usable Privacy and Security - SOUPS, pp. 1–12. USENIX Association, Santa Clara, CA (2017)

47. Selker, T.: Understanding considerate systems - UCS (pronounced: You see us). In: 2010 International Symposium on Collaborative Technologies and Systems, pp. 1–12, May 2010. https://doi.org/10.1109/CTS.2010.5478532

48. Shape: 2018 credential spill report. Technical report, Shape Security (2018)

49. Shin, S.W., Lee, M.K., Moon, D., Moon, K.: Dictionary attack on functional transform-based cancelable fingerprint templates. ETRI J. **31**(5), 628–630 (2009)

50. Singh, S., Agarwal, G.: Integration of sound signature in graphical password authentication system. Int. J. Comput. Appl. **12**(9), 11–13 (2011)

51. Sluganovic, I., Roeschlin, M., Rasmussen, K.B., Martinovic, I.: Using reflexive eye movements for fast challenge-response authentication. In: Proceedings of the 2016 ACM SIGSAC Conference on Computer and Communications Security, CCS 2016, pp. 1056–1067. ACM, New York (2016)

52. Wiedenbeck, S., Waters, J., Birget, J.C., Brodskiy, A., Memon, N.: Passpoints: design and longitudinal evaluation of a graphical password system. Int. J. Hum Comput Stud. **63**(1–2), 102–127 (2005)

53. Zviran, M., Haga, W.J.: Cognitive passwords: the key to easy access control. Comput. Secur. **9**(8), 723–736 (1990)

Collaborative Authentication Using Threshold Cryptography

Aysajan Abidin[1(✉)], Abdelrahaman Aly[1], and Mustafa A. Mustafa[1,2]

[1] imec-COSIC, KU Leuven, Kasteelpark Arenberg 10 - bus 2452,
3001 Heverlee, Belgium
{aysajan.abidin,abdelrahaman.aly}@esat.kuleuven.be
[2] Department of Computer Science, The University of Manchester,
Manchester M13 9PL, UK
mustafa.mustafa@manchester.ac.uk

Abstract. We propose a collaborative authentication protocol where multiple user devices (e.g., a smartphone, a smartwatch and a wristband) collaborate to authenticate the user to a third party service provider. Our protocol uses a threshold signature scheme as the main building block. The use of threshold signatures minimises the security threats in that the user devices only store shares of the signing key (i.e., the private key) and the private key is never reconstructed. For user devices that do not have secure storage capability (e.g., some wearables), we propose to use fuzzy extractors to generate their secret shares using behaviometric information when needed, so that there is no need for them to store any secret material. We discuss how to reshare the private key without reconstructing it in case a new device is added and how to repair shares that are lost due to device loss or damage. Our implementation results demonstrate the feasibility of the protocol.

Keywords: Collaborative authentication · Security and privacy · Threshold signatures · Secret sharing · Fuzzy extractors

1 Introduction

The increasing number of mobile and wearable devices being carried by users results in more sensitive information being stored on and/or accessed via these devices. This provides users with more flexibility in terms of accessing resources and services, thus enhancing their personal experience and convenience, as well as, it creates new opportunities for both users and service providers. However, this flexibility comes at a cost, introducing new security and privacy challenges [1]. For example, some of these personal devices, i.e., wearables (such as smartwatches and wristbands), unlike smartphones, have limited computational and interaction capabilities, thus making them unsuitable to use existing authentication protocols. The use of easily-accessible context information such as the user's location and typical behaviour causes privacy concerns too. In addition,

A. Saracino and P. Mori (Eds.): ETAA 2019, LNCS 11967, pp. 122–137, 2020.
https://doi.org/10.1007/978-3-030-39749-4_8

since these devices are small, light, and easy to carry, they are also prone to loss, theft and/or break. Nevertheless, users still expect strong security, privacy protection as well as maximum flexibility and convenience when accessing services or resources provided by the service providers. Satisfying the users' needs while minimising the associated security and privacy risks of using personal and wearable devices will require new, more collaborative, ways for users to be authenticated and granted access to a wide range of on-line services and content [2].

Existing solutions for user authentication [3–8] do not satisfy these needs: (i) users prefer password-less solutions, (ii) biometric-only solutions have security and usability tradeoff, and (iii) wearable devices have limited computational powers and are more prone to loss and theft. Thus, authentication solutions that are more user-, device- and context-tailored are necessary.

One way to achieve this is to use a collaborative approach in designing authentication schemes. Collaborative authentication schemes are the ones where multiple devices jointly authenticate to a remote server or within a device-to-device setting with minimum user effort. They are getting traction as users carry multiple devices and wearables with themselves nowadays. To limit the cost, the combination of wearables and the user's other devices, say, a smartphone, would be preferred. Such collaborative authentication schemes overcome the security problems of using a single possession factor or a knowledge factor during the authentication process. An adversary would have to compromise multiple wearables to successfully impersonate a user. Moreover, by using wearables the user is carrying anyhow, one avoids the need of employing external hardware authentication tokens, which could be quite costly.

The main concept of collaborative authentication is to transform a challenge-response protocol with a single prover and verifier, to a challenge-response protocol with multiple collaborating provers and a single verifier. To mitigate the threat of wearables being stolen or lost, and the fact that the set of wearables is dynamic (the user is not always carrying the same set of wearables), threshold-based cryptography can be used. The aim of threshold cryptography is to protect a key by sharing it amongst a number of entities in such a way that only a subset of minimal size, namely a threshold t (out of, say, $n > t$), can use the key. No information about the key can be learnt from $t - 1$ or less shares. To deal with user devices that do not have secure element to store their share, such devices can make use of fuzzy extractors to generate their shares of the secret key from users' biometric data on demand whenever they need them.

Contribution. The main contributions of this paper are summarised as follows.

- Firstly, it proposes a concrete collaborative authentication protocol that uses threshold signatures.
- Secondly, it presents mechanisms for key reshare and share repair in case some of the original shares of the key are lost or compromised. For repairing lost shares, we use a repairable threshold scheme proposed in a recent paper by Stinson and Wei in [9].

- Thirdly, it proposes a secret share generation mechanism for devices with no memory applying fuzzy extractors to behaviometric information captured by the device sensors, improving the usability of the authentication protocol. We do note that the same procedure also applies to PUFs (physically uncloneable functions) implemented in the devices.
- Lastly, it presents performance results from the implementation of the share regeneration and threshold signatures. The results show that the proposed protocol is feasible in practice.

Outline. The remainder of this paper is organised as follows: Sect. 2 presents our system model and requirements for collaborative authentication schemes. Section 3 presents security definitions of the cryptographic building blocks and our threat model. Then, Sect. 4 proposes a concrete collaborative authentication protocol that combines threshold signatures and fuzzy extractors, and introduces a share generation mechanism as well as the threshold Schnorr signature scheme using secret sharing. Sections 5 and 6 present the security analysis and the performance evaluation of our protocol, respectively. Section 7 presents the related work. Finally, Sect. 8 concludes the paper.

2   System Model and Requirements

System Model. As shown in Fig. 1, a system model of a collaborative authentication system consists of the following entities:

- *User*: a person who wants to access various services provided by a service provider. The user also carries a number of personal devices (including wearable) which can be used in the authentication procedure.
- *Personal devices*: devices owned by the user. Some of these devices such as a smartphone have secure storage where the user's secret data can be stored. However, other devices such as wearables (e.g., wristband) may not have such secure storage. Each of the user's devices may also have one or more sensors integrated to measure different (physiological) data such as location, gait, blood pressure, heart beats, etc.
- *Service provider*: a service provider to which users want to authenticate in order to access various services and/or resources.

Functional Requirements. A collaborative authentication system should support the following functional requirements:

- *Collaborative*: the user should use data (input) provided by multiple user devices.
- *Flexible*: the user should be able to use various combinations of data collected from various user devices.
- *Robust and resilient*: a failure or lack of a single user device should not result in an authentication failure.

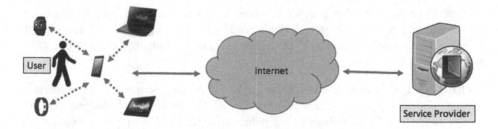

Fig. 1. A system model of a collaborative authentication scheme.

Security and Privacy Requirements. A collaborative authentication proto-col should satisfy the following security and privacy requirements.

- *Multi-factor authentication*: A user should need to use multiple factors (devices) in order to authenticate successfully to the service provider.
- *No authentication key stored*: None of the user's personal devices should store the secret authentication key in its entire form. They should either store shares of the key or generate these shares on demand.
- *Lost and/or stolen device resistance*: Loss of a certain number of a user's devices (less than a specified threshold) should still allow the user to success-fully authenticate towards the service provider, but it should not allow an attacker (in possession of those lost devices) to successfully impersonate the user.
- *No biometrics/behaviometrics information stored*: None of the user's personal devices should store any sensitive biometrics and/or behaviometrics informa-tion.
- *Device presence protection*: The service provider should not be able to identify which (combination of) personal devices the user uses in the authentication procedure.

3   Building Blocks and Their Security Definitions

Secret Sharing. Secret sharing enables the sharing of a secret S among n parties, so that any subset of t or more parties can efficiently reconstruct the secret, and any subset of $t - 1$ or less parties learn no information whatsoever about the secret. It is a key technique widely used in secure multiparty com-putation, which allows n players to compute an agreed function of their inputs in a secure way. Some secret sharing schemes, such as additive secret sharing, can offer security against dishonest majorities, whereas others, such as Shamir's secret sharing, require at least an honest majority [10]. Security in this setting means guaranteeing the correctness of the output as well as the privacy of the players' inputs, even when some players cheat. Shamir's scheme is what is typi-cally called a (t, n) (or t-out-of-n)-threshold scheme where n is the total number of parties involved in the computation and t is the size of the subset needed to reconstruct the secret.

Let P be the set of n parties involved in a computation, and let $\mathbb{Z}_q$ be a finite field and $S \in \mathbb{Z}_q$ a secret. A dealer calculates the shares S_i, $i = 1, \cdots, n$ of secret S using a polynomial $f(x)$ of degree $t-1$, by evaluating $f(i) \mod q$, $\forall i = 1, \cdots, n$, i.e., $S_i = f(i)$.

Definition 1 (Shamir Secret Sharing). *Let $S \in \mathbb{Z}_q$ be a secret to be secretly shared among n parties. Then Shamir's (t, n)-threshold secret sharing scheme works as follows. First, a degree $t-1$ polynomial $f(x) = S + a_1 x + \cdots + a_{t-1} x^{t-1}$, where $a_j \in \mathbb{Z}_q$, $j = 1, \cdots, t-1$ are randomly selected coefficients, is chosen. Then the shares S_i, $i = 1, \cdots, n$, are generated by evaluating $f(x)$ at each i, i.e., $S_i = f(i) \mod q$. Given t shares, $f(x)$ can be reconstructed using interpolation, and then the secret is equal to the evaluation of the polynomial at 0, i.e., $S = f(0) \mod q$.*

Fuzzy Extractor. A fuzzy extractor is a randomness extractor that comprises a pair of procedures known as *generation* and *reproduction* algorithms. The former algorithm generates a random string and helper data from an input. The latter algorithm reproduces the same random string using the helper data and an input that is *close* to the original input to the generation algorithm. Fuzzy extractors (and also similar concepts such as fuzzy commitments) [11–15] are commonly used as biometric cryptosystems for template protection. Formally, a fuzzy extractor is a construct that must satisfy the following properties [14].

Definition 2 (Fuzzy Extractor). *An (m, ℓ, t, ϵ)-fuzzy extractor over a metric space $(\mathcal{M}, d)$ comprises a pair of efficient randomized procedures $(\mathsf{Gen}, \mathsf{Rep})$. The generation algorithm Gen, on input $\omega \in \mathcal{M}$, outputs an extracted string $S \in \{0, 1\}^{\ell}$ and a helper string $P \in \{0, 1\}^*$. The reproduction procedure Rep takes an element $\omega' \in \mathcal{M}$ and a helper string $P \in \{0, 1\}^*$ as inputs and outputs S', such that the following two properties are satisfied:*

- *(Security) For any distribution W over $\mathcal{M}$ with min-entropy m, S is indistinguishable from a uniformly random string even when conditioned on P. That is, if the min-entropy $\mathbf{H}_\infty(W) \geq m$ and $\mathsf{Gen}(W) \to (S, P)$, then we have*

$$\mathbf{SD}((S, P), (U_\ell, P)) \leq \epsilon,$$

where $\mathbf{SD}$ is the statistical distance and U_ℓ is a uniformly distributed random string of length ℓ.
- *(Error-tolerance) If $d(\omega, \omega') \leq t$ and $\mathsf{Gen}(\omega) \to (S, P)$, then $\mathsf{Rep}(\omega', P) = S' = S$. This means that the exact value of S can be reproduced using the helper data P and any new sample ω' which is close to the originally sampled template ω from which S and P were generated.*

Threshold Signatures. The concept of threshold signatures is similar to that of secret sharing. A t out of n threshold signature scheme is one that allows any subset of t players to generate a signature, while disallowing the generation of a valid signature the number of participating players is less than t. A threshold signature scheme $\mathsf{TS} = (\mathsf{TKeyGen}, \mathsf{TSIGN}, \mathsf{VER})$ comprises three algorithms.

- The threshold key generation algorithm $\mathsf{TKeyGen}$ takes t, n and a security parameter λ as input and employs a (t, n) Shamir secret sharing to generate n shares $\mathsf{sk}_1, \cdots, \mathsf{sk}_n$ of a private key sk, and the corresponding public key pk.
- The possibly randomised threshold signature generation algorithm TSIGN further consists of signature share generation and signature construction algorithms. Each participating player i outputs its signature share upon taking a message m and its share sk_i as input. The signature construction algorithms combines all signature shares and outputs a message-signature pair (m, σ).
- The verification algorithm VER uses the public key pk to verify if a message-signature pair (m, σ) is valid.

Definition 3. *Let a $\mathsf{TS} = (\mathsf{TKeyGen}, \mathsf{TSIGN}, \mathsf{VER})$ be a threshold digital signature scheme. Then TS is called secure if no probabilistic polynomial-time adversary $\mathbf{A}$ that is allowed to corrupt up to $t - 1$ players can forge a valid signature on any message.*

Threat Model and Assumptions. The threat model used in this paper is the following. *Users* are malicious. They might try passively and/or actively to collect and alter the information stored and exchanged within the authentication system, in an attempt to gain access to services which he or she does not have permission to access. The *service provider* is honest-but-curious. It might try to learn and extract unauthorised information about the users. *External entities* (i.e., third parties) are malicious. They are active adversaries who try to impersonate legitimate users.

Assumption 1. *We assume that users' (i) personal devices (excluding wearables) are equipped with secure storage, security mechanisms to provide access control and protection against data breaches and/or malware, (ii) wearables do not have any secure storage element, and (iii) the devices can communicate with each other.*

Assumption 2. *We assume that the employed threshold signature scheme is secure, cf Definition 3.*

4   The Collaborative Authentication Protocol

In this section, we propose a collaborative authentication protocol that combines a threshold signature scheme and fuzzy extractors. Afterwards, we detail how the remaining shares could be used to regenerate a new share to replace a lost one (due to a lost device). Finally, we propose a new threshold signature scheme by combining the classical Schnorr signature scheme with the Shamir secret sharing scheme.

4.1 Protocol Overview

Below we explain how any threshold signature scheme could be used to support collaborative authentication schemes. Then we describe how these schemes could be combined with fuzzy extractors to allow some of the users' personal devices to generate the shares of the secret key on demand, rather than storing them.

Using Threshold Signatures. Suppose that sk and pk are the private and public key pair of a threshold signature scheme. Then sk is split into shares which are distributed to the personal devices of a user. To sign a challenge during the authentication process, these devices perform computations on the challenge using their shares. Then, the results of these computations are combined (by one of the user's personal devices) to form a valid signature, which will be verified by the service provider to verify the user identity. In particular:

- The user's devices share the private key using secret sharing scheme among themselves. The shares can be generated by one of the personal devices, say, a smartphone, tablet, personal computer of the user.
- To authenticate a user, the service provider sends a challenge to the user's device which initiated the authentication request or acts as a gateway device.
- Upon receiving the challenge, the devices jointly compute a signature without reconstructing the user's private key.
- The signature is sent to the service provider, which verifies the signature using the user's public key.

Using Biometrics/Behaviometrics. The authentication system can also incorporate biometrics or behaviometric information for increased security and flexibility. In this case, the shares of the key can either be accessed by the devices using the measured biometric/behaviometric information, or they can be directly generated from such sources on demand. Below we describe how such fuzzy sources can be utilised to generate the shares.

- A key is generated from the user biometrics using a fuzzy extractor in one of the user's biometric-enabled devices. The generated key will be used as one of the shares of the private key for the signature scheme. The generated public data, named helper data, is stored either in the device itself if there is sufficient storage, or in a gateway device, which can be one of user's more computationally-capable personal devices, e.g., a smartphone, in the case the device has limited storage capabilities, e.g., a wearable.
- During the authentication procedure, the behaviometric data is used to reproduce the share with the help of the helper data, and then the signature share is computed by the device. In the case of a wearable, the gateway device sends the helper data to the device which then uses it to reproduce the share, which in turn is used for calculating the signature share of the device by the device.

4.2   Share Regeneration and Repair

It may happen from time to time that a user device gets lost or damaged, which results in the loss of the share distributed to that device; or even a new device is added. In such cases, regeneration of the shares of the key using the remaining shares without reconstructing the entire private key becomes necessary. Fortunately, this is possible due to the nature of the Shamir secret sharing. Below we describe the main idea with an example; for details we refer the curious reader to [16].

Suppose that a secret S is shared among n players using the Shamir secret sharing and that the shares are $S_1, \cdots, S_n$. Also, suppose that one share, say, S_i, is lost. We want to generate new shares, $S_1', \cdots, S_n'$, of the secret S without reconstructing S. The procedure for achieving this is as follows.

- All players, except for the i-th player, generate n shares, say $S_{j1}, \cdots, S_{jn}$, of their share S_j, $j = 1, \cdots, n$ and $j \neq i$.
- The shares of S_j are distributed to all players, so each player has $n-1$ shares of the remaining shares of the original secret S.
- Each player uses t shares to interpolate a polynomial $f_i(x)$ of degree $t-1$ and evaluates the polynomial at 0.
- The new shares of the original secret S is $S_i' = f_i(0)$, for $i = 1, \cdots, n$.

Note that a distributed key generation scheme also follows the same procedures as the share regeneration. The only difference is that in distributed key generation, each and every participating player picks a random secret string and shares it with the rest of the players using a (t, n) secret sharing scheme. Then, using the shares at its disposal, each player locally computes a value that will be a share of a common secret. Later on, we will present a performance analysis for both distributed key generation and share regeneration.

This share regeneration procedure requires communication among all players and the number of messages exchanged among them is $(n-1)^2$. The required computational complexity is also $n \times t$ modular additions and $n(n-1)$ polynomial evaluations.

However, in cases where we only want to recover a single share, then there is a more efficient way to achieve this rather that regenerating the shares of all parties. In this case, we can use what is called an *enrollment repairable threshold scheme (eRTS)* proposed by Stinson and Wei [9]. This eRTS only requires a subset of k players to help repair a share, where $t \leqslant k \leqslant n$; see [17] for more on reparable threshold schemes. Below we describe how the enrollment repairable threshold scheme works.

Suppose that a secret S is shared among n players using a (t, n)-Shamir secret sharing scheme and we wish to repair the share S_ℓ for a player P_ℓ. Assume that t players $P_1, \cdots, P_t$ are helping with the recovery of S_ℓ and that $\ell > k$. Suppose that $S_\ell = f(\ell)$, where $f(x) \in \mathbb{Z}_q[x]$ is a random polynomial of degree at most $t-1$ whose constant term is the secret S. The share S_ℓ can be expressed as

$$S_\ell = \sum_{i=1}^{t} \omega_i s_i,$$

where the ω_i's are public Lagrange coefficients. The eRTS proceeds as follows:

- $\forall 1 \leqslant i \leqslant t$, player P_i picks random values δ_{ij}, $j = 1, \cdots, t$ such that

$$\sum_{j=1}^{t} \delta_{ij} = \omega_i S_i.$$

- $\forall 1 \leqslant i \leqslant t, 1 \leqslant j \leqslant t$, player P_i sends δ_{ij} to player P_j.
- $\forall 1 \leqslant j \leqslant t$, player P_j computes

$$\sigma_j = \sum_{i=1}^{t} \delta_{ij}.$$

- $\forall 1 \leqslant j \leqslant t$, player P_j sends σ_j to player P_ℓ.
- Player P_ℓ recovers S_ℓ by computing

$$S_\ell = \sum_{j=1}^{t} \sigma_j.$$

As can be seen, the eRTS requires only an exchange of t^2 messages and $2t^2 - t - 1$ modular additions. The communication complexity can further be reduced to $t(t + 1)/2$ messages and the computational complexity to $t(t + 1)/2$ modular additions by requiring that player P_i does not send anything to player P_j if $i < j$, as shown in [17].

4.3   Threshold Schnorr Signatures

As a concrete example, here we present a threshold signature scheme that can be employed in the collaborative authentication protocol proposed in this paper. Namely, we present threshold Schnorr signatures which can be obtained from the classical Schnorr signatures by using secret sharing.

Schnorr Signature Scheme. Let q be a prime. Let $\mathbb{G}$ be a group of order q in which the discrete log is (assumed to be) hard, and let g be the generator of $\mathbb{G}$. Let M be the message space. Also, let $H : \{0,1\}^* \mapsto \{1, 2, \cdots, q-1\}$ be a cryptographic hash function. The Schnorr signature scheme, which is constructed by applying the Fiat-Shamir transformation [18] to Schnorr's identification protocol [19], works as follows.

The private key sk is an integer x in the range $1 \leqslant x \leqslant q - 1$, and the public key pk is $y = g^x \mod q$.

- **Sign:** $(r, s) \leftarrow \text{Sign}(\text{sk}, m)$: A message $m \in M$ is signed using the secret key sk by first picking a random integer k in the range $1 \leqslant k \leqslant q - 1$; then $r = g^k \mod q$ and $s = H(m\|r)x + k \mod q$. Here $m\|r$ is concatenation of bit representation of m and r.
- **Verify:** $1/0 \leftarrow \text{Verify}(\text{pk}, m, s, r)$: To verify whether the signature (s, r) for m is correct, use the public key y to check if $g^s \stackrel{?}{=} y^{H(m\|r)} r \mod q$.

Threshold Schnorr Signature Scheme. The threshold scheme has a share combining algorithm which takes as input a message and t valid signature shares on the message, along with the public key, and outputs a valid signature on the message.

Suppose that there are $n \geqslant 2$ players, and that the parameters, that is, the group $\mathbb{G}$, the private secret x and the public key $(g, q, y = g^x \mod q)$, are the same as before. The secret x is partitioned into n shares $x_1, x_2, \cdots, x_n$ using an additive secret sharing scheme and distributed to the respective parties. The shares are such that at least t distinct shares would allow the reconstruction of the secret x.

Now, in order to sign a message m, each party randomly picks a random integer k_i with $1 \leqslant k_i \leqslant q-1$ and provides $g^{k_i} \mod q$ to one party, which we call the central party, which then computes $r = \prod_{i=1}^{t} g^{k_i} \mod q$ and $h = H(m||r)$, which then is sent back to each party. The devices provide $s_i = hx_i + k_i \mod q$ to the central party, which combines them to generate the signature (s, r) on the message m. So in summary, the threshold Schnorr signatures work as follows.

- The private key x is shared among the devices using Shamir secret sharing.
- Suppose that t devices are present, and let G be the set of those devices.
- To each device $i \in G$, the gateway device sends $\omega_i = \prod_{\substack{j \in G \\ j \neq i}} \frac{j}{i-j}$.
- Each device $i \in G$, picks a random k_i and provides $r_i = g^{\omega_i k_i}$ to the gateway.
- The gateway computes $r = \prod_{i \in G} r_i = g^{\sum_{i \in G} \omega_i k_i}$ and $h = H(c||r)$ and sends h to all devices in G.
- Each device $i \in G$ provides the gateway with $s_i = k_i + hx_i$
- Finally, the signature is (r, s) where

$$s = \sum_{i \in G} s_i \omega_i = \sum_{i \in G} (k_i + hx_i)\omega_i = \sum_{i \in G} k_i \omega_i + h \sum_{i \in G} x_i \omega_i = \sum_{i \in G} k_i \omega_i + hx.$$

Note that in threshold signature schemes the signing key is not reconstructed to sign a message. Instead the players compute signature shares using their share of the signing key, and the signature shares are combined to form a signature on the message.

5   Security Analysis

Our collaborative authentication protocol satisfies all the security and privacy requirements specified in Sect. 2. More specifically and informally speaking, it provides a multi-factor authentication as it requires the presence (and collaboration) of multiple user devices due to the use of secret sharing scheme. A user will not be able to authenticate successfully towards the service provider if he/she uses only one of his/her personal devices. For the same reasons, the protocol also does not require the user's private signature key to be stored in any of the user's personal devices. Instead, these devices only store (or generate) shares of the key.

In addition, the use of a threshold scheme allows the protocol to provide lost/stolen user device protection as well as device presence protection. More specifically, the nature of threshold schemes - the fact that not all of the shares, but only a subset of these shares, are required to perform a specific operation successfully - allows users to successfully generate a valid signature even if one or more of his/her devices (depending on the specified threshold) are not present due to loss or theft. For the same reason and for the fact that the user's signature is constructed locally (in one of the personal devices) and then sent to the service provider, our protocol provides protection against leakage of information about device presence. As a valid signature could be constructed using various combinations of subset of the user's personal devices, the service provider does not know exactly which devices the user carries at the time of the authentication procedure. Moreover, the use of fuzzy extractors allows users to generate some of the shares of the key without the need of storing any biometric or behaviometric information.

Formally speaking, it is obvious that for the proposed collaborative authentication protocol to be secure, the underlying threshold signature scheme has to be secure (i.e., unforgeable). There are threshold signature schemes that satisfy various security requirements, such as the practical threshold RSA signatures by Shoup [20] and more recent ones by Simoens et al. [16]. Shamir secret sharing is used in the former and verifiable secret sharing together with bilinear maps in the latter. In addition, Schnorr signatures are unforgeable and the unforgeability of (t, n)-threshold Schnorr signatures is also straightforward assuming that no more than $t - 1$ players are corrupted.

Below, we first give a security definition for a collaborative authentication protocol, and then show that our protocol is secure.

Definition 4. *We say that a collaborative authentication protocol using a (t, n)-threshold signature scheme is secure against active attacks if for all efficient (i.e., probabilistic polynomial time) adversaries $\mathbf{A}$ that can corrupt up to $t - 1$ players, the advantage of $\mathbf{A}$ in the following game between a Challenger and $\mathbf{A}$ is negligible.*

- Key generation. *The Challenger runs $(pk, sk_1, \cdots, sk_n) \leftarrow TKeyGen(\lambda, n, t)$, and sends pk and a randomly chosen $t - 1$ shares of sk to $\mathbf{A}$.*
- Active attack phase. *The adversary interacts with the prover (i.e., the user) and gets the prover to produce signatures for a polynomial number of challenges. In this case, $\mathbf{A}$ plays the role of the verifier and the Challenger that of the prover.*
- Impersonation attempt. *The Challenger and $\mathbf{A}$ interact with $\mathbf{A}$ playing impersonating the prover. The Challenger requests $\mathbf{A}$ to produce a signature for a challenge c, and $\mathbf{A}$ responds with (c, σ).*

The adversary wins the game if σ is a valid signature for c. The adversary's advantage is defined as the probability that $\mathbf{A}$ wins the game.

Theorem 1 (Security). *Let M be the space of all authentication challenges, and assume that the size $|M|$ of M is super-poly. Assume further that Assump-*

tions 1 and 2 holds. Then the presented collaborative authentication protocol using threshold signatures is secure against active attacks as defined in Definition 4.

Proof (Sketch). First of all, the assumption that the size of the challenge space $|M|$ is super-poly implies that in each impersonation attempt, the probability that **A** gets challenge that it has previously asked the prover in the attack phase is negligible. Assumption 1 is necessary for security for obvious reasons. To prove that Assumption 2 (i.e., the assumption that the threshold signature scheme is unforgeable) implies the security of the authentication protocol, we show that a successful attack on the authentication protocol can be converted in a blackbox way into a successful attack on the signature scheme. This is also straightforward. Suppose that an adversary **A** can break the authentication protocol. This means that **A** can generate a valid signature on an authentication challenge. Now, suppose that another adversary **A'** is attempting to forge a valid signature for a message. Then **A'** first simulates the authentication protocol of **A** using the threshold signature scheme. Then **A'** presents **A** with the message as an authentication challenge. **A**'s response will be a valid signature (for the message) that **A'** was attempting to forge.

Therefore, either the adversary gets the same challenge that it previously used in the attack phase, or it successfully forges a signature. The probability for both is negligible. □

In the case of using fuzzy extractors for generation of some of the shares, the fuzzy extractor must satisfy Definition 2. The fuzzy extractors introduced by Dodis et al. [15] already satisfy that definition. Security of fuzzy extractors also implies the privacy of behaviometric data, as the public helper data does not reveal information on the behaviometric data or the extracted key. Lastly, the share regeneration procedure is information-theoretically secure against honest majority, as it is the Shamir secret sharing, cf. Definition 1.

6   Performance Analysis

To evaluate the performance of our authentication protocol, we first have prototyped and tested our basic scheme for share regeneration and distributed key generation on relatively small key sizes (1024 bits). We implemented our test cases using C++ and the secret sharing tools (Shamir Secret Sharing [10]) implemented by the *mpcToolkit*[1] introduced in [21]. The library was implemented over NTL (Library for doing Number Theory) [22] and natively supports 63-bit inputs. Hence, we further adapted it to support longer key sizes. We run our tests over a $2 \times 2 \times 10$-cores Intel Xeon E5-2687 server at 3.1 GHz. We simulated a three-device scenario over our server, and averaged the results of 10000 executions. The computational times are depicted in Table 1. As can be seen from the table, both procedures for distributed key generation and share regeneration are efficient.

---

[1] https://github.com/abdelrahamanaly/mpcToolkit.

Table 1. CPU running times.

Protocol	Time in seconds	Key sizes
Key generation	3.57×10^{-4}	1024
Share reconstruction	7.60×10^{-5}	1024

We then tested the performance of a python implementation of threshold Schnorr signatures in a simulated network environment on the same server. With parameters for 128-bit level security (chosen according to ECRYPT II recommendations [23]), the total runtime for calculating the signature shares, communicating them and combining them to form a signature is approximately 0.022 s, for 3-out-of-5 devices.

7   Related Work

Shamir [10] was the first to introduce the concept of secret sharing. Feldman [24] extended this concept by introducing verifiable secret sharing. Pedersen [25] then used this idea to construct the first Distributed Key Generation (DKG) protocol. To increase the resilience in threshold schemes, the number of devices included in the scheme should be maximized. Therefore, Simoens et al. [16] presented a new DKG protocol and demonstrated how this allows wearables not capable of securely storing secret shares to be incorporated. Peeters et al. [26] used this idea to propose a threshold distance bounding protocol. In this paper, we consider a threshold-based authentication protocol, where the secret key is shared among a set of user devices such as mobile phone and wearables.

Ever since the introduction of the general notion of threshold signatures by Desmedt [27], threshold signature schemes have been extensively studied in the literature. For example, Desmedt and Frankel [28] and Harn [29] respectively presented a non-robust and a robust threshold ElGamal signature scheme [30] based on secret sharing [10]. These schemes have small share size and require synchronized interaction among the players. Gennaro et al. [31] presented a robust threshold digital signature standard scheme. Shoup [20] showed how RSA signatures could be transformed into a robust and practical threshold-based variant.

On the collaborative continuous authentication front, there have been a recent surge in interest and the industry demand due to the significantly increased use of smartphones, tablets and wearables. Martinovic et al. [32] introduced a new biometric based on the human body's response to an electric square pulse signal, called pulse-response. It is proposed to enhance security in the context of two example applications: (1) an additional authentication mechanism in PIN entry systems, and (2) a means of continuous authentication on a secure terminal. As the authors show, the pulse-response biometric is effective because each human body exhibits a unique response to a signal pulse applied at the palm of one hand, and measured at the palm of the other. Patel et al. [33] gave a nice survey on continuous authentication on mobile devices, and also discussed challenges and research directions in this field. This survey along with the references therein provides sufficient information on the state-of-the-practice in this field of continuous authentication. Van hamme et al. [2] reviewed emerging trends and challenges with collaborative frictionless authentication systems and identified the enrollment of users, usability as well as security and privacy of such systems as key research challenges. Mustafa et al. [34] provided a comprehensive threat analysis of such a system and specified a list of security and privacy requirements. The authors also suggested three high-level solutions to address these requirements, however, without providing any specific design or implementation details.

8   Conclusions

In this paper, we proposed a collaborative authentication protocol based on the use of threshold signature schemes. In particular, the user devices store the shares of the signing key (i.e., the private key) of a threshold signature scheme, and the private key is never reconstructed to minimise the security threats. In case a share of the key is lost, the remaining shares can be used to (i) generate new shares of the key for each party or (ii) repair only the lost share without reconstructing the entire key. Furthermore, we showed how the shares of the key can also be generated using contextual and/or behavioral information using fuzzy extractors. Finally, our performance results demonstrate the practical feasibility of our collaborative authentication protocol.

Acknowledgments. We thank the anonymous reviewers for their valuable comment. This work was supported by imec through ICON DiskMan, the Security & Privacy Centre projects on Biometrics & Authentication and Secure Distance Bounding. It was also funded by the Flemish government through the FWO SBO project SPITE S002417N.

References

1. Sagiroglu, S., Sinanc, D.: Big data: a review. In: International Conference on Collaboration Technologies and Systems (CTS 2013), pp. 42–47 (2013)
2. Van hamme, T., Rimmer, V., Preuveneers, D., Joosen, W., Mustafa, M.A., Abidin, A., Argones Rúa, E.: Frictionless authentication systems: emerging trends, research challenges and opportunities. In: the 11th International Conference on Emerging Security Information, Systems and Technologies (SECURWARE 2017). IARIA (2017)
3. Bhargav-Spantzel, A., Squicciarini, A., Bertino, E.: Privacy preserving multi-factor authentication with biometrics. In: Proceedings of the Second ACM Workshop on Digital Identity Management (DIM 2006). ACM, New York (2006) 63–72
4. Bonneau, J., Herley, C., Oorschot, P.C.V., Stajano, F.: The quest to replace passwords: a framework for comparative evaluation of web authentication schemes. In: Proceedings of the 2012 IEEE Symposium on Security and Privacy (S&P 2012), pp. 553–567. IEEE Computer Society, Washington (2012)

5. Grosse, E., Upadhyay, M.: Authentication at scale. In: In: Proceedings of the 2013 IEEE Symposium on Security and Privacy (S&P 2013), vol. 11, no. 1, pp. 15–22 (2013)
6. Guidorizzi, R.P.: Security: active authentication. IT Prof. **15**(4), 4–7 (2013)
7. Preuveneers, D., Joosen, W.: SmartAuth: dynamic context fingerprinting for continuous user authentication. In: Proceedings of the 30th Annual ACM Symposium on Applied Computing (SAC 2015), pp. 2185–2191. ACM, New York (2015)
8. Abidin, A., Argones Rúa, E., Peeters, R.: Uncoupling biometrics from templates for secure and privacy-preserving authentication. In: Proceedings of the 22nd ACM on Symposium on Access Control Models and Technologies, pp. 21–29. ACM (2017)
9. Stinson, D.R., Wei, R.: Combinatorial repairability for threshold schemes. Des. Codes Crypt. **86**(1), 195–210 (2018)
10. Shamir, A.: How to share a secret. Commun. ACM **22**(11), 612–613 (1979)
11. Juels, A., Wattenberg, M.: A fuzzy commitment scheme. In: ACM Conference on Computer and Communications Security, pp. 28–36. ACM (1999)
12. Juels, A., Sudan, M.: A fuzzy vault scheme. IACR Cryptology ePrint Archive (2002)
13. Juels, A., Sudan, M.: A fuzzy vault scheme. Des. Codes Cryptogr. **38**(2), 237–257 (2006)
14. Dodis, Y., Reyzin, L., Smith, A.: Fuzzy extractors: how to generate strong keys from biometrics and other noisy data. In: Cachin, C., Camenisch, J.L. (eds.) EUROCRYPT 2004. LNCS, vol. 3027, pp. 523–540. Springer, Heidelberg (2004). https://doi.org/10.1007/978-3-540-24676-3_31
15. Dodis, Y., Ostrovsky, R., Reyzin, L., Smith, A.: Fuzzy extractors: how to generate strong keys from biometrics and other noisy data. SIAM J. Comput. **38**(1), 97–139 (2008)
16. Simoens, K., Peeters, R., Preneel, B.: Increased resilience in threshold cryptography: sharing a secret with devices that cannot store shares. In: Joye, M., Miyaji, A., Otsuka, A. (eds.) Pairing 2010. LNCS, vol. 6487, pp. 116–135. Springer, Heidelberg (2010). https://doi.org/10.1007/978-3-642-17455-1_8
17. Laing, T.M., Stinson, D.R.: A survey and refinement of repairable threshold schemes. eprint:2017/1155
18. Fiat, A., Shamir, A.: How to prove yourself: practical solutions to identification and signature problems. In: Odlyzko, A.M. (ed.) CRYPTO 1986. LNCS, vol. 263, pp. 186–194. Springer, Heidelberg (1987). https://doi.org/10.1007/3-540-47721-7_12
19. Schnorr, C.P.: Efficient identification and signatures for smart cards. In: Brassard, G. (ed.) CRYPTO 1989. LNCS, vol. 435, pp. 239–252. Springer, New York (1990). https://doi.org/10.1007/0-387-34805-0_22
20. Shoup, V.: Practical threshold signatures. In: Preneel, B. (ed.) EUROCRYPT 2000. LNCS, vol. 1807, pp. 207–220. Springer, Heidelberg (2000). https://doi.org/10.1007/3-540-45539-6_15
21. Aly, A.: Network flow problems with secure multiparty computation. Ph.D. thesis, Universté catholique de Louvain, IMMAQ (2015)
22. Shoup, V.: NTL: a library for doing number theory (2001)
23. ECRYPT II NoE: ECRYPT II yearly report on algorithms and key lengths (2011–2012) (2012). ECRYPT II deliverable D.SPA.20-1.0
24. Feldman., P.: A practical scheme for non-interactive verifiable secret sharing. In: FOCS 1987, pp. 427–437. IEEE Computer Society (1987)
25. Pedersen, T.P.: Non-interactive and information-theoretic secure verifiable secret sharing. In: Feigenbaum, J. (ed.) CRYPTO 1991. LNCS, vol. 576, pp. 129–140. Springer, Heidelberg (1992). https://doi.org/10.1007/3-540-46766-1_9

26. Peeters, R., Singelee, D., Preneel, B.: Toward more secure and reliable access control. IEEE Pervasive Comput. **11**(3), 76–83 (2012)
27. Desmedt, Y.: Society and group oriented cryptography: a new concept. In: Pomerance, C. (ed.) CRYPTO 1987. LNCS, vol. 293, pp. 120–127. Springer, Heidelberg (1988). https://doi.org/10.1007/3-540-48184-2_8
28. Desmedt, Y., Frankel, Y.: Threshold cryptosystems. In: Brassard, G. (ed.) CRYPTO 1989. LNCS, vol. 435, pp. 307–315. Springer, New York (1990). https://doi.org/10.1007/0-387-34805-0_28
29. Harn, L.: Group-oriented (t, n) threshold digital signature scheme and digital multisignature. IEE Proc.-Comput. Digit. Tech. **141**(5), 307–313 (1994)
30. ElGamal, T.: A public key cryptosystem and a signature scheme based on discrete logarithms. IEEE Trans. Inf. Theory **31**(4), 469–472 (1985)
31. Gennaro, R., Jarecki, S., Krawczyk, H., Rabin, T.: Robust threshold DSS signatures. Inf. Comput. **164**(1), 54–84 (2001)
32. Rasmussen, K.B., Roeschlin, M., Martinovic, I., Tsudik, G.: Authentication using pulse-response biometrics. In: NDSS (2014)
33. Patel, V.M., Chellappa, R., Chandra, D., Barbello, B.: Continuous user authentication on mobile devices: recent progress and remaining challenges. IEEE Signal Process. Mag. **33**(4), 49–61 (2016)
34. Mustafa, M.A., Abidin, A., Argones Rúa, E.: Frictionless authentication system: security & privacy analysis and potential solutions. In: The 11-th International Conference on Emerging Security Information, Systems and Technologies (SECURWARE 2017). IARIA (2017)

MuFASA: A Tool for High-level Specification and Analysis of Multi-factor Authentication Protocols

Federico Sinigaglia[1,2][✉], Roberto Carbone[2], Gabriele Costa[3],
and Silvio Ranise[2]

[1] DIBRIS, Università degli Studi di Genova, Genova, Italy
[2] Security & Trust Research Unit, Fondazione Bruno Kessler, Trento, Italy
`{sinigaglia,carbone,ranise}@fbk.eu`
[3] SysMA Unit, IMT School for Advanced Studies, Lucca, Italy
`gabriele.costa@imtlucca.it`

Abstract. In recent years, the usage of online services (e.g., banking) has considerably increased. To protect the sensitive resources managed by these services against attackers, Multi-Factor Authentication (MFA) has been widely adopted. To date, a variety of MFA protocols have been implemented, leveraging different designs and features and providing a non-homogeneous level of security and user experience. Public and private authorities have defined laws and guidelines to guide the design of more secure and usable MFA protocols, but their influence on existing MFA implementations remains unclear.

We present MuFASA, a tool for high-level specification and analysis of MFA protocols, which aims at supporting normal users and security experts (in the design phase of an MFA protocol), providing a high level report regarding possible risks associated to the specified MFA protocol, its resistance to a set of attacker models (defined by NIST), its ease-of-use and its compliance with a set of security requirements derived from European laws.

Keywords: Multi-Factor Authentication · Security protocols · Legal compliance · Threat models

1 Introduction

Nowadays an enormous amount of our sensitive data is managed by various service providers. To properly protect them, new mechanisms have been introduced. Among these mechanisms, Multi-Factor Authentication (MFA) has been increasingly adopted. MFA is based on security protocols that are specifically

This work has been partially supported by the EU Horizon 2020 projects FINSEC (grant agreement No 786727) and SPARTA (grant agreement No 830892), by the IMT PAI (Programma di Attività Integrata) project VeriOSS, and by the activity 19183 Teîchos of the action line *Digital Finance* of the AT Digital.

© Springer Nature Switzerland AG 2020
A. Saracino and P. Mori (Eds.): ETAA 2019, LNCS 11967, pp. 138–155, 2020.
https://doi.org/10.1007/978-3-030-39749-4_9

designed for providing a higher level of security that traditional protocols cannot reach. In particular, they leverage multiple identity proofs for authenticating the user.

However, poor design choices (and consequent implementations) can potentially nullify the theoretical strength of these protocols. Therefore, assessing the security of MFA protocols becomes of paramount importance. To this aim, formal analysis represents the highest guarantee of correctness, since it relies on rigorous, mathematical properties. Unfortunately, in the case of MFA protocols, modeling an MFA protocol is a very challenging task due its complexity.

Public and private authorities have defined laws and guidelines to drive the design of more secure and usable MFA solutions. Nevertheless, their influence on existing MFA implementations remains unclear. Among these standardization initiatives, one of the most relevant is the Special Publication on Digital Authentication, published by the NIST [12]. There, the NIST identifies the so-called *authenticators*, i.e., the objects providing the identity proofs, as fundamental parts of an MFA and specifies their main features. Understanding whether a real MFA protocol complies with the existing specifications is an open challenge.

In this paper we propose a methodology—and its implementation in the MuFASA (**Mu**lti-**F**actor **A**uthentication **S**pecification and **A**nalysis) tool—to generate and analyze a high-level specification of an MFA protocol. Our specification language abstracts from many internal details of the protocol and focuses on the user experience. In this way, even non-experts can define the behavior of an MFA protocol. Yet, the specification language is expressive enough to allow the automatic comparison of the protocol against a set of rules, including the NIST directives. The final report generated by our tool provides several information about the protocol features and, in particular, on the most relevant attacker models.

More in detail, MuFASA automatically checks the following aspects of an MFA protocol.

- Its exposure w.r.t. (most of) the attacker models defined in [12].
- Its compliance w.r.t. a set of guidelines and best practices defined by the European Central Bank (EBA).
- Its complexity in terms of basic user actions.

Moreover, to assess our tool we applied it to a set of real-world MFA protocols employed by 30 major international banks.

2   Background on MFA

Our first step is to revise the existing definitions and specifications of the building blocks of MFA. Unfortunately, the literature on MFA shows a general lack of standard definitions and terminology (e.g., see [1,3,8–10,13]). In our work we align with the definitions given by the *National Institute of Standards and Technology* (NIST) in [12].

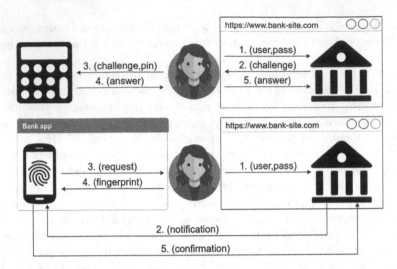

Fig. 1. Two alternative MFA protocols adopted by Nordea

Authentication Factors and Protocols. An *authentication protocol* is a sequence of actions that allows the *digital authentication* of a user. The authentication occurs by verifying that the user can exhibit her *authentication factors* (AF). An AF can be of three different types, i.e., (*i*) *knowledge* (something the user knows), (*ii*) *ownership* (something the user possesses) and (*iii*) *inherence* (something the user is).

An MFA protocol is an authentication protocol that leverages more than one AF. The user starts the MFA protocol from her *endpoint*, e.g., a web browser or a mobile phone, and she must provide the necessary AFs to correctly execute the protocol and be authenticated.

Authenticators. The authenticators are specific objects that allow for attesting the possession and control of authentication factors.

There exists a wide range of authenticators whose features may vary significantly. Common examples include OTP generators, smart card readers and even passwords. The output of the authenticator is an *evidence* for the authentication service that the user controls the AF.

When an authenticator generates an evidence from more than one AF (as a piece of hardware generating an OTP after being unlocked by a code), we call it a *multi-factor authenticator*.

3   Motivations and Overview of the Approach

In this section we discuss the motivations behind our proposal. Moreover, we provide an overview of the main workflow of MuFASA. We start by presenting a motivating example.

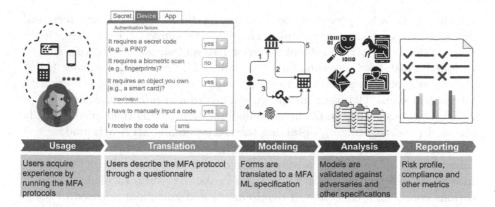

Fig. 2. Flow of the proposed approach.

Motivating Example. Let us consider a real-world example. Nordea[1] is a major, international bank based in Sweden. Its customers can opt, among others, for two MFA protocols for authenticating, leveraging a physical device[2] and a mobile application[3]. We schematically depict them in Fig. 1.

In the first MFA protocol the user is in possession of a device to authenticate. Initially, she connects to the website of the bank and she logs in with her credentials (1). Then (2) she is prompted with a challenge, i.e., a code that only the device can process, and (3) she submits the challenge to the device (together with the card and the pin code that unlocks it). Finally, the device returns an answer code (4) that the user copies in her browser (5).

The second protocol is slightly different. Again, the process starts with the user authenticating to the website (1). However, in this case the remote service sends a notification (2) to a mobile application running on the user's smartphone. The application displays the authentication request (3) to the user that, to confirm, touches the fingerprint reader of the phone (4). The protocol terminates (5) with the mobile app sending a confirmation code to the bank server.

Few questions arise when considering these two MFA protocols.

(A) Can the user, according to her personal experience, be aware of the specific risks of each protocol? **(B)** Do the protocols differ in terms of the provided level of security? **(C)** Is it possible to easily assess the compliance of the protocols with common criteria (e.g., requirements or guidelines)? **(D)** What is their complexity in terms of user effort?

Overview of our Approach. Our proposal is based on the modeling and analysis process schematically depicted in Fig. 2. Our working assumption is to obtain a description of the MFA protocol from the experience of common users, acquired

---

[1] https://www.nordea.se/.

[2] https://www.nordea.se/Images/154-21252/quickguide-cardreader.PDF.

[3] https://www.nordea.se/Images/154-300029/Broschyr_skaffa_Mobilt_BankID.
pdf.

by running the MFA protocol (*usage* phase), without requiring any technical
skills (e.g., the customers of a bank). Therefore, we convert the user knowledge
into a model of the MFA protocol behavior (*translation* phase). To this aim we
developed a high-level modeling language, called *MFA modeling language* (MFA
ML). We rely on a questionnaire to support the modeling process for users with
no technical skills. The users fill the questionnaire and provide a description of
the MFA protocols they use. The compiled questionnaire is then automatically
processed (*modeling* phase), obtaining the corresponding MFA ML model.

The model then passes through an *analysis* phase, in which it is validated
against both a set of built-in adversaries and a list of specifications. The adversaries model a set of capabilities identified in the literature. Instead, the specifications consist of a collection of requirements and guidelines released by some
authorities. At present, our implementation supports a list of adversaries inspired
to those described in [12] and specifications from [12], [6] and [7].

The final result of the process is a report, i.e., the output of the *reporting*
phase. The report contains the results of the security analysis as well as other
metrics of interest. In particular, we provide (*i*) a risk profile (in terms of the
adversaries that might compromise the protocol), (*ii*) a compliance checklist
(i.e., what are the requirements and guidelines that the protocol meets) and
(*iii*) a complexity score (i.e., how many operations must be correctly executed
by the user to authenticate).

All in all, MuFASA answers the four questions given above by (**A**) supporting
unskilled users to define the protocols they use in order to automatically evaluate
them (**B**) against the relevant attacker models, in terms of (**C**) compliance with
the relevant security criteria and (**D**) complexity of use.

In the following sections, we detail the peculiarities of the *modeling* and the
analysis phases. The description of a real implementation of the whole workflow
presented in Fig. 2 is then presented in Sect. 6.

4   Modeling an MFA Protocol

In this section we present our specification language for MFA protocols. Our
goal is to model each MFA protocol in terms of the authenticators it involves.
Moreover, below we discuss the expressiveness of our language and we show that
it captures the definitions given in [12].

4.1   MFA Modeling Language

We specify an MFA protocol as a finite sequence of authenticators.[4] In our
framework, an authenticator is uniquely characterized by three main features,
i.e., its (*i*) type, (*ii*) I/O channels, (*iii*) data. The general definitions of an
authenticator is

$$\delta \gg_\gamma \tau[\bar{a}] \gg_{\gamma'} \delta' \tag{1}$$

---

[4] We use ";" to separate the elements of the sequence.

where δ, δ' are data items, γ, γ' are channels and τ is an authenticator type. Below we detail our specification language and we explain how it models these three aspects. In addition, an authenticator type may be optionally labeled with **?** to indicate that, for each operation, it requires the review and confirmation of the users (see below).

Authenticator Types. The type of an authenticator is defined by its physical and behavioral features. We distinguish among three categories of authenticators, i.e., *secrets*, *hardware* and *software*. Below we describe them in details.

Secrets. A secret is the simplest form of authenticator. Basically, it consists of some information, e.g., a secret number, that the user exhibits at a certain point of the protocol. We distinguish between *memorized secrets* (🔑) and *look-up secrets* (⊞). The main difference between these two types is that a memorized secret represents a pure knowledge factor, e.g., a secret pin number, while a look-up secret is stored on some physical support such as a device or a piece of paper. For instance, look-up secrets include matrices where each cell contains an access code.

Hardware. Hardware authenticators (▦) are devices that carry out some computation, e.g., cryptographic operations. Hardware authenticators can either work in isolation (i.e., only interacting with the user) or connect to some other device (e.g., through a USB cable). Nevertheless, they consist of dedicated hardware and they cannot carry out any task other than that specified by their embedded program.

The AFs of a hardware authenticator can vary significantly. For instance, a card reader may also require a secret pin, i.e., it attests both an ownership (the smart card) and a knowledge (the pin) factor. Notice that the pin of the card reader is not considered a memorized secret (see above) if it cannot be used as a stand-alone authenticator, e.g., when its purpose is only to protect the hardware from unauthorized users. We denote with ▦ $[\bar{a}]$ a hardware authenticator that attests the AFs $\bar{a} \subseteq \{O, K, I\}$. For instance, (the type of) the card reader mentioned above is ▦ [O,K].

Software. Software authenticators (🔓) are the counterpart of hardware authenticators. Their distinguishing feature is that they consist of programs that run on some general-purpose computing platform, e.g., a tablet or a smartphone. As for the hardware authenticators, also software authenticators can attest different AFs. Hence, we apply the same notation introduced above. For instance, 🔓 [O] stands for (the type of) a software authenticator that attests an ownership factor.

Example 1. Both the MFA protocols of Fig. 1 start with the user entering her credentials. This corresponds to a memorized secret 🔑. Instead, the two protocols differ on the second authenticator. In the first case, there is a hardware authenticator that is *owned* by the user and is activated by a pin that she only *knows*. In our language this corresponds to ▦ [O,K]. In the second protocol, the second authenticator is a software running on the smartphone of the user that the user activates through her fingerprint. In symbols this amounts to ⊛ [O,I].

Data Channels. MFA protocols often rely on more than one communication channel. There are several types of channels that are commonly adopted and we list them below.

h *Human beings* are part of the MFA protocols. Their role is often to provide the authenticators with the proper input and collect their output. For this reason we model them as communication channels.

o Sometimes an authenticator acquires its input through some *optical* scan interface, e.g., a bar code or QR code reader.

n The *network* is the primary communication channel for most internet protocols. The network channel includes all IP-based communications independently from the link medium (e.g, WiFi or 4G).

i Sometimes two processes directly communicate through some *inter-process* channel. For instance, this is very common on the modern smartphones where two apps can directly share a piece of data.

m The *mobile telephony network* is also commonly adopted to send authentication codes through an SMS of a phone call.

Example 2. Let us consider again the two MFA protocols presented in Sect. 3. In the first protocol every piece of information is transmitted by the user, i.e., user, password, challenge, pin and answer. Thus, all these operations occur on the h channel. In the second protocol, the user only inserts her credentials. All the other communications pass through the network (n channel).

Data Items. Data items represent the information that an authenticator receives and generates. Although the internal structure of the communications may be obscure, e.g., because messages are encrypted, the content of a data item is commonly well-understood. For instance, a hardware authenticator may return a number to be submitted on a website in order to authorize an operation. Such a number can be generated through various algorithms (e.g., via RNG or hashing). From our perspective, all these numbers have the same features, i.e., they are unforgeable, unrepeatable evidences that only the authenticator can generate. As a matter of fact, a user cannot perceive any observable difference between them. Therefore, we distinguish between data items only depending on their role in the protocol. In particular, here we consider three possible data items that one can infer from the behavior of the authenticator.

ε We use ε to denote that the authenticator receives/sends no data or when the transmitted data play no role in the authentication protocol.

opid An *operation identifier* is a piece of information that univocally defines the ongoing operation.

otp A *one time password* is a code generated with some (assumed cryptographically perfect) algorithm that only the authorized parties can compute and verify.

Example 3. Both the protocols of Fig. 1 terminate with the bank server receiving a response code. In the first case it amounts to the challenge answer. In the second case it is the confirmation code generated after the notification. In both cases we assume that the authenticators receive an identification code, i.e., opid, and return an encrypted confirmation code, i.e., otp.

Further Notation and Restrictions. The specification given in (1) provides a general definition of an authenticator. Nevertheless, we apply few restrictions to the structure of *well-formed* authenticators.

We already mentioned that a distinguishing feature of (software and hardware) authenticators is whether they inform the user about the ongoing operation. In general, these authenticators prompt the user with a message with the operation to be authorized, e.g., "transfer 100\$ to account 1234". Then the user has to confirm the operation. This fact denotes the generation of an output (an otp in our setting) that is uniquely associated to a specific operation. Such an association is also called *dynamic linking* [6,7]. The definition of dynamic linking given there also states that the user must be aware of the ongoing operation and she has to explicitly agree on it. We use the label **?** to denote an authenticator type that informs the user and asks for her authorization as discussed above, e.g., $\boxplus$**?** [O]. Reasonably, in order to display the operation details, the authenticator must receive an input, i.e., $\gamma \neq \varepsilon$. Well-formed authenticators must respect this requirement.

The Secret authenticator type consists of pure data objects, e.g., passwords or other information that can be stored on some support. As such, they do not have a proper input/output interaction (we assume that the user copies the information on some endpoint such as a web browser). For this reason $\mathbf{Q}$ and $\boxplus$ are not annotated with channels and data items.

Finally, we introduce two abbreviations that will simplify the discussion about the out-of-band authenticators (see Sect. 4.2 below). In particular we define $\blacksquare \triangleq \boxplus[O]$ and $\blacksquare \triangleq \otimes[O]$. Moreover, to apply these abbreviations two conditions must be satisfied:

- $\blacksquare$ $\gamma = m \lor \gamma' = m$; i.e., input or output are transmitted through mobile channels and,
- $\blacksquare$ $\gamma = n \lor \gamma' = n$, i.e., input or output are transmitted through network channels.

Example 4. We combine the observations of Examples 1, 2 and 3 to provide the specification for the two protocols of our working example. The first protocol corresponds to the following specification.

$$\mathbf{Q}; \text{opid} \gg_h \boxplus[\text{O,K}] \gg_h \text{otp} \tag{2}$$

For the second protocol, we replace $\otimes[\text{O,I}]$ with the abbreviation introduced above, i.e., $\blacksquare[\text{I}]$. Moreover, we notice that the authenticator informs the user about the ongoing operation (**?**). Thus, the resulsng specification for the second protocol is as follows.

$$\text{⚷}; \text{opid}»_n \; \square^? [I] »_n \text{otp} \tag{3}$$

4.2 Compliance w.r.t. the NIST Classification

In [12] a classification of the authenticators is provided. Such a classification is highly influential and most manufacturers and service providers comply with it. In this section we show that our modeling language is expressive enough to include the definitions given there. Each definition amounts to a constraint over the structure of a generic authenticator as defined in (1). The mapping between the definitions and our modeling language is presented in Table 1. Below we discuss our encoding (with the exception of ⚷ and ⊞ which are straightforward).

Out-of-Band Devices. According to [12, §5.1.3] out-of-band authenticators are physical devices that are uniquely addressable and communicate over a distinct, namely *secondary*, channel (w.r.t. the *primary* channel used by the endpoint). Out-of-band devices include both dedicated and general purpose hardware as far as they satisfy one of the following conditions.

1. The secondary channel is used to receive a data item for the user.
2. The secondary channel is used to transmit a data item from the user.
3. The secondary channel is used to send and receive a data item on which the user must agree.

For instance, a common practice is to receive an SMS containing an `otp`. This case complies with the first condition, i.e., it relies on the mobile telephony network as a secondary channel. Similarly, some MFA protocols require the user to call a secure number from their mobile. This behavior matches the second condition. Finally, the second protocol presented in Sect. 3 is an instance of the third case. As a matter of fact, the user receives a notification on her smartphone. The smartphone connection is a secondary channel w.r.t. the browser connection.

Single and Multi-Factor OTP Device. In [12, §5.1.4 and §5.1.5] these authenticators are defined as devices embedding some seed number used for the generation of OTPs. This category includes both hardware devices and software-based OTP generators installed on devices such as mobile phones. They are distinguished from the out-of-band authenticators as they do not rely on a secondary channel. Moreover, their output can either directly go to the endpoint through an inter-process connection (i) or be copied by the user (h).

Single and Multi-Factor Cryptographic Device. A single or Multi-factor cryptographic device [12, §5.1.7 and §5.1.9] is a hardware device that performs some cryptographic operation (e.g., digital signature) on the operation identifier and directly interacts (I/O) with the user endpoint.

Single and Multi-Factor Cryptographic Software. Basically, these authenticators [12, §5.1.6 and §5.1.8] are the software counterparts of the previous category.

Table 1. Mapping NIST definitions to patterns

Name	Constraints	Example
Memorized Secret	🔑	🔑
Look-up Secret	▦	▦
Out-of-Band Device	$\vee \begin{cases} \tau \in \{ ▣, ▣^?, ▢, ▢^? \} \wedge \delta \neq \varepsilon \wedge \gamma' = h \\ \tau \in \{ ▣, ▣^?, ▢, ▢^? \} \wedge \delta \neq \varepsilon \wedge \gamma \in \{h, o\} \\ \tau \in \{ ▣, ▣^?, ▢, ▢^? \} \wedge \delta \neq \varepsilon \wedge \gamma, \gamma' \in \{n, m\} \end{cases}$	otp $\gg_m$ ▣$^?$ $\gg_h$ otp
Single-Factor OTP Device	$\tau \in \{ ▦, ▦^?, 🎛, 🎛^? \} \wedge \bar{a} = \{O\} \wedge \gamma \notin \{n, m\} \wedge \gamma' \in \{h, i\}$	opid $\gg_o$ ▦$^?$[O] $\gg_h$ otp
Multi-Factor OTP Device	$\tau \in \{ ▦, ▦^?, 🎛, 🎛^? \} \wedge (O \in \bar{a} \wedge |\bar{a}| > 1) \wedge \gamma \notin \{n, m\} \wedge \gamma' \in \{h, i\}$	$\varepsilon \gg_h$ 🔒[O,I] $\gg_h$ otp
Single-Factor Cryptographic Device	$\tau \in \{ ▦, ▦^? \} \wedge \bar{a} = \{O\} \wedge \gamma = i \wedge \delta = \text{opid} \wedge \gamma' = i$	opid $\gg_i$ ▦$^?$[O] $\gg_i$ otp
Multi-Factor Cryptographic Device	$\tau \in \{ ▦, ▦^? \} \wedge (O \in \bar{a} \wedge |\bar{a}| > 1) \wedge \gamma = i \wedge \delta = \text{opid} \wedge \gamma' = i$	opid $\gg_i$ ▦[O,K] $\gg_i$ otp
Single-Factor Cryptographic Software	$\tau \in \{ 🔒, 🔒^? \} \wedge \bar{a} = \{O\} \wedge \gamma = i \wedge \delta = \text{opid} \wedge \gamma' = i$	opid $\gg_i$ 🔒$^?$[O] $\gg_i$ otp
Multi-Factor Cryptographic Software	$\tau \in \{ 🔒, 🔒^? \} \wedge (O \in \bar{a} \wedge |\bar{a}| > 1) \wedge \gamma = i \wedge \delta = \text{opid} \wedge \gamma' = i$	opid $\gg_i$ 🔒$^?$[O,I] $\gg_i$ otp

Observations. It is worth noticing that our definitions admit intersections between the authenticators. For instance, according to Table 1, opid $\gg_i$ ▦[O] $\gg_i$ otp is both an OTP and a cryptographic device. This is not actually allowed by the classification of [12]. The reason is that the distinction between these two authenticators is based on an internal feature, i.e., whether they use cryptography or not, that the user cannot observe. As a consequence, our language does not perfectly comply with the categories of [12]. This is expected as, under our working assumptions, we are only interested in classifying authenticators that the user can recognize.

5   Protocol Analysis

In this section we present our approach for the analysis of MFA protocols specified using MFA ML. In particular, we compare each protocol against a set of attackers and a list of common security criteria. In addition, we evaluate the complexity of the MFA protocol.

5.1   Attacker Models and Applicability

In our analysis, we evaluate the risk profile of an MFA protocol by comparing it against a set of attackers. An attacker operates by targeting the authenticators

Table 2. Excerpt of two attackers of MuFASA.

Device thief (expt.)		Shoulder surfer (expt.)	
Authenticator	Effect	Authenticator	Effect
$\delta \gg_\gamma \boxplus[O,\ldots] \gg_{\gamma'} \delta'$	$\cancel{\varnothing}$	⚷	☠
		$\delta \gg_\gamma \boxplus[K,\ldots] \gg_{\gamma'} \delta'$	$\cancel{K}$

Table 3. Attacker models defined by NIST covered by our tool

Assertion Manufacture or Modification	Theft	Duplication	Eaves-dropping	Offline Cracking	Side Channel Attack	Phishing or Pharming	Social Engineering	Online Guessing	Endpoint Compromise	Unauthorized Binding
✘	✔	✔	✔	✘	✘	✔	✔	✘	✔	✘

of the MFA protocol execution. In particular, an attacker can *compromise* an authenticator either entirely or partially.

An attacker partially compromises an authenticator when she can attest the control over a subset of the authenticator's AFs. Said differently, the presence of the compromised AFs is immaterial from the point of view of the attacker. In general, we denote with $\cancel{a}$ when the AF a is compromised, e.g., $\cancel{\varnothing}$. We say that an authenticator is entirely compromised, denoted by ☠, all of its AFs are so.

MuFASA includes a number of attackers. Each of them is modeled as a function that removes the compromised AFs and authenticators from a protocol specification. Attacker collusion is modeled as function composition. A set of attackers win against a protocol if, by applying their functions, the protocol specification is reduced to nil.

To clarify our approach, we propose the following example and we present an excerpt of two attackers supported by MuFASA.

Example 5. Consider again the MFA protocols specified in (2) and (3). We discuss the application of two attackers supported by MuFASA, i.e., the *device thief* and the *shoulder surfer*.

A device thief can steal something. For instance, she can take an authenticator away from the user. In our settings, this corresponds to compromise the ownership factor of an authenticator. Instead, a shoulder surfer can leak data from the user when she run the protocol. For instance, a pin or a password can be eavesdropped. Notice that this does not apply to the OTP, since - in this case - it is generated from the opid, hence associated to a specific operation. In our model, a shoulder surfer entirely compromises secrets and partially compromises authenticators relying on a knowledge factor. The rules described above are schematically reported in Table 2.

By applying the two attackers to the protocol specifications (2) and (3) we obtain the following effects.

Target	Attacker	Result
$\mathbf{Q}$; opid$\gg_h$ ▦[O,K] $\gg_h$ otp	Device thief	$\mathbf{Q}$; opid$\gg_h$ ▦[K] $\gg_h$ otp
$\mathbf{Q}$; opid$\gg_h$ ▦[O,K] $\gg_h$ otp	Shoulder surfer	☠;opid$\gg_h$ ▦[O] $\gg_h$ otp
$\mathbf{Q}$; opid$\gg_n$ ▯?[I] $\gg_n$ otp	Device thief	$\mathbf{Q}$; opid$\gg_n$ ☻?[I] $\gg_n$ otp
$\mathbf{Q}$; opid$\gg_n$ ▯?[I] $\gg_n$ otp	Shoulder surfer	☠;opid$\gg_n$ ▯?[I] $\gg_n$ otp

Since no ☠;☠ appears on the right column, neither the device thief nor the shoulder surfer can entirely compromise the protocol. However, the first protocol can be entirely compromised by a colluded attack, i.e., the composition of the two attackers. As a matter of fact, the application of the device thief (first row) results in a single-factor protocol (only relying on knowledge). Such a protocol can be entirely compromised by the shoulder surfer.

Compliance w.r.t. NIST Attacker Models. In [12] a list of attacker models is provided. Here we put their attackers in correspondence with the attacker models included in MuFASA. Table 3 reports the list of the attackers of [12]. We denote by ✔ those that are currently supported by MuFASA.

Five attackers are not supported (✖). This is due to our working assumptions. In particular, our approach is designed to only rely on the user experience. Thus, the expected input only includes details about the MFA protocol that a (non expert) user can observe. This entails, for instance, that we cannot model the internal structure of an authenticator device or software.

The assertion manufacture and modification attack applies to the service infrastructure that handles the authentication process. Such infrastructure is usually totally transparent to the user. Also, attackers such as offline cracking, side channel and online guessing exploit flaws in the implementation of the authenticators. Under our assumptions, the user is not aware of these internal and remote implementation details. Finally, the unauthorized binding attack applies to the delivery and activation of a new authenticator. This phase takes place before any execution of the MFA protocol. Hence, it is out of scope for the present work.

5.2 Security Criteria and Complexity

Due to their general interest for the modern society, the security of MFA protocols have been considered by several authorities. These authorities released criteria, e.g., guidelines and requirements, to drive the security assessment. By relying on our modeling language, some of these criteria can be encoded through a pattern matching procedure. Below, we discuss some of the criteria that are currently supported by our implementation.

In the last years, the European Central Bank (EBA) published several directives [4–7] about the correct implementation of MFA protocols. These directives are mainly oriented to the e-banking and e-payment services, but most of them apply to the MFA protocols in general. Among the supported criteria we have the following two.

- MFA protocols should use at least two types of AFs [4, §1 - Guiding Principles].
- MFA protocol must keep the user aware of the operation she is authorizing, hence employing dynamic linking [7, Article 5, paragraph 2, letter a].

Example 6. Consider the two requirements given above. The first one amounts to requiring that the model of an MFA protocol includes some authenticators using at least two different AFs. This is obviously true for both the protocols (2) and (3). Instead, the second requirement states that ? must appear in the protocol, which is not true for (2).

Another key aspect of MFA protocols is their usability. As several studies [2, 11, 14] point out, the users may tend to misuse an MFA protocol if it is too difficult. In our analysis we consider the *complexity*. Our notion of complexity is based on three scores, i.e., *memory*, *operations* and *devices*. The memory score measures what the user has to memorize, the operations score measures how many steps she has to do and the devices score measures how many objects she has to carry. More in detail, the memory score counts the number of knowledge factors used in an MFA protocol (i.e., $\mathbf{Q}$ and [K]). The operations score counts the manual input/output operations ($\gg_h$) that the user has to perform. Finally, the devices score corresponds to the number of physical devices (i.e., ▦ and ▦) that the user has to carry to execute the MFA protocol. The complexity score is the sum of these three scores.

Example 7. Let us consider again protocol (2). It requires the user to memorize (and employ during the protocol execution) her credentials and the pin for unlocking the second authenticator (i.e., the OTP generator - ▦). Therefore, the score related to the *memory* effort is 2. Moreover, the user has to *(a)* manually transfer the code displayed on her browser to the OTP generator and *(b)* to copy the obtained OTP back on the browser: the value for the *operations* score is 2. Finally, for executing the protocol, the user is required to carry a specific hardware device (i.e., the OTP generator): the value of the *devices* score is 1. Hence, the overall complexity score for protocol (2) amounts at 5. On the contrary, protocol (3) only requires the user to memorize her credentials, check the correctness of the data sent to her smartphone (after tapping the push notification) and use her fingerprint to confirm. In this case, the complexity cost is only given by memory efforts, since no manual operations and specific hardware devices are present. Therefore, the overall complexity score for protocol (3) amounts at 1.

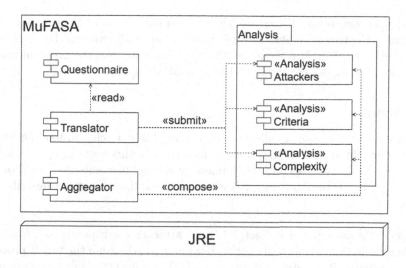

Fig. 3. Architecture of MuFASA

6   Implementation

In this section we describe the implementation of MuFASA. Figure 3 depicts its abstract architecture. MuFASA is a Java application consisting of four main modules. Below we discuss them in detail.

6.1   Questionnaire

This module implements the user interface of MuFASA. The user is prompted with high-level questions about her experience with the MFA protocol she wants to model. Each round of questions aims at precisely identify an authenticator. The rounds are iterated until the user describes all the authenticators in the protocol.

The actual questions presented at each round are determined by the previous answers. For instance, the first question is

"What is your nth operation?" (where n is the round counter)

The user can pick one of four answers, i.e., "I insert some secret credentials", "I use a device", "I use a software" and "I send/receive something on my mobile phone (e.g., an SMS)". Some questions can be also accompanied by some pictures. The pictures show several elements and the user has to select the one that more resembles her experience. An example questionnaire is reported in Appendix A.

6.2   Translator

The Translator module reads the answers to the questionnaire and converts them to a model of the MFA protocol. The module follows an interpretation tree that exhaustively represents all the possible answers to a round of the questionnaire. Each leaf of the tree is labeled with the model of an authenticator. By combining all the authenticators in a sequence, the Translator obtains the protocol model. Eventually, the model is submitted to the analysis module.

6.3   Analysis

This module consists of a collection of sub-modules. Each sub-module implements a common interface: the *Analysis* interface. In this way, the set of analysis carried out by MuFASA can be extended by adding new sub-modules. For the time being, the three built-in analyses implement the operations described in Sect. 5.

Attackers. As anticipated in Sect. 5.1, each attacker corresponds to a function. Attackers' functions remove the authenticators and AFs from the target protocol until, eventually, it is entirely compromised. When an attacker cannot compromise a protocol, its function behaves as the identity. Moreover, applying the same attacker, i.e., the same function, twice on the same protocol has no effect. Thus, the module iterates until a fixed point is reached, i.e., the protocol is entirely compromised or all the attacks reduce to the identity. Eventually, the list of the attacks is returned. The list contains all the groups of attackers together with their effect on the protocol.

Criteria. The security criteria evaluation amounts to a pattern matching between the protocol and the rules encoding each criterion. Each comparison results in a boolean value indicating whether the protocol matches the rule. The final result is a list of the criteria that the protocol matches.

Complexity. This module evaluates the complexity score of the specified MFA protocol. The complexity score is computed as the sum of three scores, i.e., memory, operations and devices (see Sect. 5.2).

6.4   Aggregator

The Aggregator module retrieves the output of each analysis module and combines them into a unified report. The report is then returned to the user in the form of a PDF document.

7   Discussion and Future Directions

We assessed MuFASA by applying it to real-world e-banking MFA protocols. In particular, we used MuFASA to analyze 61 MFA protocols adopted by 30 international banks. More information is available online at https://sites.google. com/fbk.eu/mufasa. The reports generated by MuFASA show that the landscape is very heterogeneous. As a matter of fact, most of the considered MFA protocols significantly differ in terms of the compatible attackers and compliance with the security criteria.

Future developments include the adoption of automated reasoning techniques for verification and refinement. Such techniques are commonly based on formal specification languages. Hence we are interested in defining a formal semantics for our language. In particular, we plan to map our specification language into the formal language of an existing verification framework for the analysis of security protocols.

Moreover, although we focused on the user experience so far, it is reasonable to expect that further information exist about the protocol. For instance, official documentation or usage examples and tutorials are often available. These sources might expose internal details about the protocol that we cannot model with the current version of our modeling language. Also, these details might support a more precise security analysis.

Another interesting direction is to extend our experiments. In particular, we plan to assess the usability of MuFASA by publicly releasing it as a web application. Moreover, we are interested in comparing the actual attacks to MFA protocols against the results of our analysis process. The goal is to check whether our attacker models comply with the real-world attacks.

8   Conclusion

We proposed MuFASA, a tool for the security assessment of MFA protocols. We showed that MuFASA can effectively model actual MFA protocols and evaluate them against several attacker models of interest. Moreover, MuFASA supports the user to evaluate an MFA protocol in terms of compliance with a set of relevant security criteria and complexity of use. The primary goal of our tool is to raise the awareness of users having no technical skills. For instance, the customers of a bank can analyze the MFA protocol they use daily. As a result, they gain a better understanding of the kind of attackers they are most exposed to. Furthermore, we advocate that MuFASA can be also useful for the security experts. As a matter of fact, MFA protocol developers can use it to make a preliminary evaluation, at design-time.

A   Example Input

Here we provide an example of how the user fills the questionnaire to obtain protocol (2). Notice that the sequence of the reported questions only represent a specific path in the interpretation tree.

1. What is your 1st operation?
   - ⊘ I insert some secret credentials (e.g., a password on a website)
   - ○ I use a device (e.g., a card reader)
   - ○ I use a software (e.g., an app on my smartphone)
   - ○ I send/receive something on my mobile phone (e.g., an SMS)

◯ None, I am authenticated
(a) Where are the secret credentials stored?
    ◯ On a physical support (e.g., a piece of paper)
    ⊘ Nowhere, I remember them
2. What is your 2nd operation?
    ◯ I insert some secret credentials (e.g., a password on a website)
    ⊘ I use a device (e.g., a card reader)
    ◯ I use a software (e.g., an app on my smartphone)
    ◯ I send/receive something on my mobile phone (e.g., an SMS)
    ◯ None, I am authenticated
(a) Is the device personal? Can you use others' devices?
    ⊘ Yes, it is personal
    ◯ No, they are all exchangeable
(b) Among the followings, what do you need to use the device?
    ⊘ I must insert a secret code/pin
    ◯ I must scan a part of my body (e.g., my fingerprint)
    ◯ Nothing
(c) Is your device connected to something?
    ◯ Yes, to my PC (e.g., through a USB cable)
    ◯ Yes, to the internet (e.g., through the WiFi)
    ⊘ No, it is isolated
(d) Does it read some sort of input code?
    ◯ Yes, it scans an optic code (e.g., barcode or QR code)
    ⊘ Yes, I personally digit it (e.g., a code displayed on a website)
    ◯ No
(e) Does it recap the ongoing operation and ask for your confirmation?
    ◯ Yes (e.g., "Your are paying x\$ to y. Confirm?")
    ⊘ No
(f) Does it return some code that you have to copy somewhere?
    ⊘ Yes
    ◯ No
3. What is your 3rd operation?
    ◯ I insert some secret credentials (e.g., a password on a website)
    ◯ I use a device (e.g., a card reader)
    ◯ I use a software (e.g., an app on my smartphone)
    ◯ I send/receive something on my mobile phone (e.g., an SMS)
    ⊘ None, I am authenticated.

References

1. Armando, A., Carbone, R., Zanetti, L.: Formal modeling and automatic security analysis of two-factor and two-channel authentication protocols. In: Lopez, J., Huang, X., Sandhu, R. (eds.) NSS 2013. LNCS, vol. 7873, pp. 728–734. Springer, Heidelberg (2013). https://doi.org/10.1007/978-3-642-38631-2_63
2. Cristofaro, E.D., Du, H., Freudiger, J., Norcie, G.: Two-Factor or not Two-Factor? A Comparative Usability Study of Two-Factor Authentication. CoRR abs/1309.5344. University College London (2013)

3. DeFigueiredo, D.: The case for mobile two-factor authentication. IEEE Secur. Priv. **9**, 81–85 (2011)
4. European Banking Authority: Recommendations for the Security of Internet Payments (2013). https://www.ecb.europa.eu/pub/pdf/other/recommendationssecuri tyinternetpaymentsoutcomeofpcfinalversionafterpc201301en.pdf
5. European Banking Authority: Recommendations for the Security of Mobile Payments - DRAFT (2013). https://www.ecb.europa.eu/paym/cons/pdf/131120/reco mmendationsforthesecurityofmobilepaymentsdraftpc201311en.pdf
6. European Banking Authority: Directive 2015/2366 of the European Parliament and of the Council on payment services in the internal market (PSD2) (2015). https://eur-lex.europa.eu/legal-content/en/TXT/?uri=CELEX:32015L2366
7. European Banking Authority: Regulatory Technical Standards on Strong Customer Authentication and common and secure communication under Article 98 of PSD2 (2017). https://eur-lex.europa.eu/legal-content/EN/TXT/PDF/?uri=CELEX:32018R0389&from=EN
8. Furst, K., Lang, W.W., Nolle, D.E.: Internet banking: Developments and prospects. Economic and Policy Analysis Working Paper No. 2000-9, Office of the Comptroller of the Currency (2000)
9. Hao, F., Clarke, D.: Security analysis of a multi-factor authenticated key exchange protocol. In: Bao, F., Samarati, P., Zhou, J. (eds.) ACNS 2012. LNCS, vol. 7341, pp. 1–11. Springer, Heidelberg (2012). https://doi.org/10.1007/978-3-642-31284-7_1
10. Kennedy, E., Millard, C.: Data security and multi-factor authentication: analysis of requirements under EU law and in selected EU Member States. Comput. Law Secur. Rev. **32**, 91–110 (2016)
11. Krol, K., Philippou, E., Cristofaro, E.D., Sasse, M.A.: "They brought in the horrible key ring thing!" Analysing the Usability of Two-Factor Authentication in UK Online Banking. CoRR abs/1501.04434. University College London (2015)
12. NIST: Special Publication - Digital Identity Guidelines (2017). https://pages.nist.gov/800-63-3/
13. Sciarretta, G., Carbone, R., Ranise, S., Viganò, L.: Design, formal specification and analysis of multi-factor authentication solutions with a single sign-on experience. In: Bauer, L., Küsters, R. (eds.) POST 2018. LNCS, vol. 10804, pp. 188–213. Springer, Cham (2018). https://doi.org/10.1007/978-3-319-89722-6_8
14. Weir, C.S., Douglas, G., Richardson, T., Jack, M.: Usable security: user preferences for authentication methods in eBanking and the effects of experience. Interact. Comput. **22**(3), 153–164 (2010)

A Risk-Driven Model to Minimize the Effects of Human Factors on Smart Devices

Sandeep Gupta[1]([✉]) [iD], Attaullah Buriro[1]([✉]) [iD], and Bruno Crispo[1,2]([✉]) [iD]

[1] Department of Information Engineering and Computer Science (DISI), University of Trento, Trento, Italy
{sandeep.gupta,attaullah.buriro,bruno.crispo}@unitn.it
[2] Department of Computer Science, imec-DistriNET, KULeuven, Leuven, Belgium

Abstract. Human errors exploitation could entail unfavorable consequences to smart device users. Typically, smart devices provide multiple configurable features, e.g., user authentication settings, network selection, application installation, communication interfaces, etc., which users can configure according to their need and convenience. However, untrustworthy features configuration could mount severe risks towards the protection and integrity of data and assets residing on smart devices or to perform security-sensitive activities on smart devices. Conventional security mechanisms mainly focus on preventing and monitoring malware, but they do not perform the runtime vulnerabilities assessment while users use their smart devices. In this paper, we propose a risk-driven model that determines features reliability at runtime by monitoring users' features usage patterns. The resource access permissions (e.g., `ACCESS_INTERNET` and `ACCESS_NETWORK_STATE`) given to an application requiring higher security are revoked in case users configure less reliable features (e.g., open `WIFI` or `HOTSPOT`) on their smart devices. Thus, our model dynamically fulfills the security criteria of the security-sensitive applications and revokes resources access permission given to them, until features reliability is set to a secure level. Consequently, smart devices are secured against any runtime vulnerabilities that may surface due to human factors.

Keywords: Human factors · Risk-driven model · Smart devices

1 Introduction

Smart devices such as smartphones, tablets, smart-watches, smart TVs, smart speakers and many more, indeed, bring rich digital experiences to their users. Users can perform many personalized services, e.g., banking, emailing, navigation, shopping, social networking, video conferencing, etc., on their smart devices. Similarly, users can access data stored on cloud servers or to control appliances and gadgets paired with their smart devices. Typically, smart devices

© Springer Nature Switzerland AG 2020
A. Saracino and P. Mori (Eds.): ETAA 2019, LNCS 11967, pp. 156–170, 2020.
https://doi.org/10.1007/978-3-030-39749-4_10

amass a huge amount of their users' private data, and any security breach could result in unfavorable consequences to their users [1]. Thus, dedicated security mechanisms are required to address threats, vulnerabilities, and insecure features usage on smart devices.

Conventional security mechanisms address threats by deploying automatic tools (e.g., anti-malware applications), which can discriminate between malicious- and healthy apps, or mobile device management tools, which can wipe data remotely and provide device-level controls. Generally, these anti-malware applications apply strategies like signature-based malware detection, behavior-based malware detection and sandboxing, to protect devices from malicious software [2]. Likewise, system vulnerabilities could be addressed proactively by applying threat modeling techniques or reactively by upgrading or patching the system [3]. However, these existing security mechanisms have shown to be incapable of addressing insecure features usage patterns on smart devices posed by human factors.

A study by Google has revealed that maximum cyber-attacks on smart devices occurred due to the users own errors, and in the last two years, the victims have spent more than 25 million USD to recover their data [4]. Several techniques have been proposed for human reliability assessment (HRA) because humans are found to be the weakest link in a system security chain [5]. Some of these techniques deploy qualitative and quantitative methods to estimate human errors in sensitive tasks [6] whereas, some techniques focus on human reliability and their performance, such as the ability of a human to complete a given task, in given conditions, in a given time period, without any errors [7]. However, targeting smart devices is such a lucrative affair for attackers that they become more sophisticated and motivated to exploit human factors for accessing smart devices [8].

In this paper, we analyze various scenarios that could make features available on smart devices unreliable due to insecure usage patterns by the end users. Then, we propose a risk-driven model that determines the features' reliability during runtime by monitoring users usage pattern to configure each feature on their smart devices. Accordingly, the resources access permissions given to security-sensitive applications are revoked unless features reliability level is configured to fulfill the applications security criteria set by the users. Thus, our model tackles possible human errors and secures smart devices against vulnerabilities that may surface due to human factors.

The rest of the paper is structured as follows: Sect. 2 briefly, describes some commonly used security terminologies, risk factors and security strategies for smart devices, and methods for human reliability assessment. Sections 3 and 4 presents the problem and the solution, respectively. The proposed security model performs a risk assessment on the basis of feature reliability level and application security level to grant system resources access to an application. Finally, Sect. 5 concludes the paper with the expected outcome of this research work.

2   Background

This section describes some commonly used security related terminologies, various risk factors affecting smart devices, existing security strategies for smart devices, and available methods for human reliability assessment.

2.1   Terminologies

- **Smart devices:** Smart devices are the portable electronic gadgets with user-friendly interfaces that offer multiple services and controls to their users anytime anywhere. Moreover, their features can be easily configured to provide better user experiences.
- **Threats:** Threat refers to the source and means of a particular type of attack that might be potentially hazardous to system's security [9]. In simple words, threat can be define as something that can exploit a system, intentionally or unintentionally.
- **Vulnerabilities:** Vulnerability refers to the weaknesses in a system that could expose the integrity, availability, or confidentiality of the system in a hostile environment [10]. Human factors can introduce or expose the vulnerabilities at the device or application level, which can be further exacerbate attack surfaces.
- **Risk:** Risk refers to the likelihood of exposure or exploitation of a system in case of threats being materialized as a result of an attack [9].
- **Reliability:** The ISO/IEC 25010:2011 standards define the degree to which a system, product or component performs specified functions under specified conditions for a specified period of time. Limitations in reliability are due to faults in requirements, design, and implementation, or due to contextual changes [11].
- **Human Factors:** The ISO 6385:2004 standards define human factors as a scientific discipline concerned with the understanding of interactions among human and other elements of a system and the profession that applies theory, principles, data, and methods to design in order to optimize human well-being and overall system performance [12]. In simple words, human factors can be collectively defined as (lack of) awareness, (risky) belief, (risky) behavior, (lack of) motivation, (inadequate) knowledge of technology while a user uses the security mechanisms [13].
- **Threat agent:** Threat agent (source) refers to an individual or group that can manifest a threat [14].

2.2   Risk Factors for Smart Devices

Figure 1 illustrates the overall risk to a smart device from threat agents having capabilities and intentions to cause an adverse impact on it. Threat agents can pose threats: (1) either directly, or (2) by exploiting vulnerabilities, or (3) by discovering insecure usage patterns of system features.

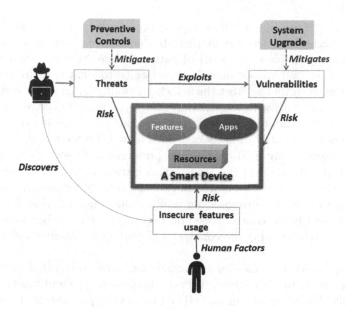

Fig. 1. Risk factors: threats, vulnerabilities, and insecure features usage

2.3   Security Strategies for Smart Devices

Security strategies for a given system fundamentally involve steps like identification, characterization, and assessment of various risk factors. However, a
common strategy to address risks due to threats, vulnerabilities, and untrustworthy feature configurations, does not suffice for smart devices considering their
asymmetrical characteristics.

- **Threats:** Threats reported on smart devices are generally value-driven [2].
  Unethical wireless carriers and malicious third-party apps may use persis-
  tent malware to steal users' data to trade the data in open markets [15].
  Also, casual attackers, hackers, device harvesters, or espionage professionals may gain access to smart devices to retrieve users' information and sell
  data to spammers and spear-phishers [15]. Ransomware attacks could infect
  devices by encrypting or scrambling files so they can no longer be readable
  or accessible [16]. Similarly, attacks like DoubleLocker distributed through a
  fake Adobe flash player apps lock smart devices by changing their PIN and
  encrypts all the data stored in that device, compelling victims to pay a ransom [17]. Another scammer exploited a bug in Apple's Mobile Safari browser
  to extort ransom from users [18].
  For smart devices, traditional anti-malware and third-party anti-virus software could not work effectively to monitor other applications and system
  properties due to their inherent increased security model (e.g., sandboxing).
  Iqbal et al. [19] proposed a secure anti-malware framework (SAM) for smartphone operating systems that prevent malicious activities of the third-party
  apps and malware.

Yang et al. [20] proposed a two-stage approach that unifies data states and software execution on the critical path. In the first stage, a pilot static analysis identifies the possible attack critical path based on APIs and existing attack patterns. Then, a dynamic analysis is performed to identify a directed path to execute the program to detect the attack possibility by checking conformance of the detected path with the existing attack patterns. In the second stage, a runtime dynamic analysis reports the type of attack scenarios with respect to the type of confidential data leakage such as web browser cookie and others without accessing any real critical and protected data sources in the mobile device. Typically, most of the applications installed on Android-based smart devices can access the data stored in external storage (emulated Sdcard storage). Hong et al. [21] proposed an application, Sdguard, that incorporated fine-grain permission control based on Linux DAC mechanism to detect ransomware, which encrypts the content of file stored in external storage or lock user screen.

Commonly used strategies for threat management on smart devices are: (1) automatic tools to discriminate between malicious apps and healthy apps, or (2) mobile device management (MDM) tools that provide device-level password controls and remote data wipe commands.

- **Vulnerabilities:** Security surveys for smart devices have shown that the presence of vulnerabilities and flaws in a system is inevitable [22,23]. Technically, vulnerabilities could be introduced by native applications and platform APIs, third-party apps and open APIs, voice and image capturing hardware, network interfaces like WiFi, Bluetooth, NFC, rooted or jail-broken OS, etc. [15]. From the risk perspective, vulnerabilities pose risk to a system only in the event of being exploited by threat agents causing an adverse impact on the system users [3].

  Vulnerabilities can be addressed proactively by using threat modeling techniques from the early stages of the software development life cycle (SDLC) [3]. However, in most cases, vulnerabilities are fixed reactively by upgrading the system, or by applying software patches, periodically [3].

- **Features Usage Decisions:** Any smart devices security critically depends on features configuration information conveyed to users, their decisions to operate them, and the interpretation of their actions by the system to configure those features [24]. To address security and privacy compromises, popular operating systems for smart devices have introduced application-specific permissions that can be specified by users to restrict resources access by the applications [25,26].

  Shabtai et al. [27] demonstrated the likelihood and impact of 16 Android features usage. Attacks based on permissions abuse can exploit the system resources, if permissions are granted, carelessly. For example, malware can send SMS messages to stored numbers without the user's knowledge by exploiting READ_CONTACT permission. In fact, there are only a few numbers of users pay attention to the permissions while installing the applications [28]. Lindorfer et al. [29] proposed a hybrid static and dynamic feature set method that extracts the class names, permissions, intents, publisher identification from a manifest file. The APK and manifest are checked to confirm their validity and then extracted the user permissions, sensitive API calls and native code from the APK, followed by the examination of APK certificate and resources as indicators. Finally, the application was run in a sandbox to observe operations, such as file activity, network traffic, phone calls, exposed data, runtime code and registered broadcasts.

Studies have shown that humans are the weakest link in the security chain and users carelessly take risky usage decisions [30]. Consequently, attackers simply target human factors in setting traps to take control of the user's device. Thus, features management strategies must include attributes to assert users decisions.

2.4   Human Reliability Assessment Methods

Typically, a feature can be defined as an interface that enables users to configure the resources present in a system. Similarly, resources are used by applications to perform tasks or activities for the benefit of the users. It could be inferred that the reliability of a feature directly depends on the usage pattern of a user. Thus, how a user decides to use a particular feature can be characterized by associating an attribute with that feature, to assert its reliability [31]. Figure 2 shows the connection between features, resources, and applications along with their normal interaction paths for a smart device.

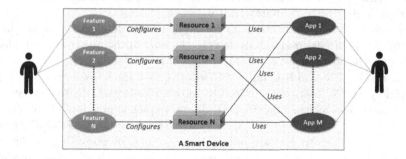

Fig. 2. Connection between features, resources, and applications in a smart device

A number of approaches, e.g., task analysis, error identification, and quantification of human error probabilities, etc., have been proposed for human reliability assessment. Current human reliability assessment (HRA) methods such as THERP (Technique for Human Error Rate Prediction), HCR (Human Cognitive Reliability), STAHR (Socio-technical assessment of human reliability), ATHEANA (A Technique for Human Event Analysis), are based on qualitative and quantitative assessment of human contribution to risk in productive tasks [6]. These methods are successfully deployed in high-reliability industries such as petrochemical, nuclear and aviation.

3 Problem Description

We analyze the various features usage scenarios available on various smart devices that may introduce risk to the system if users do not adhere to features usage guidelines as prescribed by the system providers.

- *Scenario 1:* "No user authentication is enabled" - According to a web-report [32], average users open ≈76 phone sessions per day while heavy users (the top 10%) open ≈132 sessions per day. This is clearly the case of lack of motivation where the PIN or password-based schemes to secure the access (typing pin-numbers (76 x 4) times or alphanumeric (76 x 8) time per day) are annoying to users [33]. Consequently, smart devices become vulnerable to direct attacks.
- *Scenario 2:* "Apps/activities/services active or running in background" - Along with apps opened by a user, several processes/services are also running in the background on smart devices, this is a case of inadequate use of technology. While using any sensitive operation these active apps/services must be stopped to averse possible threats.
- *Scenario 3:* "Apps installed from untrustworthy source" - Users install third-party apps on their device, which is a risk behavior. Just because this application promises to do everything a user required, it doesn't mean it isn't malicious. And many such apps may be infested with spying capabilities including activity monitoring, collecting sensory data of user's behavioral biometrics (keystrokes, gait, touch-strokes), data harvesting (account information, logins, financial data), and more.
- *Scenario 4:* "USB debugging is ON" - When USB debugging [34] is enabled intruders can access user's data despite the user authentication is enabled or disk encryption is in place. This is a case of lack of awareness.
- *Scenario 5:* "Bluetooth is on" - Bluetooth [35] connections are simply protected by a PIN. Users are required to enter a passkey or PIN to connect their wireless devices for the first time. Often, users pick simple four-digit code like "0000", "1111", "9999" or "1234", which can be easily cracked [36,37]. Exposing smart devices to eavesdropping, bluesnarfing, bluebugging, or denial of service, showing user's lack of awareness, risky belief or inadequate knowledge of technology.
- *Scenario 6:* "Open Hotspots and WIFIs" - Hotspots are very common in airports, hotels and coffee shops [38]. They are also starting to appear on public transport, such as trains and buses, in supermarkets and in other establishments. However, smart device users who unwittingly connect to them can be the victim of snooping. Their user names, passwords, and even the credit card details can be stolen easily. Hackers can label their Wi-Fi connection impersonating as a genuine service provider, so users may think they are on a secure connection but in reality, all their personal information they are entering on their device is high-jacked. This is also known as Evil Twin, designed to make illegitimate access points look identical to legitimate ones, making it difficult for users to determine which one is correct. Once users join the rogue network,

the hacker can launch a man-in-the-middle attack and intercept information between the user and another party. Therefore, it is advisable not to use your online banking or anything sensitive on a public Wi-Fi network and such risky behavior should be avoided.

– *Scenario 7:* "Mirroring the device" - Many applications track a user using unique identifiers such as smartphone's UDID (Unique Device Identifier - the equivalent of a phone's serial number) or IMEI (International Mobile Station Equipment Identity - the unique number mobile networks use to identify subscribers). Hackers can gain access to this information and mirror the device and see everything on it, or install malware that will enable them to siphon data from it due to inadequate knowledge of technology or lack of awareness.

– *Scenario 8:* "Pairing a smart device with another devices" - The flexibility to pair the smart devices to other devices might be a value addition but this might be risky believe. The feature offers easiness to watch Youtube video on the smart TV, listen to choice of music on paired speakers or headphone, or to get directions of the desired location by pairing with smart navigation system of a car, but it's also providing cyber-criminals and hackers another attack surface they could use to target the smart devices for vicious activities.

– *Scenario 9:* "Location, trusted place" - The authentication can be enforced as per the user location. If a user is at home, explicit authentication can be avoided in favor of continuous authentication using behavioral biometrics like gait recognition [39] or keystroke dynamics [40]. Whereas, if the user is at some unfamiliar location explicit authentication along with the second factor can be added and some high-risk activities, like transferring a significant amount of money using mobile banking, might be disabled. Smart devices save the user's latitude and longitude, along with a time and date stamp. It then copies the data to the owner's computer whenever the two are synchronized. This means anyone who stole the phone or gained access to the computer it is paired with could build a detailed picture of the owner's movements.

– *Scenario 10:* "Disable anti-malware or anti-virus apps" - This is a case of inadequate use of technology. Disabling anti-malware or anti-virus apps will stop the periodic scan and check for the potentially unwanted programs like viruses and malware including Trojans, Worms, Spyware, Rootkits, and Keyloggers.

Thus, security issues arising due to irregular and unpredictable features usage decision induced by human factors can be tackled by computing the features reliability at runtime. Appendix A summarizes the available features on smart devices and their insecure usage patterns that could expose the resources associated with those features.

4 Our Solution

We conceptualize a risk-driven model that dynamically monitors users' usage patterns of various features available on smart devices. Subsequently, a reliability level assigned to each feature at runtime to assess the risk involved in the usage patterns of those features with respect to the application. The model, then, compares the user-defined application security level with the features reliability level and revokes the resources permission associated with the less reliable features to fulfill the security criteria of that application.

For example, a user assigned her banking app the highest security level and the banking app requires the network feature to offer its services to the user. If the user connects to an open WIFI or HOTSPOT, which could be risky in the light of various cyber attacks. The model assigns the LOW reliability to the network feature. Hence, the model automatically revokes the ACCESS_INTERNET and ACCESS_NETWORK_STATE permissions associated with the banking app to prevent threats due to the unsecured network connection.

4.1   Model Description

Figure 3 illustrates the design of our model that is implemented within the Application and Application Program Interface (API) Framework layers of the device stack. The model establishes a relationship between installed applications, system features, and human factors.

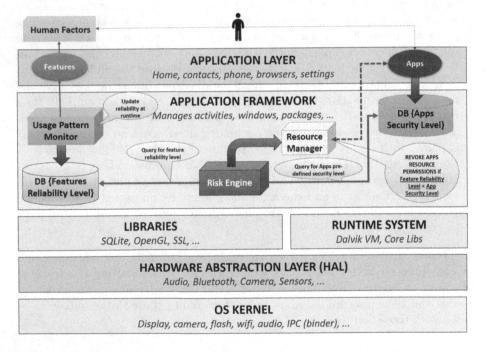

Fig. 3. Our model design for smart devices OS framework

The first step requires the user to assign the desired security level, i.e., high, medium or low, to the applications installed on their smart devices, which is store in the App Security Level (ASL) database in the API Framework layer. The second step requires to determine the reliability of each feature (refer to Appendix A). To achieve this, we assign a dedicated attribute, namely, FEATURE_RELIABITY_LEVEL to each feature that stores the reliability of the feature in the Features Reliability Level (FRL) database.

Initially, FEATURE_RELIABITY_LEVEL for each feature is set to LOW. At the runtime, Usage Pattern Monitor (UPM) module dynamically update the reliability level, i.e., high, medium or low as per the user's usage patterns of each feature. This reliability assignment process varies from feature to feature. It could be fully automated or depends on user input. For example, if a user sets a PIN/PASSWORD or FINGER_PRINT for [AUTH] feature, FEATURE_RELIABITY_LEVEL is automatically set to MEDIUM or HIGH, respectively. Similarly, in the case of [CONNECT2NW] feature, the model relies on the user's input to set the FEATURE_RELIABITY_LEVEL, every time the user connects to a new network.

4.2   Risk Assessment Process

Risk Engine (RE) periodically queries the ASL and FRL databases to fetch the required security level of each application and current reliability level of features. In the next step, the model generates a map between application security level (APP_i_ASL) and feature reliability levels (F_j_FRL) used by each application at an instance t_k, as shown in Table 1.

Table 1. Application security level and feature reliability levels map

#	Application	App security level	Features reliability level
1	APP_1	$APP_1\_ASL = HIGH$	$F_1\_FRL = HIGH$ $F_2\_FRL = LOW$ $F_3\_FRL = MEDIUM$ ... $F_{N-2}\_FRL = HIGH$
2	APP_2	$APP_2\_ASL = LOW$	$F_2\_FRL = LOW$ $F_{15}\_FRL = MEDIUM$ ... $F_{N-1}\_FRL = HIGH$
...	...	...	...
M	APP_M	$APP_M\_ASL = MEDIUM$	$F_1\_FRL = HIGH$ $F_3\_FRL = MEDIUM$ $F_6\_FRL = MEDIUM$ ... $F_N\_FRL = HIGH$

With reference to Table 1, APP_1 requires HIGH security level and it users features F_1, F_2, F_3, and F_{N-2}. The model revokes the APP_1 permission to use resources associated with F_2, and F_{N-2}, as their FRL is not HIGH as required by APP_1. Similarly, APP_2 and APP_M require LOW and MEDIUM security level, respectively. The model verifies the apps security level criteria is satisfied. Therefore, permissions to use resources in both apps remain unchanged.

4.3   Resource Revocation Process

The model revokes the application permission to use resources by processing the map generated at runtime as described in Sect. 4.1. The model iterates for each application APP_i and reads required security level and determines F_j_FRL for all the features used by them. If F_j_FRL is less APP_i_ASL, models send the instruction to Resource Manager (RM) to revokes permission of resources associated with that feature as explained in Algorithm 1.

Algorithm 1. Resource revocation process

1: **procedure** READMAP
2:     **while** $i \leq M$ **do**
3:         Read APP_i_ASL ▷ Reads required security level
4:         **for** $j = 1$ *to* N; j++ **do**
5:             **if** $F_j\_FRL < APP_i\_ASL$ **then**
6:                 *Revoke Resource Permission* $\in F_j$ ▷ Sends instruction to RM
7:             **end if**
8:         **end for**
9:     **end while**
10: **end procedure**

---

5   Conclusions

A balance between security and convenience is the most critical requirement for smart devices. Moreover, there is always a contest between threat agents and security professionals, where human factors swing the balance one way or the other. Security mechanisms in smart devices, technically, get affected by human factors that influence users' usage patterns to use various features available on a smart device. Unarguably, the irregular and unpredictable features usage decisions by users can make smart devices unreliable to perform security-sensitive activities or to store private data.

Our risk-driven model dynamically determines the features configuration reliability by monitoring users usage patterns of various features available on smart devices. The user-defined application security levels and features reliability levels are compared at runtime, and the permission of the resources associated with the less reliable features are revoked to fulfill applications security criteria. Thus, this user-centric approach mitigates security risks caused by insecure features usage patterns without affecting the user experience.

Acknowledgement. This project has received funding from the European Union's Horizon 2020 research and innovation programme under the Marie Sklodowska-Curie grant agreement No. 675320. Also, this work has been supported by the EU H2020-SU-ICT-03-2018 Project No. 830929 CyberSec4Europe.

A   Summary of features, their incorrect usage patterns, and resources exposed

Features	Feature incorrect usage patterns	Resources exposed
[AUTH]	Do not enable authentication, Do not set a strong password for accessing sensitive information	All resources
[APPINBG]	Leave Apps/activities/ services running in background	Memory, broadcast messages, battery-life [41]
[APPINSTALLATION]	Install third-party applications from unknown/untrusted sources	Device ID, contracts, call log, and locations [42]
[USBDEBUG]	Leave the USB debugging, using public USB charging stations [43]	File system [44], private user data, phone calls and massages, Keystrokes, SIM informations [45]
[BLUETOOTH]	Leave the Bluetooth is on, Use of an easy password, Giving BLUETOOTH_ADMIN permissions to other devices	Any Bluetooth devices [46], discovery services, and launch camera, mail, music and phone system applications [47]
[CONNECT2NW]	Connect to open Hotspots and WIFIs	Network traffic [48], wireless data [49]
[PHONEMIRRORING]	Leave the smart device mirrored	Multimedia and documents, online streaming [50]
[DEVICEPAIRING]	Leave the smart device paired with another device	Multimedia and documents [51]
[AVT]	Disable anti-virus or anti-malware applications	File system [2]
[FIRMWAREUPDATE]	Installing upgrades from untrusted source	Device management tools [52]

References

1. Gupta, S., Buriro, A., Crispo, B.: Demystifying authentication concepts insmart-phones: ways and types to secure access. Mob. Inf. Syst. **2018**, 16 p. (2018)
2. He, D., Chan, S., Guizani, M.: Mobile application security: malware threats and defenses. IEEE Wirel. Commun. **22**(1), 138–144 (2015)
3. UcedaVelez, T., Morana, M.M.: Risk Centric Threat Modeling: Process for Attack Simulation and Threat Analysis. Wiley, Hoboken (2015)
4. Ward, M.: Ransomware 'here to stay', warns google study (2017). http://www.bbc.com/news/technology-40737060
5. Pieters, W.: Defining "the weakest link" comparative security in complex systems of systems. In: Proceeding of 5th International Conference on Cloud Computing Technology and Science (CloudCom), vol. 2, pp. 39–44. IEEE (2013)
6. Proctor, R.W., Van Zandt, T.: Human Factors in Simple and Complex Systems. CRC Press, Boca Raton (2018)
7. Li, P., Chen, G., Zhang, L., et al.: Research review and development trends of human reliability analysis techniques. At. Energy Sci. Technol. **45**(3), 329–340 (2011)
8. Gu, T., Li, L., Lu, M., Li, J.: Research on the calculation method of information security risk assessment considering human reliability. In: 2014 International Conference on Reliability, Maintainability and Safety (ICRMS), pp. 457–462. IEEE (2014)
9. Stoneburner, G., Goguen, A., Feringa, A.: Risk Management Guide for Information Technology Systems. NIST Special Publication 800–30 (2002)
10. Microsoft: Definition of a security vulnerability. https://msdn.microsoft.com/en-us/library/cc751383.aspx?f=255&MSPPError=-2147217396 (2018)
11. ISO/IEC 25010:2011: Reliability (2018). https://www.iso.org/obp/ui/#iso:std:iso-iec:25010:ed-1:v1:en
12. ISO: Human factors. https://www.iso.org/obp/ui/#iso:std:iso:9241:-210:ed-1:v1:en (2018)
13. Metalidou, E., Marinagi, C., Trivellas, P., Eberhagen, N., Skourlas, C., Giannakopoulos, G.: The human factor of information security: unintentional damage perspective. Soc. Behav. Sci. **147**, 424–428 (2014)
14. Vidalis, S., Jones, A.: Analyzing threat agents and their attributes. In: ECIW, pp. 369–380 (2005)
15. Fixmo: Enabling your business through mobile risk management (2018). https://www.eiseverywhere.com/file_uploads/12d988fc44b269ec828834bbaef0c6b3_Fixmo Whitepaper.pdf
16. Lord, N.: A history of ransomware attacks: the biggest and worst ransomware attacks of all time (2017). https://digitalguardian.com/blog/history-ransomware-attacks-biggest-and-worst-ransomware-attacks-all-time
17. Johar, A.: Now ransomware attacks android: doublelocker locks your smartphone by changing the pin (2017). https://economictimes.indiatimes.com/tech/internet/now-ransomware-attacks-android-doublelocker-locks-your-smartphone-by-changing-the-pin/articleshow/61247838.cms
18. Goodin, D.: Ransomware scammers exploited safari bug to extort porn-viewing IOS users. https://arstechnica.com/information-technology/2017/03/ransomware-scammers-exploited-safari-bug-to-extort-porn-viewing-ios-users/ (2017)
19. Iqbal, M.S., Zulkernine, M.: SAM: a secure anti-malware framework for the smartphone operating systems. In: Proceeding of Wireless Communications and Networking Conference (WCNC), pp. 1–6. IEEE (2016)

20. Yang, T., Yang, Y., Qian, K., Lo, D.C.-T., Qian, Y., Tao, L.: Automated detection and analysis for android ransomware. In: Proceeding of 7th International Symposium on Cyberspace Safety and Security (CSS), pp. 1338–1343. IEEE (2015)
21. Hong, S., Liu, C., Ren, B., Chen, J.: Poster: Sdguard: an android application implementing privacy protection and ransomware detection. In: Proceedings of the 15th Annual International Conference on Mobile Systems, Applications, and Services, pp. 149–149. ACM (2017)
22. Joshi, J., Parekh, C.: Android smartphone vulnerabilities: a survey. In: Proceeding of International Conference on Advances in Computing, Communication, & Automation (ICACCA) (Spring), pp. 1–5. IEEE (2016)
23. Yang, W., Hu, J., Fernandes, C., Sivaraman, V., Wu, Q.: Vulnerability analysis of iPhone 6. In: Proceeding of 14th Annual Conference on Privacy, Security and Trust (PST), pp. 457–463. IEEE (2016)
24. Yee, K.-P.: User interaction design for secure systems. In: Deng, R., Bao, F., Zhou, J., Qing, S. (eds.) ICICS 2002. LNCS, vol. 2513, pp. 278–290. Springer, Heidelberg (2002). https://doi.org/10.1007/3-540-36159-6_24
25. Apple: IOS requesting permission (2018). https://developer.apple.com/design/human-interface-guidelines/ios/app-architecture/requesting-permission/
26. Google: Android permissions overview (2018). https://developer.android.com/guide/topics/permissions/overview
27. Shabtai, A., Fledel, Y., Kanonov, U., Elovici, Y., Dolev, S., Glezer, C.: Google android: a comprehensive security assessment. IEEE Secur. Priv. 8(2), 35–44 (2010)
28. Wang, Y., Zheng, J., Sun, C., Mukkamala, S.: Quantitative security risk assessment of android permissions and applications. In: Wang, L., Shafiq, B. (eds.) DBSec 2013. LNCS, vol. 7964, pp. 226–241. Springer, Heidelberg (2013). https://doi.org/10.1007/978-3-642-39256-6_15
29. Lindorfer, M., Neugschwandtner, M., Platzer, C.: Marvin: efficient and comprehensive mobile app classification through static and dynamic analysis. In: 39th Annual Computer Software and Applications Conference (COMPSAC), vol. 2, pp. 422–433. IEEE (2015)
30. Aytes, K.: Computer security and risky computing practices: a rational choice perspective. In: Information Security and Ethics: Concepts, Methodologies, Tools, and Applications, pp. 1994–2011. IGI Global (2008)
31. Modarres, M., Kaminskiy, M.P., Krivtsov, V.: Reliability Engineering and Risk Analysis: A Practical Guide. CRC Press, Boca Raton (2016)
32. Winnick, M.: Putting a finger on our phone obsession - mobile touches: a study on humans and their tech (2016). https://blog.dscout.com/mobile-touches
33. Harbach, M., Von Zezschwitz, E., Fichtner, A., De Luca, A., Smith, M.: It's a hard lock life: a field study of smartphone (un) locking behavior and risk perception. In: Symposium on usable privacy and security (SOUPS), pp. 213–230 (2014)
34. Summerson, C.: What is USB debugging, and is it safe to leave it enabled on android? (2016). https://www.howtogeek.com/258788/what-is-usb-debugging-and-is-it-safe-to-leave-it-enabled-on-android/
35. Padgette, J.: Guide to Bluetooth Security. NIST Special Publication 800-121 (2017)
36. Shaked, Y., Wool, A.: Cracking the Bluetooth Pin. In: Proceedings of the 3rd International Conference on Mobile Systems, Applications, and Services, pp. 39–50. ACM (2005)
37. Dunning, J.: Taming the blue beast: a survey of Bluetooth based threats. IEEE Secur. Priv. 8(2), 20–27 (2010)
38. kaspersky: How to avoid public WiFi security risks (2018). https://usa.kaspersky.com/resource-center/preemptive-safety/public-wifi-risks

39. Muaaz, M., Mayrhofer, R.: Smartphone-based gait recognition: from authentication to imitation. IEEE Trans. Mob. Comput. **16**(11), 3209–3221 (2017)
40. Traore, I., Woungang, I., Obaidat, M.S., Nakkabi, Y., Lai, I.: Online risk-based authentication using behavioral biometrics. Multimed. Tools Appl. **71**(2), 575–605 (2014)
41. Google: Background execution limits (2018). https://developer.android.com/about/versions/oreo/background
42. Zhou, Y., Zhang, X., Jiang, X., Freeh, V.W.: Taming information-stealing smartphone applications (on android). In: McCune, J.M., Balacheff, B., Perrig, A., Sadeghi, A.-R., Sasse, A., Beres, Y. (eds.) Trust 2011. LNCS, vol. 6740, pp. 93–107. Springer, Heidelberg (2011). https://doi.org/10.1007/978-3-642-21599-5_7
43. Shiroma, T., Nishio, Y., Inoue, H.: A threat to mobile devices from spoofing public USB charging stations. In: Proceeding of International Conference on Consumer Electronics (ICCE), pp. 88–89. IEEE (2017)
44. Google: Android debug bridge (adb) (2018). https://developer.android.com/studio/command-line/adb
45. Hwang, S., Lee, S., Kim, Y., Ryu, S.: Bittersweet ADB: attacks and defenses. In: Proceedings of the 10th ACM Symposium on Information, Computer and Communications Security, pp. 579–584. ACM (2015)
46. Demetriou, S., Zhou, X.-Y., Naveed, M., Lee, Y., Yuan, K., Wang, X., Gunter, C.A.: What's in your dongle and bank account? Mandatory and discretionary protection of android external resources. In: NDSS (2015)
47. Kywe, S.M., Li, Y., Petal, K., Grace, M.: Attacking android smartphone systems without permissions. In: 2016 14th Annual Conference on Privacy, Security and Trust (PST), pp. 147–156. IEEE (2016)
48. Spaulding, J., Krauss, A., Srinivasan, A.: Exploring an open WiFi detection vulnerability as a malware attack vector on IOS devices. In: Proceeding of 7th International Conference on Malicious and Unwanted Software (MALWARE), pp. 87–93. IEEE (2012)
49. Wasil, D., Nakhila, O., Bacanli, S.S., Zou, C., Turgut, D.: Exposing vulnerabilities in mobile networks: a mobile data consumption attack. In: Proceeding of 14th International Conference on Mobile Ad Hoc and Sensor Systems (MASS), pp. 550–554. IEEE (2017)
50. Sharma, K., Gupta, B.B.: Attack in smartphone Wi-Fi access channel: state of the art, current issues, and challenges. In: Lobiyal, D.K., Mansotra, V., Singh, U. (eds.) Next-Generation Networks. AISC, vol. 638, pp. 555–561. Springer, Singapore (2018). https://doi.org/10.1007/978-981-10-6005-2_56
51. Sun, D.-Z., Mu, Y., Susilo, W.: Man-in-the-middle attacks on secure simple pairing in Bluetooth standard v5. 0 and its countermeasure. Pers. Ubiquit. Comput. **22**(1), 55–67 (2018)
52. Zeiter, K.: Hackers can control your phone using a tool that's already built into it (2014). https://www.wired.com/2014/07/hackers-can-control-your-phone-using-a-tool-thats-already-built-into-it/

A Formal Security Analysis of the $p \equiv p$ Authentication Protocol for Decentralized Key Distribution and End-to-End Encrypted Email

Itzel Vazquez Sandoval$^{(\boxtimes)}$ and Gabriele Lenzini (iD)

University of Luxembourg, Luxembourg City, Luxembourg
{itzel.vazquezsandoval,gabriele.lenzini}@uni.lu

Abstract. To send encrypted emails, users typically need to create and exchange keys which later should be manually authenticated, for instance, by comparing long strings of characters. These tasks are cumbersome for the average user. To make more accessible the use of encrypted email, a secure email application named $p \equiv p$ automates the key management operations; $p \equiv p$ still requires the users to carry out the verification, however, the authentication process is simple: users have to compare familiar words instead of strings of random characters, then the application shows the users what level of trust they have achieved via colored visual indicators. Yet, users may not execute the authentication ceremony as intended, $p \equiv p$'s trust rating may be wrongly assigned, or both. To learn whether $p \equiv p$'s trust ratings (and the corresponding visual indicators) are assigned consistently, we present a formal security analysis of $p \equiv p$'s authentication ceremony. From the software implementation in C, we derive the specifications of an abstract protocol for public key distribution, encryption and trust establishment; then, we model the protocol in a variant of the applied pi calculus and later formally verify and validate specific privacy and authentication properties. We also discuss alternative research directions that could enrich the analysis.

Keywords: Formal verification · Authentication protocols · Software security analysis · Privacy-by-default · Secure email · End-to-end encryption

1 Introduction

Despite the success of *instant messaging* (IM) applications, email prevails as the principal means for written communication [24]; yet, communication over email remains largely insecure nowadays [11]. Solutions for securing email have however been proposed. For instance, OpenPGP [1] is arguably the most widely used email encryption standard. Derived from the PGP software, it proposes

© Springer Nature Switzerland AG 2020
A. Saracino and P. Mori (Eds.): ETAA 2019, LNCS 11967, pp. 171–187, 2020.
https://doi.org/10.1007/978-3-030-39749-4_11

the use of symmetric and asymmetric cryptography plus data compression to encrypt communication, and digital signatures for message authentication and integrity.

Unfortunately, severe usability drawbacks have been identified and highlighted in the standard (e.g. [27]). Along with the need for users to understand at least general cryptographic concepts regarding encryption—which inevitably narrows down the scope of the audience—the principal issue is the need for verifying the ownership of public keys, i.e., that a public key claimed to be of an entity A does indeed belong to A exclusively. Various approaches tackle this problem, e.g., fingerprint comparisons, public key infrastructure, certificate authorities, and the notion of web of trust, which involves individuals signing each other's public keys, thus forming a chain of certifications [28]. However, these approaches have encountered limited adoption mostly due to usability or scalability issues [11].

Attempting to overcome OpenPGP's usability issues related to trust establishment, an open source commercial software, called $p \equiv p$ (Sect. 3), proposes the use of so called *trustwords* (detailed in Sect. 3.1) to carry out peer-to-peer entity authentication via an out-of-band channel—e.g., in-person, video-call. This approach argues to introduce an improvement to usability and security of the PGP word list.

In this work we present a formal security analysis of the core protocols implemented in $p \equiv p$, focusing particularly in authentication and privacy goals.

1.1   Contributions

First, we derive from the open source code the specifications of $p \equiv p$'s abstract protocols for key distribution and trust establishment, and present them as Message Sequence Charts (MSC). From now on, we will refer to this abstraction as the $p \equiv p$ *protocol*. This is the first detailed technical documentation of such protocol.

Second, we provide a symbolic formal security analysis of the $p \equiv p$ protocol with respect to authentication and privacy goals, under a Dolev-Yao threat model. The analysis validates the security claims of $p \equiv p$ and the correct assignment of privacy ratings to messages.

2   Context and Approach

The application of formal methods for verifying that specific security properties hold in cryptographic protocols in the presence of a certain adversary is a well-established research area. Both the detection of flaws in a protocol (or, contrariwise, the proof of security) and the nature of those flaws depend on different factors, such as the verification approach and the phase of the system in which it takes place (e.g., design, implementation, compilation). An introductory reference for the topic is [21].

A variety of tools and formalizations have been used to successfully analyze, amongst others, authentication scenarios in real world and authentication standards (e.g., [6,7,13]). Important flaws have been discovered even in well-established protocols years after their publication and while being used (e.g., [19]). Therefore and because the design of protocols is by default an error-prone task, to effectively protect a system, security protocols need to be not only carefully designed and rigorously implemented but also strictly verified.

Here, we carry out a symbolic formal analysis of the $p \equiv p$ protocol specification. The symbolic approach assumes cryptographic primitives to work as perfect black boxes and focuses on the description of the logic of the protocol, the interaction among participants and the exchange of messages [10]. The resulting models allow to seek for attacks that rely on logical flaws in the protocol while taking advantage of mature automated tools for protocol analysis (e.g., ProVerif [9], Tamarin [5]).

Our work concerns remote human-to-human authentication, where human A wants to be sure that human B is who he claims to be and vice versa—in $p \equiv p$, the owner of a specific public key—, in a global communication scenario where A and B might not know each other.

2.1 Methodology

At the time when we started studying the $p \equiv p$ protocol there was not substantial documentation regarding neither the protocol specifications nor the source code. In consequence, the work presented here relies on the open source code of $p \equiv p$ [22], together with online documentation mainly for users [23]. Recently some internet drafts have been released [17,18], which has helped clarifying our models.

Our security analysis consists of the following steps, which we detail in the rest of the paper:

1. Extract the specifications of the key distribution and handshake protocols from the available sources [22,23].
2. Describe the protocol in MSC notation.
3. Formalize in the *applied pi calculus* the MSC specifications of the previous step, along with the attacker model.
4. Specify and formalize in the *applied pi calculus* the properties to be verified.
5. Verify the satisfiability of the properties formalized in 4, in the model resulting from step 3.
6. Analyze and interpret the results of the verification.

We start by introducing the $p \equiv p$ software and its relevant features in Sect. 3. Then, steps 1 and 2, which deal with specifying the $p \equiv p$ protocol, are presented in Sect. 4. In Sect. 5, we define the security properties related to privacy and authentication that concern our analysis. Section 6 covers steps 3 and 4 of the methodology, i.e., the formalization of the protocol and of the security properties introduced informally in Sect. 5. The results of the execution of step 5 and the analysis in step 6 are discussed in Sect. 6.4; we also discuss limitations of the analysis in Sect. 6.5. Further directions and conclusions are presented in the last section.

3   Background: Pretty Easy Privacy ($p \equiv p$)

Pretty Easy Privacy ($p \equiv p$)[1] is a software that claims to provide privacy-by-default in email communications via end-to-end opportunistic encryption. Roughly, this means that the software encrypts outgoing email messages without any intervention from the user, whenever a secure or trusted public key of the intended receiver is available.

$p \equiv p$ attempts to automate tasks that would otherwise require specialized-knowledge from non-expert users, while informing the user of the privacy rating assigned to messages in an intuitive way. Hence, its more relevant features are: (1) a fully automated process for the generation and management of encryption keys and for the encryption of emails; (2) an algorithm to determine the strongest privacy level that can be assigned to a message for a specific partner—this level is further communicated to the user by colored visual icons; (3) a fully decentralized architecture for key storage—this design decision eludes relying on possibly untrusted central authorities by having the users perform the trust establishment task via out-of-band channels.

$p \equiv p$ is distributed as a standalone application for Android and as plugins for desktop installations of some existing email clients, e.g., Outlook, Enigmail. In this work we consider a general abstraction of the $p \equiv p$ protocols that represent improvements to PGP by means of the features described above. Comparing and discussing specific implementations is out of the scope of this paper.

3.1 $p \equiv p$ Trustwords

Manual key-fingerprint comparison is a well-established method for entity authentication in messaging protocols; yet, the approach has been shown to perform poorly for the intended goal (e.g., [14]). As a solution, in addition to hexadecimal numbers, PGP allows fingerprints to appear as a series of so-called "biometric words", which are phonetically different English words that intend to ease the comparison for humans and to make it less prone to misunderstandings [2].

Trustwords in $p \equiv p$ follow the same idea; they are natural language words mapping hexadecimal strings that are used to authenticate a peer after having exchanged public keys in an opportunistic manner. In short, such hexadecimal strings represent a combined fingerprint obtained by applying an XOR operation to the fingerprints associated to the public keys being authenticated. Each block of 4 hex characters of the combined fingerprint is mapped to a word in a predefined trustwords dictionary. For instance, F482 E952 2F48 618B

---

[1]   https://www.pep.security.

01BC 31DC 5428 D7FA could be mapped to kite house brother town juice school dice broken.

The main difference with the "biometric words" is the availability of trust-words in different languages, which improves the security for non-English speakers, and the use of longer words, which presumably increases the entropy as the dictionary is larger and therefore the likelihood for phonetic collision is decreased [17]. Considerations regarding the number of words in the dictionaries and the length of the words themselves are discussed also in [17].

3.2 Trust Rating and Visual Indicators

In agreement with the privacy-by-default principle, $p \equiv p$ assigns a specific privacy rating to each email exchange. Such a rating is determined per message and per identity depending on certain criteria and is shown to the users by colored icons in the message. The ratings are:

- MISTRUSTED: the system has evidence that the communication partner is not who (s)he claims to be, e.g., when the user explicitly mistrusts a peer.
- UNKNOWN/UNSECURE/UNRELIABLE (UNSECURE): encryption/decryption of a message cannot be properly executed, e.g., when the recipient does not use any secure email solution. The message is sent in plain text.
- SECURE: the user has a valid public key for the recipient, however it has not been personally confirmed. The message is encrypted/decrypted.
- TRUSTED: the user has the recipient's public key and it has been validated with the peer. The message is encrypted/decrypted and authenticated.

3.3 Technical Specifications of $p \equiv p$

The core component of $p \equiv p$ is pEpEngine, a library developed in C99 where the automation of cryptographic functionalities (e.g., key generation) is implemented relying on existing standards and tools for secure end-to-end encrypted communications (PGP, GnuPG). The $p \equiv p$ protocols are built upon those functionalities, therefore pEpEngine is the component from which we extracted the specifications hereby presented.

Each installation of $p \equiv p$ creates a local database of $p \equiv p$ peers, their corresponding keys and privacy ratings. Additionally, it creates a database from which the trustwords for mutual authentication are retrieved; the trustwords database contains the exact same data in all the distributions. To securely store private and public keys in the devices, $p \equiv p$ uses GnuPG². A more detailed description of $p \equiv p$ can be found in [18].

4   The $p \equiv p$ Protocol

In order to carry out a security analysis it is essential to clearly understand the logic of the protocol, to know the cryptographic primitives used, the parties

---

² https://www.gnupg.org/.

involved and the messages exchanged between them. Our case study required us to obtain this information mainly from the source code of $p \equiv p$.

Following the approach in [26], we executed the first step of the methodology proposed here in Sect. 2.1 by reverse engineering a fragment of the source code files. We then represented the output of such a process by means of MSC diagrams (step 2) which $p \equiv p$ confirmed to be accurately representing their protocol.

Here, we present and describe such diagrams which correspond to our abstracted version of the key distribution and authentication protocols used by $p \equiv p$ to engage in end-to-end private and authenticated communications.

In the rest of the paper, we will use sk_x and pk_x to refer to secret and public keys owned by agent x, respectively. As well, we use $\mathcal{A}$ and $\mathcal{B}$ to refer to honest participants and $\mathcal{M}$ for the malicious agent trying to prevent the honest parties from achieving the security goals.

4.1 Public Key Distribution and Encrypted Communication

Let $\mathcal{A}$ and $\mathcal{B}$ be two partners that do not know each other's public key. $\mathcal{A}$ installs $p \equiv p$ from scratch without having any cryptographic keys. She wants to privately communicate with $\mathcal{B}$ who is already a $p \equiv p$ user owning a pair of keys (sk_B, pk_B). We denote the $p \equiv p$ instances running in $\mathcal{A}$'s and $\mathcal{B}$'s devices as pEp$_A$ and pEp$_B$ respectively.

So that the key distribution protocol (Fig. 1) can take place, when $p \equiv p$ is installed, pEp$_A$ generates a pair of keys (sk_A, pk_A) for $\mathcal{A}$ (step 1). The protocol starts when $\mathcal{A}$ sends a message m to $\mathcal{B}$; pEp$_A$ creates an identity for $\mathcal{B}$ (2) and stores his contact details (3); then, pEp$_A$ sends m as plain text along with pk_A (4). When pEp$_B$ receives the message, it displays m to $\mathcal{B}$ with the privacy rating UNSECURE (5); additionally, pEp$_B$ creates an identity for $\mathcal{A}$ (6) and stores her email address and pk_A (7); finally pEp$_B$ assigns the privacy rating SECURE to $\mathcal{A}$'s identity (8). When $\mathcal{B}$ replies to $\mathcal{A}$, pEp$_B$ attaches pk_B to his response $resp$; this message is then signed with $\mathcal{B}$'s secret key sk_B (9) and encrypted using pk_A (10). The signed and encrypted message is sent to $\mathcal{A}$ (11); pEp$_B$ shows to $\mathcal{B}$ his message as SECURE. At reception, pEp$_A$ decrypts $\mathcal{B}$'s message using sk_A (12); then it stores pk_B as the public key of $\mathcal{B}$ (13) and assigns to his identity the SECURE rating (14). $\mathcal{B}$'s response is finally shown as SECURE to $\mathcal{A}$.

Note that the identifiers created for $\mathcal{A}$ and $\mathcal{B}$ do not need to coincide in pEp$_A$ and pEp$_B$, since they are only used by the corresponding $p \equiv p$ instance. Also, pk_A and pk_B sent in steps (4) and (11) are only attached to the first communication between $\mathcal{A}$ and $\mathcal{B}$ or whenever they are updated.

The key distribution protocol allows making the communication secret to everyone but the receiver, however, it does not guarantee that the receiver is the intended person. Man-in-the-middle attacks are still possible, as we will discuss in Sect. 6.4.

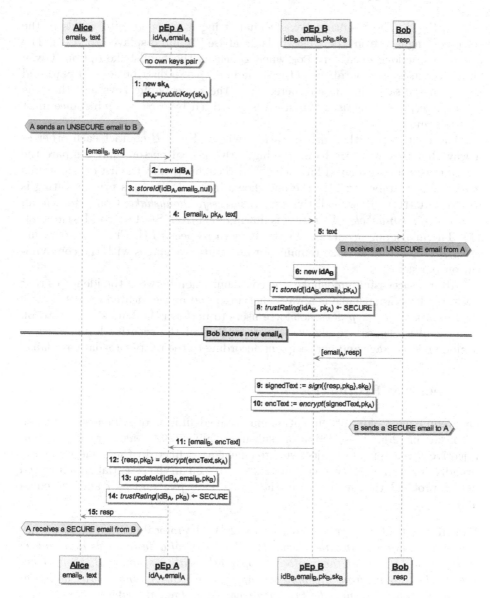

Fig. 1. $p \equiv p$ key distribution protocol

4.2 Authentication and $p \equiv p$ Privacy Rating Assignment

Trust establishment is achieved via the $p \equiv p$ Handshake protocol (Fig. 2), which consists in $\mathcal{A}$ and $\mathcal{B}$ comparing a list of trustwords via a communication channel assumed to be secure and that needs to be used only once.

When $\mathcal{A}$ selects the option to perform a handshake with $\mathcal{B}$ (1), pEp$_\mathcal{A}$ generates a combined fingerprint based on applying an *xor* function to the fingerprints of

$\mathcal{A}$ and $\mathcal{B}$ (2). The resulting hexadecimal string is mapped onto words in the selected language from the trustwords database (3) and displayed to $\mathcal{A}$ (4). The analogous actions occur in pEp$_\mathcal{B}$ when $\mathcal{B}$ selects the handshake option. Given that the trustwords database is the same in all $p \equiv p$ distributions, if pEp$_\mathcal{A}$ and pEp$_\mathcal{B}$ use the same input parameters, i.e., the same public keys and thus the same fingerprints, the list of trustwords generated by each $p \equiv p$ instance must be the same.

The next step is the authentication, where $\mathcal{A}$ and $\mathcal{B}$ contact each other in a way that they are sure to be talking with the real person, and compare the list of trustwords displayed for each (5). If $\mathcal{B}$ confirms that the list of trustwords given by $\mathcal{A}$ matches exactly the one shown in his device, $\mathcal{A}$'s privacy rating is set to TRUSTED (6); we call this case a *successful handshake*. Conversely, in an *unsuccessful handshake* $\mathcal{A}$'s rating is downgraded from SECURE to MISTRUSTED (7). The analogous occurs in $\mathcal{A}$'s device with respect to $\mathcal{B}$. The privacy rating assigned after a handshake remains for all future exchanges with the communication partner.

After a successful handshake, the communication between the identities that performed the handshake is always encrypted and authenticated (8–12).

Remark that $p \equiv p$ does not force users to perform the handshake protocol. The email messages are always sent regardless of the security level, which is decided per message and per recipient according to the recipient's data available.

5   Security Properties

Our requirements for authentication match the definition of *full agreement* given by Lowe in [20]. This definition subsumes aliveness, weak agreement, non-injective agreement and injective agreement as defined in the same reference; broadly, it requires the two participants to agree on all the essential data involved in the protocol run, in our case, the public keys pk_A and pk_B and the email addresses.

Definition 1 (Full agreement, from [20]**).** *A protocol guarantees to an initiator A full agreement with a responder B on a set of data items ds if, whenever A completes a run of the protocol, apparently with responder B, then B has previously been running the protocol, apparently with A, and B was acting as responder in his run, and the two agents agreed on the data values corresponding to all the terms in ds, and each such run of A corresponds to a unique run of B. Additionally, ds contains all the atomic data items used in the protocol run.*

Here we redefine this property in terms of $p \equiv p$ and introduce informally other properties in which we are interested.

Property 1 (Full agreement). A full agreement between $\mathcal{A}$ and $\mathcal{B}$ holds on pk_A, pk_B, $email_A$ and $email_B$ if, whenever $\mathcal{A}$ completes a successful handshake with $\mathcal{B}$, then: $\mathcal{B}$ has previously been running the protocol with $\mathcal{A}$, the identity data of $\mathcal{A}$ is $(email_A, pk_A)$ and the identity data of $\mathcal{B}$ is $(email_B, pk_B)$.

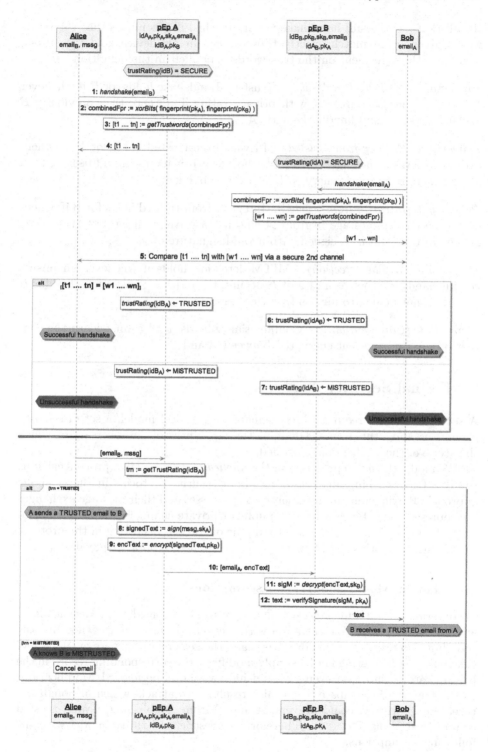

Fig. 2. $p \equiv p$ handshake protocol for authentication

Recall that a successful handshake is only reached if B confirms that the trustwords given by A match exactly those shown in his device, and vice versa; therefore, the agreement on the trustwords is implicit in the definition.

Property 2 (Trust-by-Handshake). Trust-by-Handshake holds for B if whenever B receives a message from A with privacy rating TRUSTED, then previously B executed a successful handhsake with A.

Property 3 (Privacy-from-trusted). Privacy-from-trusted holds for B if, whenever B receives a message m from A who has a privacy rating TRUSTED, then A sent m to B and m is encrypted with B's public key.

Property 4 (Integrity-from-trusted). Integrity-from-trusted holds for B if, whenever B receives a message m from A who has a privacy rating TRUSTED, then A sent m to B and m is signed with a valid signature of A.

Property 5 (MITM-detection). MITM-detection holds if whenever an unsuccessful handshake between A and B occurs, then A has registered a key for B that does not belong to him and/or vice versa.

Property 6 (Confidentiality). Confidentiality holds if M cannot learn the content of any message sent encrypted between A and B.

6   Formal Security Analysis

A security analysis requires three elements: a protocol model, a set of security properties, and a threat model defining the capabilities of the adversary by which the scope of the verification is framed.

We model the $p \equiv p$ protocols in the *applied pi calculus* [4], a process calculus suitable for describing and reasoning about security protocols in the symbolic approach. Participants are represented as processes and their message exchanges are represented by terms sent over public or private channels. A so called equational theory defines how the cryptographic operations occurring in the protocol relate with each other, and how they can be applied to obtain equivalent terms.

6.1   Threat Model and Trust Assumptions

To determine a relevant attacker model we need to consider the decentralized architecture of $p \equiv p$. To an attacker with access to the user's device, not only the code but also the application databases and the keys repository are available. M can thus have B trusting her by simply modifying the corresponding record in the privacy ratings database, even if a handshake was never performed. Modifications to the trustwords database would also result in an attack, which although not threatening privacy, could prevent A and B from establishing a valid trusted communication as TRUSTED. Therefore, we restrict the threat model with the following assumptions:

1. $p \equiv p$ users are honest participants and their devices are secure;
2. The adversary cannot modify exchanges over the trustwords channel;
3. The adversary has complete control over the network used to exchange emails (Dolev-Yao attacker [15]);
4. The users execute the comparison of trustwords correctly, i.e., they confirm the trustwords in the system only when they match in the real world and they mistrust them only in the contrary case.

These assumptions allow $\mathcal{M}$ to eavesdrop, remove, and modify emails exchanged between $\mathcal{A}$ and $\mathcal{B}$, as well as to send them messages of her choice; this includes learning their public keys exchanged by email. $\mathcal{M}$ cannot however interfere with the channel used to corroborate trustwords. Remark that this is a secondary channel such as the phone or in-person, thus, not intended to replace the email communication channel. We elaborate on assumption 4 in Sect. 7.

6.2   Modeling the $p \equiv p$ Protocol

The $p \equiv p$ protocol consists of the sequential execution of the key distribution and the trust establishment protocols presented in Sect. 4.

$\mathcal{A}$ and $\mathcal{B}$ are represented by two processes, senderA and receiverB, whose parameters symbolize the knowledge that they have. To communicate with $\mathcal{B}$, $\mathcal{A}$ needs to know his contact details, which here we abstract with the type *userId*; in turn, $\mathcal{B}$ only needs to know his own id and his secret key. The actions for each participant come from the diagrams in Figs. 1 and 2. We run multiple instances of $\mathcal{A}$ as well as of $\mathcal{B}$, to simulate communication with multiple peers.

For the exchange of emails we use a public channel; on the contrary, a private channel models the trustwords' validation channel. In order to prove confidentiality of encrypted and authenticated communication, we introduce a private message *mssg* representing a message whose content is initially unknown to $\mathcal{M}$; then, we model $\mathcal{A}$ sending *mssg* to $\mathcal{B}$ via the public channel after a successful handshake between them. Since $\mathcal{B}$ is trusted, *mssg* is sent signed and encrypted (steps 8–9, Fig. 2), and thus, expected to remain unreadable by $\mathcal{M}$ at the end of the protocol.

According to the symbolic model assumption, our equational theory models a perfect behavior of asymmetric encryption and digital signatures. These equations capture the relationships allowed among the cryptographic primitives involved, determining the ways in which any participant, the attacker included, can reduce terms. Then, for M a message and SK a secret key:

$$adec(aenc(M, pubKey(SK)),\ SK) = M \tag{1}$$
$$verifSign(sign(M, SK),\ pubKey(SK)) = M \tag{2}$$
$$getMssg(sign(M, SK)) = M \tag{3}$$

Equation (1) expresses that a message M encrypted with a certain public key can be decrypted with the corresponding secret key; moreover, this is the only way to obtain M from a ciphertext since there is no other equation involving the *aenc* primitive. Analogously, Eq. (2) returns M only if it was signed with the secret key associated to the public key used for the verification. Equation (3) allows the recovery of a message without verification of a digital signature and we introduce it here to model the capability of $\mathcal{M}$ for learning messages without the need of verifying the signature.

Also, we model a correct trustwords comparison as per assumption 4 in Sect. 6.1. We abstract fingerprints as public keys since a PGP fingerprint is uniquely derived from a public key. Then, for two public keys PK_1, PK_2, two trustwords lists W_1, W_2 and the trustwords generation function *trustwords*:

$$trustwordsMatch(trustwords(PK_1, PK_2), trustwords(PK_1, PK_2)) = true$$
$$trustwordsMatch(trustwords(PK_1, PK_2), trustwords(PK_2, PK_1)) = true$$

During its computations, $\mathcal{M}$ is allowed to apply all and only these primitives. Additionally, she has access to all the messages exchanged via the public channels and to any information declared as public. This models for instance $\mathcal{M}$'s real-life capability of generating the trustwords, which is possible because all the elements are public knowledge: the source code of the function, the trustwords database, $\mathcal{B}$'s public key and $\mathcal{A}$'s public key.

6.3   Privacy and Authentication Properties of $p \equiv p$

We formalize the properties introduced in Sect. 5 as correspondence and reachability queries based on events. Correspondences have the form $E \implies e_1 \wedge ... \wedge e_n$; they model properties expressing: *if an event E is executed, then events $e_1, ..., e_n$ have been previously executed.* Events mark important states reached by the protocol and do not affect the protocol's behavior. Our properties are defined in terms of the next events, where s and r represent two $p \equiv p$ users:

- *endHandshakeOk(s,r,pk$_s$,pk$_r$,e$_s$,e$_r$)*: s and r completed a successful handshake with the public keys and emails (pk_s, e_s) and (pk_r, e_r) respectively.
- startHandshake(s,r): s starts a handshake via a second-channel with r
- *userKey(s,pk$_s$)*: the agent s is the owner of the key pk_s
- *userEmail(s,e$_s$)*: the agent s owns the email address e_s
- *receiveGreen(r,s,m)*: r received the message m from s as TRUSTED
- *receiverTrustsS(r,s)*: the contacted peer r sets the privacy rating of s as TRUSTED after confirming that the trustwords match
- *sendGreen(s,r,m)*: s sent the message m to r as TRUSTED
- *decryptionFails(r,s,m)*: r cannot decrypt a message m from a trusted peer s
- *signVerifFails(r,s,m)*: r cannot verify the signature attached to m as a valid signature of s
- *endHandshakeUnsucc(s,r,pk$_s$,pk$_r$)*: s and r completed an unsuccessful handshake with the public keys pk_s and pk_r respectively.
- *attacker(m)*: the adversary knows the content of the message m

Then, for a private message $mssg$ and for all $p \equiv p$ users a and b, messages m and public keys ka, kb, pk_A, pk_B:

Full Agreement. For email addresses e_A and e_B,

$$endHandshakeOk(a, b, pk_A, pk_B, e_A, e_B) \implies startHandshake(a, b) \land startHandshake(b, a)$$
$$\land \; userKey(a, pk_A) \land userKey(b, pk_B)$$
$$\land \; userEmail(a, e_A) \land userEmail(b, e_B)$$

In our model the email address is abstracted as the identity itself, since we consider the case of one account per user. Therefore, in the verification the *userEmail* predicates are disregarded. We include them here for completeness.

Trust-by-Handshake

$$receiveGreen(b, a, m) \implies receiverTrustsS(b, a)$$

This formula matches exactly the definition of Property 2.

Privacy-from-Trusted. For a message z,

$$\big(receiveGreen(b, a, z) \implies sendGreen(a, b, z) \land z = aenc(m, pk_B)$$
$$\land \; userKey(b, pk_B)\big) \land$$
$$\big(decryptionFails(b, a, m) \implies \neg\, sendGreen(a, b, m)\big)$$

This formula is the conjunction of two correspondence assertions. The first one expresses Property 3; the second correspondence enforces the first by saying that it cannot be otherwise, i.e., when b receives a message m from a which for any reason cannot be decrypted—e.g. m is not encrypted—, then a did not send m to b.

Integrity-from-Trusted. For a message z and a secret key sk_A

$$\big(receiveGreen(b, a, z) \implies sendGreen(a, b, z) \land z = aenc(sign(m, sk_A), kb)$$
$$\land \; userKey(a, sk_A)\big) \land$$
$$\big(signVerifFails(b, a, m) \implies \neg\, sendGreen(a, b, m)\big)$$

Analogous to the previous formula, in this one we express Property 4 and reinforce it by proving that whenever the verification of the signature fails in message m, then a did not send m.

MITM-detection

$$endHandshakeUnsucc(a, b, ka, kb) \implies (userKey(a, pk_A) \land pk_A \neq ka) \lor$$
$$(userKey(b, pk_B) \land pk_B \neq kb)$$

This formula matches exactly the definition of Property 5.

Confidentiality. *attacker* is a built in predicate in ProVerif, which evaluates to TRUE if by applying the derivation rules to the knowledge of the adversary, there exists a derivation that results in $mssg$. Therefore, the protocol achieves confidentiality if

$$\neg\, attacker(mssg)$$

6.4   Verification Results and Analysis

In order to determine whether or not the protocol satisfies the specified security properties we use ProVerif [9], an automatic symbolic cryptographic protocol verifier. We executed the verification[3] with ProVerif 2.0 on a standard PC (Intel i7 2.7GHz, 8GB RAM). The response time was immediate.

We analyzed three different models: of the key distribution protocol, of the trust establishment protocol and of the key distribution followed by the trust establishment (the $p \equiv p$ protocol).

For the key distribution protocol, the results confirmed its vulnerability to MITM attacks. The weakness resides in the exchange of public keys via a channel where $\mathcal{M}$ has complete access. An attack proceeds as follows: $\mathcal{M}$ can intercept the initial message from $\mathcal{A}$ to $\mathcal{B}$ and send him a new message attaching her own public key, pk_E, instead of $\mathcal{A}$'s one. pEp$_\mathsf{B}$ will then link $\mathcal{M}$'s key with $\mathcal{A}$'s email in step (7) of Fig. 1, i.e., $storeId(idA_B, email_A, pk_E)$. When $\mathcal{B}$ replies, the message in step (10) is encrypted with pk_E, and thus $\mathcal{M}$ can intercept it again and decrypt it with her secret key, therefore obtaining pk_B attached. From this point, $\mathcal{M}$ can send encrypted emails to $\mathcal{B}$ using $\mathcal{A}$'s email address and she will be able to intercept and decrypt the responses sent by $\mathcal{B}$. In an analogous way, $\mathcal{M}$ can have $\mathcal{A}$ linking $\mathcal{M}$'s public key to $\mathcal{B}$'s identity, by sending her pk_E encrypted with pk_A obtained by intercepting the first message.

Regarding the trust establishment protocol, encryption and authentication hold since the trustwords comparison never mismatches due to the assumptions of the peer devices being secure and of a previous key distribution successfully executed.

The subsequent analysis of the $p \equiv p$ protocol determined that the six properties, full agreement, trust-by-handshake, privacy-from-trusted, integrity-from-trusted, MITM-detection and confidentiality are satisfied.

Regarding unsuccessful handshakes, even if $\mathcal{A}$ has the correct public key of $\mathcal{B}$, the handshake will fail if $\mathcal{B}$ has a key of $\mathcal{A}$ that does not correspond to her. Both partners will mistrust each other because the communication with those keys is threatened, however, once a peer is mistrusted, by $p \equiv p$ design such a privacy rating can not be reverted. This might be an issue, for instance if in the future $\mathcal{A}$ and $\mathcal{B}$ meet in person and exchange their public keys; they can then perform the handshake and $\mathcal{B}$ would be able to trust $\mathcal{A}$, but $\mathcal{A}$ would not be able to trust $\mathcal{B}$ in her device. In this case though, $\mathcal{M}$ misleading $\mathcal{A}$ to mistrust the intended partner is closer to a Denial of Service (DoS) attack but does not represent a threat to privacy.

We conclude that the execution of the $p \equiv p$ protocol fulfills the claimed security goals, i.e., after a successful handshake there is no undetectable way for $\mathcal{M}$ to modify the exchanges between $\mathcal{A}$ and $\mathcal{B}$, given that every message between them is always sent encrypted and signed with the corresponding keys. As a consequence, the privacy, authentication and integrity of the messages is preserved. Also, entity authentication is achieved by the $p \equiv p$ trust establishment protocol. These results depend on the assumptions of $p \equiv p$ residing in a

---

[3]   https://www.dropbox.com/s/ste22xe2zfj9bnt/fullPepProtocol.pv?dl=0.

secure environment, of a secure second channel for the trustwords comparison and of $p \equiv p$ users owning a single instance of $p \equiv p$ with a single email account.

6.5 Limitations

This analysis focuses solely on the technical specification of the key distribution and handshake protocols. Social attacks such as impersonation or phishing are however still possible; for instance $\mathcal{M}$ can create a fake email account related to $\mathcal{A}$'s name and then use it to send $\mathcal{B}$ an email attaching $\mathcal{M}$'s public key and contact details. If $\mathcal{B}$ has never met $\mathcal{A}$, a handshake via trustwords comparison with $\mathcal{M}$ would succeed given that both partners are indeed executing the protocol, but the human $\mathcal{B}$ thinks that he is interacting with the human $\mathcal{A}$.

The assumption of perfect cryptography implies that we consider the libraries implementing cryptographic operations to be correct. Implementation flaws in $p \equiv p$ and side-channel attacks are not considered either; however, we highlight the requirement for the software to ensure that the trustwords database provided contains exactly the same data in all the distributions, to prevent introducing false mismatches during the trustwords generation.

7 Further Directions and Concluding Remarks

We reported a symbolic security analysis of the specifications of $p \equiv p$ protocols for key distribution and authentication, validating the exchange of authenticated end-to-end encrypted email between two $p \equiv p$ trusted peers. Here, we conclude by discussing some approaches that we have considered to extend our analysis.

How humans behave when comparing trustwords is not considered in this work; yet, incorrect input from users, such as mistrusting a trusted peer or vice-versa, might introduce security flaws. These situations happen, for instance, when users verify only the first two words of the list or when they click the trustwords confirmation button without comparing the trustwords. A formal model of human errors in human-to-machine authentication protocols is proposed in [8]; adapting such an approach to studying further the mentioned scenarios could give insights into how flaws introduced by users can be prevented. Understanding the causes and frequency of incorrect behavior requires a different kind of analysis mainly in the scope of usable security.

Regarding the decentralization of keys, we observe that trusting the user device instead of a third party key server could represent an issue, for instance if the user misplaces his device and does not have a protected repository. A comprehensive systematization and evaluation of current architectures and protocols for securing email is presented in [11], where authors discuss approaches achieving the strongest guarantees and their adoption decisions.

Since protocols for IM in general provide stronger security guarantees than those for email [11,25], we speculate whether solutions for automating IM security can be applied in the context of email. The Signal protocol [3], for instance, performs key agreement by mixing multiple Diffie-Hellman shared keys (X3DH) and refreshing keys for every message exchange (double-ratchet), so that earlier keys cannot be calculated from later ones. The protocol has been formally analyzed and proved secure regarding secrecy and authentication of message keys [12]. The underlying reason preventing $p \equiv p$ from adopting a similar approach, hence upgrading security guarantees while relying less on the user, is Signal' use of a central server as a deposit for all the public keys involved and which is assumed to be trusted. This contradicts the decentralized paradigm adopted in $p \equiv p$'s design.

Following $p \equiv p$'s line of automating the processes as reasonably as possible, an idea to consider is how to automatically derive the trust from shared contacts with peers already trusted; a sort of an automatic web of trust. While there are many important considerations, for instance, how to get knowledge of shared contacts without violating privacy, we believe that this could be a direction worth studying.

As in the case of $p \equiv p$, in many systems that involve human-to-human authentication such a task is not mandatory to provide a service, but rather used to upgrade the security; therefore, users tend to neglect this step. Studying causes and solutions for those problems could be interesting from a usability perspective.

Finally, given that the human-to-human authentication relies on the trustwords shown to the user, as a next step we plan to verify $p \equiv p$'s trustwords generation function. Our approach considers taking advantage of the protocol verifier Tamarin, which recently added support for XOR operations [16]. Additionally, we foresee a verification closer to the implementation in the computational model.

Acknowledgments. Authors are supported by the project pEp Security SA/SnT "Protocols for Privacy Security Analysis".

References

1. OpenPGP. https://www.openpgp.org/
2. PGP word list. https://en.wikipedia.org/wiki/PGP_word_list
3. Signal technical specifications. https://signal.org/docs/
4. Abadi, M., Fournet, C.: Mobile values, new names, and secure communication. In: Acm Sigplan Notices, vol. 36, pp. 104–115. ACM (2001)
5. Basin, D., Cremers, C., Dreier, J., Meier, S., Sasse, R., Schmidt, B.: Tamarin prover. https://tamarin-prover.github.io/
6. Basin, D., Cremers, C., Meier, S.: Provably repairing the ISO/IEC 9798 standard for entity authentication. J. Comput. Secur. **21**(6), 817–846 (2013)
7. Basin, D., Dreier, J., Hirschi, L., Radomirovic, S., Sasse, R., Stettler, V.: A formal analysis of 5G authentication. In: Proceedings of the 2018 ACM SIGSAC Conference on Computer and Communications Security, pp. 1383–1396. ACM (2018)
8. Basin, D., Radomirovic, S., Schmid, L.: Modeling human errors in security protocols. In: 2016 IEEE 29th Computer Security Foundations Symposium (CSF), pp. 325–340. IEEE (2016)

9. Blanchet, B.: An efficient cryptographic protocol verifier based on prolog rules. In: 14th IEEE Computer Security Foundations Workshop, pp. 82–96. IEEE (2001)
10. Blanchet, B.: Security protocol verification: symbolic and computational models. In: Degano, P., Guttman, J.D. (eds.) POST 2012. LNCS, vol. 7215, pp. 3–29. Springer, Heidelberg (2012). https://doi.org/10.1007/978-3-642-28641-4_2
11. Clark, J., van Oorschot, P.C., Ruoti, S., Seamons, K., Zappala, D.: Securing email. arXiv preprint arXiv:1804.07706 (2018)
12. Cohn-Gordon, K., Cremers, C., Dowling, B., Garratt, L., Stebila, D.: A formal security analysis of the signal messaging protocol. In: 2017 IEEE European Symposium on Security and Privacy (EuroS&P), pp. 451–466. IEEE (2017)
13. Cremers, C.: Key exchange in IPsec revisited: formal analysis of IKEv1 and IKEv2. In: Atluri, V., Diaz, C. (eds.) ESORICS 2011. LNCS, vol. 6879, pp. 315–334. Springer, Heidelberg (2011). https://doi.org/10.1007/978-3-642-23822-2_18
14. Dechand, S., Schürmann, D., Busse, K., Acar, Y., Fahl, S., Smith, M.: An empirical study of textual key-fingerprint representations. In: 25th {USENIX} Security Symposium ({USENIX} Security 16), pp. 193–208 (2016)
15. Dolev, D., Yao, A.C.: On the security of public key protocols. In: Proceedings of the 22nd Annual Symposium on Foundations of Computer Science, SFCS 1981, pp. 350–357. IEEE Computer Society, Washington, DC (1981)
16. Dreier, J., Hirschi, L., Radomirovic, S., Sasse, R.: Automated unbounded verification of stateful cryptographic protocols with exclusive OR. In: 2018 IEEE 31st Computer Security Foundations Symposium (CSF), pp. 359–373. IEEE (2018)
17. (IETF), I.E.T.F.: IANA registration of trustword lists. https://tools.ietf.org/html/draft-birk-pep-trustwords-03
18. (IETF), I.E.T.F.: pretty Easy privacy (pEp): privacy by default. https://www.ietf.org/id/draft-birk-pep-03.txt
19. Lowe, G.: Breaking and fixing the Needham-Schroeder Public-Key Protocol using FDR. In: Margaria, T., Steffen, B. (eds.) TACAS 1996. LNCS, vol. 1055, pp. 147–166. Springer, Heidelberg (1996). https://doi.org/10.1007/3-540-61042-1_43
20. Lowe, G.: A hierarchy of authentication specifications. In: Proceedings 10th Computer Security Foundations Workshop, pp. 31–43. IEEE (1997)
21. Mauw, S., Cremers, C.: Operational Semantics and Verification of Security Protocols. Springer, Heidelberg (2012)
22. Pretty Easy Privacy: pep source code. https://pep.foundation/pep-software/index.html
23. Pretty Easy Privacy: pep user documentation. https://www.pep.security/docs/index.html
24. The Radicati Group: Email Statistics Report, 2018–2022. Technical report (2018)
25. Unger, N., et al.: SoK: secure messaging. In: 2015 IEEE Symposium on Security and Privacy, pp. 232–249. IEEE (2015)
26. Vazquez-Sandoval, I., Lenzini, G.: Experience report: how to extract security protocols' specifications from C libraries. In: IEEE 42nd Annual COMPSAC 2018, Tokyo, Japan, Vol. 2, pp. 719–724 (2018)
27. Whitten, A., Tygar, J.D.: Why Johnny can't encrypt: a usability evaluation of PGP 5.0. In: USENIX Security Symposium, vol. 348 (1999)
28. Zimmermann, P.R.: The Official PGP User's Guide. MIT Press, Cambridge (1995)

Author Index

Abidin, Aysajan   122
Aldini, Alessandro   1
Aly, Abdelrahaman   122

Blanchard, Nikola K.   104
Buriro, Attaullah   156

Carbone, Roberto   138
Costa, Gabriele   138
Crispo, Bruno   156

Dajsuren, Yanja   16
Daoudagh, Said   35

Genç, Ziya Alper   69
Gupta, Sandeep   156

Heutelbeck, Dominic   52
Higo, Haruna   86

Isshiki, Toshiyuki   86

Kachanovich, Siargey   104
Karkhanis, Priyanka   16

Lenzini, Gabriele   69, 171
Lonetti, Francesca   35

Marchetti, Eda   35
Mustafa, Mustafa A.   122

Nara, Masahiro   86

Obana, Satoshi   86
Okamura, Toshihiko   86

Ranise, Silvio   138
Ravidas, Sowmya   16
Ryan, Peter Y. A.   69

Selker, Ted   104
Sinigaglia, Federico   138

Tagliaferri, Mirko   1
Tamiya, Hiroto   86

Vazquez Sandoval, Itzel   171

Waligorski, Florentin   104

Zannone, Nicola   16

Printed in the United States
By Bookmasters